# Corky Meyer's
# *FLIGHT*
# *Journal*

## A Test Pilot's Tales of Dodging Disasters –
## *Just in Time*

**By Corwin H. M**

GW00771941

**specialty**press
PUBLISHERS AND WHOLESALERS

ISBN-13   978-1-58007-093-5
ISBN-10   1-58007-093-0

Item #SP093

**specialty**press
PUBLISHERS AND WHOLESALERS

39966 Grand Avenue
North Branch, MN 55056 USA
(651) 277-1400 or (800) 895-4585
www.specialtypress.com

Printed in China

Distributed in the UK and Europe by:
Midland Publishing
4 Watling Drive
Hinckley LE10 3EY, England
Tel: 01455 233 747 Fax: 01455 233 737
www.midlandcountiessuperstore.com

Library of Congress Cataloging-in-Publication
    Data
Meyer, Corwin H.
  Corky Meyer's flight journal / by Corwin H.
    Meyer.
      p. cm.
  ISBN 1-58007-093-0
  1.  Meyer, Corwin H. 2.  Test pilots--United
    States--Biography. 3.  Airplanes, Military--
    United States--Testing--History. I. Title.

TL540.M4123A3 2006
623.7'46'092--dc22
    2005024692

**Cover Captions**

*Main image: Number one Super Tiger flying over the Majove Desert in California. One of the main armament differences between the Tiger and Super Tiger was the capability of doubling the range of the radar in the nose of the aircraft to 35 miles. This asset could have given the Navy a much greater combat air patrol range for carrier protection. (Credit Northrop Grumman History Center)*

*Top left image: On 7 November 1997 I was given a checkout in the Navy F/A-18B at NAS Jacksonville, Florida. I had a chance to evaluate this great new Navy fighter as a test pilot and I enjoyed every minute of it. When I arrived home I discovered in my logbook that that day was the 60th anniversary of my first solo flight. (Corwin H. Meyer Collection)*

*Bottom image: This P-40N picture illustrates the 20-inch extension on the aft fuselage to move the fin and rudder further behind the horizontal tail assembly in order to improve directional stability and to reduce blanking of the vertical tail in spins. Unfortunately, it was grossly insufficient to cure the very bad handling characteristics in the slow-speed stall-spin regime for a very dull-witted pilot on 30 June 1943. (USAAC)*

# Table of Contents

# Foreword

Flight-testing of military aircraft from 1940 to 1950 was in transition from being an art performed by very experienced company test pilots, while being observed by government chase-pilots, to gradually becoming an accepted science, which could be validated by electronic recording of pertinent in-flight data. It was during that time period that I was privileged to become acquainted with a number of individuals who were either experienced commercial test pilots, for the most part, or pilots who were in the process of becoming bona-fide test pilots. As part of the acquisition process of each new aircraft type, the contractor test pilots were required to demonstrate that the aircraft was structurally sound and could be flown safely throughout the contract flight envelope. Those of us in the Flight Test Section of the Naval Air Test Center at Patuxent River, Maryland, were then assigned the task of making certain that the various aircraft met all of the BIS (Board of Inspection and Survey) performance and handling characteristics as spelled out in the government contracts. During the early portions of this era much of the verification of the required tests was still done by having the Navy chase pilot observe the contractor demonstration flights and confirm that the tests were performed satisfactorily using the approved techniques and maneuvers. In the late 1940s and early 1950s, photo-panels installed in the test aircraft recorded the data, and in turn they were eventually replaced by today's sophisticated telemetry systems.

Upon completion of Naval Test Pilot School, I had the good fortune to be assigned to duty in the Flight Division of the Naval Air Test Center, and it was at this point of my career that I became acquainted with Corwin H. "Corky" Meyer, an eager and aspiring young test pilot for Grumman Aircraft. Since I was assigned as the project officer for a number of Grumman fighter acquisitions during the next several years (including the F6F-3 Hellcat, F7F-1 Tigercat, F8F-1 Bearcat, F9F-2 and -5 Panther jet, F9F-6 Cougar, F11F-1 Tiger and Super Tiger, up to the F-14 Tomcat) we had ample opportunity to become intimately acquainted, both socially and professionally, while we were both striving to make certain that the Navy would be getting the best possible aircraft for use in the fleet. During this era most of the demonstration flights were considered fairly routine. The one exception was the "rolling pullout maneuver" in which Corky, as the demonstration pilot, was required to apply the maximum "G" force while simultaneously applying full roll control in one direction or the other in less than one-tenth of a second! All these were vaunted products of "The Grumman Ironworks" and this maneuver required a great number of attempts before successful completion. It was very taxing on Corky as the demonstration pilot while we chase pilots enjoyed the show from the front-row seats.

Corky realized his lack of Navy carrier background shortly after he was hired as an experimental test pilot at Grumman in 1942. At his request, his boss, a former Navy test pilot, arranged for him to go through complete Navy operational training under Commander Swede Vejtasa at NAS Atlantic City in Grumman Hellcats in early 1943. This was followed with 12 arrested landings and catapult shots at Naval Air Test Center (NATC) Patuxent and finally eight carrier catapults and arrestments on the USS *Lake Champlain* in a Cougar with VF-61. Corky thus became the first civilian pilot to qualify as a carrier jet pilot.

As the author covers the details of his colorful career in aviation, he has simultaneously provided us with some valuable insights into the ever-changing and often maligned world of the military/industrial complex. His firsthand accounts of some of the critical decisions affecting military history portions of our international relations and defense policies make for interesting reading. His detailed accounts of certain events reveal why and how our military/industrial complex had been so successful in providing the free world with such highly effective and versatile forces for democracy for over a half century. The intimate knowledge of each partner's strengths and capabilities results in a team effort that continues in the world of today and for the foreseeable future.

I am still in debt to Corky for his very fast response to my frantic appeal for some last-minute info during the final phases of the F-14 fighter Source Selection process in 1969. I had learned that our Navy Seniors were greatly concerned that Grumman's F-14 proposal was woefully short of data that demonstrated their ability to actually build and produce a modern aircraft of such sophistication and complexity as the F-14. After a thorough discussion with some of my troops, I decided that we needed immediate help and that was the reason Corky received an invitation to have lunch with Mac Snowden, Carl Colloquist, and me. We all knew that Grumman was well equipped to handle the problem, but we needed someone to light the fire under Grumman management to get us factual information for presentation to the Navy decision makers. I will never understand how he accomplished the miracle but still remember my great sense of relief when he called two days later and justified my faith in his ability to do the impossible by inviting us to review the presentation, which was exactly the information that was not included in any of Grumman's F-14 proposal. As a result of his efforts, the Navy has had a fantastic fighter since 1969 that will not be retired until 2007. Our country has benefited from the performance of one of the world's most versatile and capable fighter aircraft.

I thoroughly enjoy Corky's numerous contributions to aviation history via journalism and will look forward to many more in the future. Just remember to make sure that they are factual. He and I know the true story and I will not be bashful in holding his feet to the fire.

F. L. Feightner
Rear Admiral USN (Ret.)

# Dedication

This book is dedicated to Dorky, my lovely wife of 41 years. When she married me she knew that as a test pilot I could never pass the annual FAA flight physical depth perception eye exam legally. She never raised her voice and when making suggestions always did it with a great sense of humor. In our early years she and I worked together without outside help on five very large home restorations, which took me out of an inferiority complex and gave me the confidence to believe I could tackle any job successfully. After test flying for 20 years, this asset provided me with a 32-year career in five aviation corporation management overhauls.

# Acknowledgments

John Bishop elevated my writing from third-grade level to college level when I first started writing 10 years ago. Judy Betz and Elizabeth Weaver each dedicated many hours to editing this book from its beginning to completion. My son John Meyer gave his father much time and computer knowledge when I had to switch over from a friendly but ancient word processor to a computer when the book was less than half complete. Wayne Fieldhouse and Chuck Truthan tolerated my many calls 24 hours a day when I lost several battles with that tricky computer. My daughter Sandra Royal suggested that I write a book on what I did for a living many years ago. John Joss, Paul Gilchrist, Larry Shelly, and Walter Boyne placed their marks of approval on my eight chapter submissions to publishers, which resulted in two acceptances out of three submittals. I am indebted to my many friends at the Northrop Grumman History Center for the multitude of pictures that they dug out of the Grumman files during the last 10 years. I am also beholden to Captain Paul Stevens, who suggested that I write some memoirs, Captain E. Earle Rogers II USN (Ret.), VP of Communications for the Navy Foundation publication, and Hill Godspeed of the Naval Air Museum at Pensacola, Florida, Budd Davisson, Editor in Chief, Roger Post, Editor of *Flight Journal*, Steve Ginter, Publisher of *Navy and Air Force Legends*, Michel Benichou, Editor, and Xavier Meal of the French magazine *The Aviation Fanatic*, for their training and assistance in making me an author of sorts.

# Introduction

I have been asked many times what I did for a living and how I spent my life. When I answer that I was an experimental test pilot for 22 years they invariably look askance and tell me that I must have been crazy. When I go on and tell them how much I thoroughly enjoyed my work, they reply that I must REALLY have been crazy. Usually I end up quoting astronaut Alan Shepard. Someone asked him if he was scared sitting atop a Redstone rocket preparing to become the first man ever launched into outer space. He replied, "You bet your life I was scared stiff that some other S.O.B. would take my place, and if he did, I would have slit his throat!" That about sums up how most of my fellow test pilots and I viewed our careers. I will always be grateful to the Lord above that I was born in just the right time and place to pursue a fulfilling life in aviation. A shocking number of my contemporaries, I'm sorry to say, didn't survive the hazards of the game.

My wife Dorky's continuous enthusiasm and backing encouraged me to enjoy my aviation passion ever since the day I met her. Without her whole-hearted sponsorship, however, I could never have had a career flying magic carpets. The reader will be the co-pilot in those machines with me.

Perhaps my fortune became complete when I joined Grumman, the builder of excellent combat, carrier-based aircraft for the Navy. Grumman's unique reputation was built on conservatism, expertise, and intelligent management of its top officers, with Mr. Grumman himself a test pilot. I found a happy niche for 36 years in this fabulous company.

The following chapters will describe in some detail my attraction to aviation early in life, the challenges I faced in getting started as a pilot and engineer, and eventually the wringing out of warplanes, which enabled the United States to prevail in World War II, Korea, the Cold War period, and from Vietnam to the present day.

This book does not strictly follow my life chronologically because I was always flying more than one Navy fighter demonstration program at a time. In order not to have a mixture of several new models of aircraft in one chapter requiring the reader to continuously identify, I have put each new aircraft in a separate chapter. You will find the time period of each chapter under the chapter's title. This should provide a continuity of my biography.

Chapter 1

# The P-40 Talked,
# But Only God Listened

## 30 July 1943

My first exposure to a Curtiss P-40 came during my second year at MIT while training for my Commercial and Instructor pilot ratings. It was 12 August 1941, a hot and sticky day at the East Boston airport. I was watching my Stinson Reliant SR-7 (NC 17124) taxi into position for takeoff on a three-hour cross country flight. This was the cross country course of my MIT-sponsored Civilian Pilot Training Program. I should have been aboard, but my trolley ride from MIT was late in getting me to the airport. My instructor had replaced me with another student. I stood there envying him, but a few seconds later my envy turned to dismay.

As the Stinson got a green light from the tower (there were no radios in towers yet) and began its takeoff roll, I saw a P-40B start its takeoff roll from another corner of the field. Stunned, I watched both aircraft inexorably meet at the center of the field. The P-40 clawed its way

*The P-40B after the accident with the Stinson SR-8D. The P-40 pilot was unhurt but his propeller blades cut the wing off the Stinson, killed the instructor, maimed two of the other students in the rear of the cabin, and left the third student pilot unhurt. I was scheduled to be one of the student pilots that day, but I was a half hour late and another student pilot took my place. (Bob Fogg via Corwin H. Meyer)*

The wingless cabin of the SR-8D Stinson Reliant that was hit by the USAAC Curtiss P-40B during both of their take-offs in the middle of the East Boston airport on 12 August 1941. The P-40B propeller ended up destroying the cabin area. I was supposed to be the student pilot on that flight. The student who took my place was killed. There but for the grace of God it would have been me. (Bob Fogg via Corwin H. Meyer)

through the Stinson, killing the instructor pilot and maiming two of my student-pilot friends. The third student and the Air Corps pilot were miraculously unhurt. Both aircraft came to a stop without catching fire.

P-40 accidents were becoming all too frequent. There had been two local P-40 spin crashes after takeoff in the previous several weeks. I had not seen these accidents but had read about those events on the front pages of the *Boston Globe*. A lot of U.S. Army Air Corps pilots had been killed in these spin-prone aircraft. I walked back into Wiggins Airways operations office in a daze to find out if or when I would be flying again.

## Fast Forward 22 Months

In June 1943 my boss, Bud Gillies, told me that there was to be a cross swapping of Army Air Corps and Navy fighters for test pilot familiarization and evaluation. We soon received the latest U.S.

Army Air Corps P-51B Mustang, P-40N Warhawk, P-38G Lightning, and P-39 Airacobra fighters.

When a young pilot is 23 years old, he has several strikes against himself. With 500 hours flight time he believes that he is invulnerable and immune to any accident that he has seen. He just knows it was caused by the other pilot's complete stupidity. It couldn't happen to him. I had had only one major accident in the Wildcat so far and it couldn't possibly have been my fault, because I wasn't fired, so I was still invulnerable. Enlightenment was just around the corner.

The Curtiss P-40N arrived on 30 July 1943. Vice President of Flight Operations Bud Gillies and Chief Test Pilot Connie Converse checked themselves out in it before me. When my turn came I thought I was fully informed about its quirks. I only had scanned the very skimpy handbook... once!

I sat in the cockpit, spent 15 minutes familiarizing myself with its details, start-

This was the P-40N I flew on 30 June 1943. From this angle it is easy to see why the aircraft absolutely must be S-turned both on the ground and in climb-outs for the pilot to have safe and clear forward visibility. (Northrop Grumman History Center via Corwin H. Meyer)

ed the engine, and taxied the bird for take-off. During the taxiing I noted that the throttle had two pieces of soft aluminum safety wire across the throttle slot; one was an inch and the other was a half-inch from the full-throttle position. I did not remember reading about set-up in the pilot's handbook. It was just a minor detail, so I took off amidst the clatter of the mighty Allison V-1710-99's impressive 1,360 horsepower.

I had learned that the first thing a good test pilot does in a new aircraft is to check out the landing condition stall carefully so he will understand the aircraft's characteristics and airspeed numbers before landing. I promptly checked these stalls and found that it had large and abrupt wing dropping either way when flying just a little out of straight directional flight. It was sharp and accompanied by prompt and rapid alternate rolling in either direction, causing a considerable loss of altitude during recovery. My only thought was that this is an inferior Army

Air Corps aircraft with unacceptable stall characteristics. That damn fool Army Air Corps would just add acres of additional cement to their runways to cure their much higher landing speeds. Navy carrier requirements just couldn't tolerate such wretched stall handling qualities. The P-40 had talked to me, but youthful arrogance had closed my mind ... and ears.

I then tried loops and slow rolls. Loops were easy because the P-40 had a lot of acceleration at low altitude and held it well going inverted over the top of the loop. My first 360-degree slow roll should have been an eye opener; however, it accidentally snap rolled for the last 180 degrees of the roll without any intent on my part for it to do so. I assumed my control coordination was poor, so I performed another few slow rolls and found that I had mastered the beast. The aircraft had now shouted to me, but I had not listened. I should have noted twice that without careful rudder coordination the P-40 would do unplanned and probably fatal spins without the pilot's careful use of the rudder. At 23 you know more about everything than God himself! I had filled my kneepad card with many numbers, which is a sign of a great test pilot, so I proceeded back to the Grumman Bethpage airport.

When I was on final approach a Hellcat, pilot buzzed the field, coming under me in the same direction. This was not an unusual occurrence in those days when the WAR EFFORT syndrome allowed test pilots to get away with murder when it came to breaking the CAA (now FAA) rules.

Having previously determined that the Warhawk had much better power/thrust acceleration than the Hellcat, I decided to pull up my wheels and flaps and give him a go at a rat race (which was also covered by the same syndrome). I pushed the throttle forward without breaking the two wires I had previously noted and pulled up into a steep fighter climb as the wheels and flaps were retracting. My eyes were focused only on the other aircraft. I was probably not using enough right rudder deflection to offset the torque caused by the large and abrupt change in engine power I had just applied.

At about 700 feet, in a tight turning climb to catch the Hellcat, my exuberance ended most abruptly. I had pulled the aircraft into an accelerated stall. The control stick and rudder pedals gave no response to my inputs and flapped loosely around the cockpit. This caused the P-40 to snap roll back and forth. The last event I remember coherently was that the P-40 was deep into the stall and buffeting quite violently. It then snapped into a spin, shaking like a dog getting rid of his bathwater. I could see the hangars below with great clarity and eerie detachment. I was stupefied, mesmerized, and seemed to be sitting on the sidelines watching this unbelievable panorama unfolding. My

mind was blank as to any actions I should take to remove this horrible kaleidoscope. I was watching it as if I didn't have a concern in the world. It just couldn't be happening to ME!

The next thing I remembered was that the spin had stopped. I was in level flight about 50 feet above the potato fields west of the Grumman airport. The ground was whizzing under me at 225 mph. Mentally, I was still only riding, not flying. The maneuver the P-40 had just done was completely out of my frame of reference, even in nightmares. I finally noted that the throttle was pushed through both of the wires and the engine was straining with much more power than I had heard or felt during takeoff. It was now delivering the full 1,350 horsepower of War Emergency Power. After a few seconds I came to my senses, retarded the throttle, and climbed to 1,500 feet. I immediately turned back to the airport because the sun had almost set and it was rapidly getting dark.

Were I a test pilot of greater experience I might have calmed down, remembered all instructions in the handbook about spins, jotted some meaningful notes about the "incident," and made a nonchalant, smooth, three-point landing. I was totally without any of these movie-star test pilot proclivities. I was still stupefied. I flew around the airport without calling the tower and talked to myself like a Dutch uncle. I said, "You stupid jerk! You can't land this aircraft! You are running out of gas! It is getting dark and you have to land this aircraft—soon, etc., etc." My conversation was also sprinkled with four-letter words impugning the legality of my birth and also my total stupidity regarding my abilities to properly evaluate a new aircraft.

After several circuits of the field I humbly called the tower and received landing clearance. They were charitable

THE P-40 TALKED, BUT ONLY GOD LISTENED

*British P-40 Kittyhawk pilots in North Africa painted the large mouth-like duct on the P-40 as a shark mouth long before the famed Flying Tigers of the American Volunteer Group fighting in China also used this same display. This idea caught on and many other USAAC P-40s and restored P-40s since have been so decorated. (Royal Air Force)*

and made no embarrassing commentary. I made a long, airline-style approach at a speed considerably higher than my flight notes would have suggested and landed without further ado. I taxied back to the parking area where all the pilots were still gathered. They had seen my spin and wanted to see the color of my face and pants after that farce. After the propeller stopped rotating the aircraft stopped shaking, but the idiot pilot didn't. After my nervousness ceased I hoped that I might now be able to stand on my own two feet. I got out of the cockpit to the total silence of the test-pilot mob watching.

Later they told me that I made a turn-and-a-half spin, went down below the hangars on the far side of the airport, and

zipped out to the west at 50 feet off the ground like a bat out of hell. I had no recollection of the number of turns of that spin until they told me.

That flight was the most impressive of my young test pilot career. I now learned to listen to the aircraft for everything it had to tell me. I should have become a born-again Christian after that 30-second episode in the P-40, but I didn't.

A week later Mr. H. A. Thomas, Chief Test Pilot of the P-40 program at the Curtiss Buffalo, New York, plant, called me to ask if what he had just heard about my spin was true and would I please explain just how I recovered from it. I told him it was true, that 26 Grumman test pilots had witnessed the deed, and that I had used full War Emergency Power throttle, totally unbeknownst to me, for recovery. There was a great silence for several moments. He then related that this was the only episode on record of a P-40 spinning below 5,000 feet altitude with the pilot living to tell the tale. He then suggested, as I had learned from discussing this event with Grumman aerodynamicists, that power is very destabilizing and should have increased the frenetic of the spin instead of making the recovery. It was my thought that the jolt of the fantastic acceleration thrust of the engine at War Emergency Power must have brought the aircraft out of its spin, but I didn't care if I ever found out.

Relatively speaking, my evaluation flights in the P-51B and the P-38H were unremarkable. Another Navy test pilot had demolished the Bell P-39 Airacobra before arriving at Grumman.

I was the spin demonstration pilot for seven Grumman fighters afterwards. I treated them with great respect, humility, and with my mind, eyes, and both ears wide open. The P-40 was a potent mentor.

The P-40 taught me two specific lessons that I never forgot; listen to an aircraft talk even though it may be just a whisper, and no matter how impressive you think your total time is, it is no license to be arrogant in something that has no visible means of support.

Twenty-six P-40s were lengthened to make room for a complete instructor pilot's cockpit behind the student to accelerate training of wartime pilots and lower the P-40 accident rate. The 13,483 USAAC P-40s built really needed about 1,000 of these trainers to have substantially reduced the P-40's high accident rate. (USAAC)

Col. Robert Scott titled his World War II fighter-pilot book, *God Was My Co-pilot.* In my P-40 spin He was my Command Pilot! I was also fortunate during many flights thereafter that He took over the controls when I became totally confused.

### Fast-Forward 57 Years

I received a letter dated 10 February 1998 from Bob Fogg. It stated, "The last *Flight Journal* was topped by your P-40 story regarding 12 August 1941, which made me jump the chocks! This event happened on my 15th birthday and I was at Boston Airport for the day to fly with my dad in a Curtiss A-12 attack aircraft, which the Reserves were using at that time. My father was working with Inter-City Airlines at Boston Airport but he kept his time up with the Reserves.

"I watched the P-40 on its takeoff that day and only saw the Stinson at the last moment when they collided, spinning the P-40 around and sliding it backwards, leaving the Stinson completely jack-knifed. Obviously a great shock to me, as it must have been to you and your friends. Corky, I went out to the accident site and photographed both ships after the wreck.

"It is amazing how the time has flown since that day. I wanted you to know that there was someone else still alive that saw your almost demise."

Sincerely,
Bob Fogg Jr.

A few days later I received another letter from an Inter-City Airlines mechanic who was having his lunch outside that day and saw the crash. Maybe I do still remember some "unadulterated" facts of my career after all of these years.

# Roots: Lindbergh's Magnificent Imprint

## 14 April 1920 to 9 November 1942

Several friends tell me that their first memories were seeing the light of day when they were born. I have given them a charitable benefit of the doubt. Not having a mind that well honed, my first detailed memory is of my mother listening to our RCA radio, avidly following the takeoff of some fellow flying 3,614 miles nonstop in 33 hours, 30 minutes, and 29.85 seconds from New York to Paris on 21 May 1927.

I was seven and living in Springfield, Illinois. I remember this event because my father had several emotional discussions about it with my mother. He was just as avid about his baseball programs as she was with this wild and unknown aviator. After Lindbergh made it, the radios went crazy, and my father's baseball programs were superseded for days.

On 27 June 1927, this newly famous New York-to-Paris aviator planned to visit all the state capitals in the United States. He was due to land at Springfield and my mother wanted to see him. She put my older brother John, my cousin Armin, and me into her car and drove out to our 60-acre, one-shed airport (managed by a fellow named Craig Isbell) to watch Lindbergh land.

I fell in love with his silver Ryan monoplane as it touched down and rolled to a stop. Lindbergh got out to greet a happy,

cheering crowd and got into his limousine to start his tour of the town and put a wreath on Lincoln's Tomb. My mother

*Charles Lindbergh standing with his mother, Evangeline Land Lindbergh, a school teacher from Little Falls, Minnesota, in front of his specially-designed Ryan while waiting for good weather a few days before he took off for Paris. (Corwin H. Meyer Collection)*

*After landing in Paris on 21 May 1927, Lindbergh was overwhelmed with the reception of thousands of Parisians who swarmed out onto the airport. He was worried that the crowds would try to take souvenirs of fabric from his aircraft. He stayed with the aircraft until it was locked in a hangar. (Corwin H. Meyer Collection)*

piled us into the car. Knowing his route, she bypassed the parade and stopped at four places where we could see him pass. We then went to see him lay a wreath at Lincoln's Tomb. Late that afternoon we returned to the pasture airport to see his beautiful aircraft take off and disappear northward into the skies on his way to Chicago. He knew that route. He had flown it for two years as Chief Airmail Pilot for the St. Louis-based Robertson Airlines.

In 1927, I could only see an aircraft cruising over Springfield once every six months or so, when an itinerant aircraft or the Navy Zeppelin *Los Angeles* floated over our town. Long gasbag Zeppelins were of no interest. They only looked like boats floating on the water. Aircraft were something to run outside to see. I envied their pilots while I watched them as long as possible. Fortunately, the 70- to 80-mph top speeds kept the aircraft in view long enough to let my imagination run wild enough to build a model of Lindbergh's silver beauty.

I descended into our dark, gloomy basement, found a hatchet and some kindling wood, and started chopping. After chopping for several days I had not only dulled the hatchet, but the model aircraft that was supposed to look like the Ryan, as if it was able to fly, looked more, well, more like the nailed-together pile of kindling that it was.

My mother was most helpful. Her father ran a window and sash mill in her hometown of Greenport, Long Island, and she knew a lot about sharpening tools. She showed me how to find rough and smooth cement areas and how to put the hatchet back in shape by rubbing the blade's cutting edge in circles at very low angles to the cement.

It was important to sharpen it because we both knew that it was my father's only tool for making kindling for our evening fire. At seven, I had been proud to be allowed to set these fires for him. I then asked my mother if I could buy some

*World War I Curtiss two-seat JN-4 Jenny trainers were the only aircraft that were seen in the air in the late 1920s and early 1930s because, as war surplus, hundreds available could be purchased for as little as $200 apiece. They also flew at about 60 mph, so they did not pass overhead very fast. (Corwin H. Meyer Collection)*

silver paint. Without commenting on the beauty of my nailed-together kindling, she bought me the paint and my Ryan was finished the next day.

Two days later the head carpenter who built our home delivered a 10-foot workbench, with a vise mounted at one end, for our new basement shop room. I was amazed at this gift. My older brother who was into constructing crystal sets (forerunners of radios) and I would discover that the location was poorly chosen for us, because my mother and dad sat in the room above after dinner. When they stamped three times on the floor it meant that homework came first.

I ran around the yard flying my chunky silver bird at the end of my outstretched arm, making sounds like an aircraft. My dad, upon hearing how much time I had taken to build my model, called Andy Santenan, director of the YMCA, and found out that they had a class in building simple flying models called ROGs (Rise Off Ground), taught by Bob Wood. Bob soon became the wonderful first of my many mentors.

After I finished that first model under his tutelage, it looked a lot more like an aircraft than my Lindbergh model, although it was only skinny sticks of balsa wood covered with tissue paper. But, it would actually take off from the ground, fly in a circle two times, and land on its two little wheels just like a real aircraft. After Bob Wood had taught me how to build, adjust, and fly simple hand-launched gliders, I was off and running in this mind-boggling enterprise. Now my imagination could really fly.

My parents readily saw how much my brother and I were driven by our hobbies. They told us that we could earn 25 cents apiece by cutting our lawn once a week. The only problem with that great deal was that it seemed the lawn didn't need enough cutting to feed the enthusiasm for our newfound shop endeavors. As we needed more money, we found that cleaning the basement and the garage earned more pieces of silver. Mowing neighbors' yards at those low wages seemed to fit in so well that I began building bigger and bigger models and entering contests sponsored

*An American Airlines single pilot Vultee V1-A seven-passenger airliner that I won a round trip in from Springfield, Illinois, to St. Louis, Missouri, in 1936 for winning a model airplane contest. I rode with the pilot Robert Rentz, sitting on a box next to him in the cockpit both ways. This trip convinced me that I wanted to learn to fly as soon as possible. (Corwin H. Meyer Collection)*

by the YMCA in our local Armory building. Sometimes I even won.

Stirred by Lindbergh's fantastic flight, six of us aviation nuts spawned the Springfield Model Airplane Club. To lower our costs, we had to share modeling secrets and expensive model aircraft plans that each of us had accumulated. Because the model aircraft supply store was two miles on the other side of town, I borrowed five dollars from my now-willing mother and stocked up on balsa wood, glue, colored dope, and Chinese gift tissue paper used to cover the models, with the intention of re-selling these materials to my fellow club members.

I lived so close to all the club members that the business soon became profitable. I paid off my loan to my parents' amazement. My business income also allowed me to make more models than I had ever imagined. At age 14 I had constructed and flown 98 scale models of real aircraft (mostly World War I fighters), contest machines, and gliders, which included 24 models I had constructed for the Myers Brothers Department Store during the 1934 and 1935 Christmas seasons.

I put as little time into schoolwork as I could get away with and had little urge to ogle the pretty high school girls that other fellows seemed to drool over. I was over six feet tall and the high school newspaper commented every year, saying: "Why isn't Corwin Meyer out for the football or basketball team?" The question always went unanswered. I didn't have the time, energy, or interest for any extra-curricular school events.

The May 1934 issue of *Model Airplane News* published the first plans for a gasoline-powered model aircraft, Joe Kovel's 8-foot-wingspan KG-3. It was designed by Charles Hampson Grant, thus the K and G. I had formerly devoured Mr. Grant's enlightening articles titled, "Aerodynamics of a Model Airplane." They received my complete attention. A previous issue contained an article about Maxwell Basset easily winning the top prize as the only gasoline engine-powered aircraft at the National Model Aircraft Contest.

After flying rubber band-powered models for so many years I was completely taken in by this KG-3 gasoline engine-powered behemoth. Maybe it was a subconscious feeling that this would get me closer to the real thing. I don't know. But at 14 it had totally captivated me. I just HAD to build it.

It soon dawned on me that because of its size the KG-3's materials would cost as much as 20 of my previous models. The engine cost alone was an out-of-sight $21.50 BIG DEPRESSION DOLLARS! When I counted my income, I realized that my discount on balsa wood, etc., the sales of model supplies, and the income from mowing lawns and shoveling snow might pay for this monster model aircraft. However, I didn't know where the astronomical engine money would come from.

It finally dawned on me that my father gave me one dollar a week for lunch money. It would only take me five-and-a-half months to buy the engine, if I didn't eat lunch. That was an easy decision. I could easily over-eat at breakfast. It would probably take me that long to build such a large and complicated model anyhow.

My first job was to get a 12-foot-piece of wrapping paper on which to scale up and lay out the two six-foot fuselage trusses and the 28 16-piece ribs. The time went by lickety-split, and I was almost finished with the model when I finally had enough money to purchase the engine. I was now only three short months over my optimistic time/cost schedule.

I will not describe the many long days it took me to learn how to start this cantankerous engine. Needless to say, I still have a hard lump on my right-hand middle finger where the propeller got angry with me all too many times because I did not know how to set the spark adjustment properly.

By the time my red and blue eight-foot monster KG-3 was completed and painted, I had a meager understanding of starting the engine. I was most anxious to make the first flight. I knew it would have to be a large field, not one of the parks where we flew our rubber band-powered models. After a few days the idea came to me. Having no inhibitions, I thought, why not ask Mr. Isbell, the manager of the Springfield Airport, if I could use the airport? All he could do was say no.

He agreed that I could use the airport because there were very few landings of itinerant aircraft each day. He often closed it down for an hour so we could launch our now engine-powered models. After

My 8-foot-wingspan KG-3 with its quarter-horsepower engine in the nose just after its first flight on 21 June 1935. I still hadn't learned enough about starting this engine. The third finger of my left hand still has a large knob on it to this day. One of its flights took 23 minutes to fly eight miles from the airport to the center of Springfield where it circled the state house, ran out of gas, and crashed against the high school. The story made the front page of the 8 March 1936 Illinois State Register. (Corwin H. Meyer Collection)

the launch we would jump into a car to chase them for up to a half hour across the Illinois flat farms until the models ran out of gas and glided to a landing.

I made four engine-powered models and the others in the club made quite a few, too. Mr. Isbell never refused us access to the airport.

We also learned that Mr. Isbell had worked for Robertson Airlines from 1926 to the early 1930s. He had met and worked with Charles Lindbergh during that time. Mr. Isbell told us many stories of the special times he had with Lindbergh before he became the first pilot to fly solo across the Atlantic Ocean in 1927. Lindbergh became the first great aviation hero since the Wright brothers first flew their aircraft in 1903.

To help explain why Craig Isbell was so amenable to my request, I must go back a few years to when three friends and I, all ten-year-old enthusiastic model aircraft builders, would walk the six-mile round trip to the new Springfield, Illinois, Municipal Airport to spend the day, in hopes of seeing the real stuff take off and land.

We entered the airport from the north side, a route that we thought shielded us from the management who might see us sneaking, unannounced, into the big main hangar. We were only inside a minute or so when this tall, handsome man came in, spotted us, and marched over with a seemingly gruff look on his tanned face. We were shaking with fear when he smiled and asked us if we would like to learn about the aircraft and maybe sit in the cockpit of one of them. We were stunned. We had been positive that he was going to call the police.

He showed us the Avro Avian biplane, the De Havilland Gypsy Moth, a Waco F, and his own Stinson Detroiter four-place monoplane. After we spent a long time with him, he told us he had to lock the

hangar. He then smiled and said that anytime we wanted to look into the hangar we should just come to his office first and ask him. We walked the three miles home in total ecstasy. We forgot everything else and only talked of our patron saint, Mr. Craig Isbell.

In 1930, when I was just 10 years of age, my dad asked Mr. Isbell to give my brother and me our first aircraft ride in his impressive Stinson Detroiter. It was the real icing on the cake. I bragged about it to all who would listen.

When I was 16, Mr. Isbell ran a Private Pilot Ground School at the YMCA. I was invited to join the group of adults. We listened to the oracle explain how an aircraft flew and how easy it was to become a pilot. I didn't miss a session.

One year later, still in the depth of the Depression, I taught model aircraft building for the city park and school system for 10 weeks. With the $150 that I had earned in my hot little hand I went immediately to my mother to get permission to learn to fly. She said I had to ask my father, who

*On 2 March 1930 my father took my brother John and me to the airport and told us that he had set it up for us to have our first airplane ride with the manager of the airport, Craig Isbell, as pilot. The 20-minute ride was an eye opener for a 10-year-old me. My older brother was little impressed. He followed in my father's footsteps and became a doctor. (Corwin H. Meyer Collection)*

not only said NO, but, HELL NO! My mother looked at me and moved her head slightly to indicate that the conversation was over.

That night after my brother and I had gone to bed, an argument began in the room below. It sounded like World War II had started. It soon quieted down and my brother said he thought that mother had won. The next day, at breakfast, mother said firmly: "Your father and I discussed your learning to fly." Overlooking the white-knuckled fists and grim expression on my father's face, she continued: "He agreed that you could learn to fly." I was in seventh heaven.

She then said, very positively: "There is one condition, however. Virginia Lee Rodgers (a young lady of my dreams) will not be your first passenger; I will be." I agreed heartily.

Early the next morning I went to the airport to ask Craig to teach me to fly. He said that I first needed to pass the required Civil Aeronautics Authority (CAA) physical to see if I was fit. I flunked it. I was found to be cross-eyed. Doctor Morris (who had never been up in an aircraft) told me forcefully that in an emergency landing I would see two airports and crash and be killed. I told Craig the sad news, thinking I could never be a pilot. Craig kindly said: "Why not try a few dual flight hours with me, to see if you really could fly." Elated, I took him up on his offer.

After eight hours of instruction in his Taylorcraft BLT (NC 19629) he said that I was ready to solo. He kindly said that he would reduce the dual rate from $7.50 per hour to the solo rate of $5 per hour and ride with me, now only as a non-speaking passenger. He stayed quiet until one day when, forgetting his presence, I tried to buzz Virginia Lee Rodgers' home. He became vocal: I got the message.

When I ran out of money after logging 15 hours and 46 minutes of delightfully

The two-place Taylorcraft Model A in November 1937 in which I learned to fly with Craig Isbell. I had just warmed it up and was picking Craig Isbell up for another lesson of pure delight for me, even though I was supposed to be cross-eyed and unable to fly. (Corwin H. Meyer Collection)

inspiring flights in his BLT model Taylorcraft, Mr. Isbell said that he couldn't find anything wrong with my flying ability and that I should try to pass the physical again. I, too, realized that I could fly without any of the traumatic eye problems that Dr. Morris had predicted so adamantly. I didn't try the physical again because a 40-hour Private Pilot's license would cost me a bigger fortune than I could even imagine with the Depression still on.

With Mr. Isbell's encouragement and the self-confidence gained from 15 delightful flight hours, I decided to make a machine similar to Dr. Morris' eye exam apparatus to find out if I could master it with practice. With my brother acting as doctor, I spent days working at it without being able to come close to passing that simple five-minute test. I was about to give up when I had a great idea.

I determined that I should put tension on the strings when my brother, playing the doctor, showed me, as Dr. Morris had done, how the rods would look to pass the test. I would then tighten the strings and immediately curl the strings around both of my index fingers, to know exactly where to bring the rods together during the test. Next I had to place the strings on the floor, when the doctor stood between me and that infernal machine, so I couldn't see which way and how far he was moving the rods away from each other. After he stepped aside I picked the strings up exactly at their curl point, tensioned them, and with a little hocus-pocus by moving the rods back and forth, as if I was having a little difficulty lining them up, I would finally line up my index fingers and the rods would obediently follow. My brother was amazed that I could now do it perfectly every time. After I told him how simple it was he remarked that I was the slyest cheater he ever knew. I instantly forgot about my eye problem.

Sixty-three years later I found out why Mr. Isbell continued to push me back to Dr. Morris to try to pass the physical again. In 2002 I phoned Mr. Isbell in Phoenix, Arizona. During our conversation he asked me why I didn't try to pass the physical again in 1938. When I told him that I really was cross-eyed, he asked me how the devil it was that I could pass the physical in 1940. When I told him about my making an eye exam machine and learning how to fake it, he was amazed and said that he always thought that my father, who he knew didn't want me to learn to fly, had told Dr. Morris to flunk me.

When it came time for mom to ride with me, we found that my mother was about three inches wider than the cabin of a Piper J-3 Cub, but we wedged her in. I never had a more wonderful and appreciative passenger. Many years later, I asked my mother why she backed me so energetically against my strong-willed father. She stated firmly, "If I had been born 10 years later than I was, I would have been Amelia Earhart!"

At the end of each school year at Springfield High they held a scale-model contest. I entered every contest with at least three models. When I was a sophomore I won first place with my Curtiss P6-E Hawk, second place with my Benny Howard DGA, *Mr. Mulligan,* and third place with my Stearman Cloudboy. After the ribbons were awarded, Mr. Deffenbaugh, my physics teacher, walked by to congratulate me. He then added a statement that quietly implied that I should look into other hobbies, sports, and extra-curricular high school events. He said I shouldn't just concentrate on one subject like model aircraft, but keep an open mind and investigate other opportunities, at least until I finished high school.

He was a very fine teacher and spoke to me as a friend. My father had said the same thing to me many times in another way. He quoted a doctoral thesis when he said: "The most difficult operation known to medical science is to implant a new idea into a closed mind." Sad to say, I didn't listen carefully to their good intentions. I stayed totally focused on aircraft for the rest of my life. I just couldn't do it any other way.

In 1938 I attended the Massachusetts Institute of Technology (MIT) with a scholarship. After a few weeks of hearing nothing but boring theory from my professors, I decided to go over to MIT's Wright Brothers Memorial Wind Tunnel to get closer to practical learning. I entered the hallowed halls. After walking around and not finding the location of the actual wind tunnel, a brusque young professor intercepted me and demanded: "Who let YOU in?" I told him that I was enrolled in Course 16, Aeronautical Engineering, and said that I just wanted to see their wind tunnel. He let me know my place in life when he said: "You are not allowed in this building! You will be allowed in here only during the last half of your junior year! Get out!" His statement discouraged me from remaining at MIT.

Other events at MIT made me feel that my previous lack of excitement for sports was on target. The curriculum required that I take a physical education course.

After reviewing the choices, I decided I would appear much more macho to the ladies if I went out for Crew.

The training had already commenced and the new crewmembers were now working out in sculls on the Charles River. It was a cold, overcast morning when I walked the mile to the boathouse and arrived by 7:00 AM. Without inside work-out on the rowing machines, I was put into a boat that was being launched. I had no idea of how an oar sweep should be manipulated.

I soon found out. I was immediately clashing oars with the fellows ahead of and behind me with regularity, and in so doing was splashing them, too. I heard some very impressive new four-letter words from almost all of my compatriots in the boat.

I soon got the rhythm down, with fewer mess-ups and four-letter words. It was the hardest work I had ever performed, and I was freezing to death. The coach soon came up to my boat, glared directly at me, and shouted, "What's your name?" After I told him he further commanded: "I want to see you out here every morning promptly at 6:30 AM from now on!" That day was the first time, and the last time, I ever participated in macho sports.

After my first year at MIT I was very discouraged, but my dad and mother's salesmanship convinced me to go back. I returned to Boston for my sophomore year. When I arrived at "Tech," as it was called, I decided I really hated it and hitch-hiked the 1,018 miles home. My parents were disappointed because I returned home after most other colleges had commenced.

Good luck prevailed and the University of Illinois accepted me for their second year course in Mechanical Engineering. My discouragement soon departed and I tried to work hard enough now to really please my parents. UI was only 65 miles from home and I could now hitchhike there and back to let my parents know that I was doing well. At the end of the year I told them I would like to return to MIT. I knew that their goal for me was to graduate from there. They agreed.

Unbeknownst to me, my very patient dad also told me he could make an appointment for us to tour the Howard Aircraft manufacturing plant in Chicago. This firm was producing a four-place DGA (Damn Good Airplane) for the Navy. It had been named *Mr. Mulligan* when Benny Howard won the Bendix race in it during the late 1930s. I had built a model of this aircraft and knew all about it. I was eager to go.

We toured the plant where I met Benny Howard and Gordon Isreal. Isreal was also a former racing pilot. He'd won racing events in a ship of his own design named *Red Head* in the mid 1930s. He was now Howard's chief engineer. I was to meet him again at Grumman two years later.

This trip revitalized me. My detailed inspection of a production line, where I could see real aircraft being produced and tested, could not have been a bigger treat for my eyes and mind. I was re-energized at the thought of returning to MIT.

Shortly after our trip I also learned of a new government-sponsored, 40-hour, private license in the Civilian Pilot Training Program (CPTP), available under Mr. Isbell's tutelage. This program had begun in the summer of 1939 in colleges around the country to better prepare us for war by turning out pilots to augment the Army Air Corps and Navy flight schools. I could now get paid for flying, and pass the physical, too.

On 1 June 1940 I signed up for the CPTP program, easily passing the flight physical. Craig was right. I could fly. I graduated and received my Private Pilot Certificate on 29 September 1940. I was in hog heaven! I kept in touch with my instructor Chick Clark until he died in 1996.

When my father talked me into returning to MIT in 1940, I found that MIT sponsored four additional CPTP courses leading up to a Commercial License and an Instructor's Certificate. The first course was in aerobatics. I jumped at that privilege and signed up. When I arrived at the East Boston airport at E. W. Wiggins Flying Service, I found out that this course was to be taught in the 220-hp Waco UPF-7. Having trained in 40-hp Taylorcrafts, I just couldn't imagine what flying a BIG 220-hp aircraft would be like.

"Dunc" McDougal, my instructor, took me for my first ride on 24 November 1940. It was a new world, and I enjoyed it from wheels off to landing. He taught me Lazy Eights, Wingovers, the Falling Leaf, Loops, Slow Rolls, Snap Rolls, Immelmann Turns, Upright Spins, and,

new to me, Inverted Spins—the whole shooting match. I was in fat-cat heaven and couldn't wait until the next flight.

My comeuppance came at the five-hour check-ride with the Chief Pilot, Charlie Scott. I was as nervous as a bride at her wedding. I taxied out to the takeoff spot, ran the engine up, and started my takeoff. At about 60 mph, just before leaving the ground, I accidentally hit the left brake hard and turned the aircraft 20 degrees. After I corrected my miserable takeoff my nervousness increased by leaps and bounds. I worried that I was doing everything wrong. I can't even remember any of the maneuvers I was tested for.

After landing I followed him back to his office like a sheep to the slaughter. He said nothing until we got to his office. I apologized for my takeoff and he immediately put me at ease by saying, "Don't worry about that, Corwin, at least you got into the correct cockpit and started the engine properly." As a friendly mentor he

*Civilian Pilot Training Program graduation class, Springfielf, Illinois, Municipal Airport, August 1940. Left to right: Keith Favorite, instructor; Adelaide O'Brien, ground school instructor; Chet Sikking; Chick Clarke, instructor; Franklin McKelvey (KIA submarine 1944); Hank Webber (KIA airplane accident 1947); unknown; Corwin H. Meyer; Jim Kurt (died of cancer 1946); unknown; all upper row unknown. (Corwin H. Meyer Collection)*

went over the good and bad points of my check ride and told me to get back with Dunc McDougal ASAP. I departed his office with his blessing, "I'll see you again when you complete the course, Corwin." After the war he flew a Grumman Mallard amphibian for Howes Leather Corporation and I had the pleasure of seeing him every time he came back to Grumman for his Mallard's maintenance checks.

I received my Commercial License and Instructor's Certificate on 7 April 1942. I was hired by Charlie Scott to teach the CPTP aerobatic course, which I thoroughly enjoyed. Now I was a salaried aviator, not just a student.

Six weeks later Gordon Brown and Tom Flanagan, two friends that had been flying with me in the Commercial Instructor's courses, came to the airport to change my life further. They had enrolled in the next CPTP course (one that I had not heard about), which provided an Instrument and a Multi-Engine Rating at Burlington, Vermont. At the end of that

*The Lockheed 10 Electra airliner that I flew to receive my Multi-engine and Instrument Ratings at Burlington, Vermont, in 1942. This gave me all the ratings that were possible to attain to begin my professional pilot career with Pan American Airways. I also learned not to make rapid decisions when solving an emergency after takeoff. However, PAA Captain Mike LaPorte was to forever better my career beyond my wildest dreams. (Corwin H. Meyer Collection)*

job they told me they would be hired by Pan American Airways flying four-engined Boeing 314 Clippers and suggested that I enroll. I did so the next day. I graduated as a Flight Officer on 15 October 1942 and received my two ratings, which, at the time, gave me all the ratings that the CAA then required for pilots.

I magically wiggled my way through the physical for 31 more years before learning that I could obtain a pilot's license with corrective glasses for my cross-eyed condition. Corrective lenses were not permissible when I started flying because of the many blustery, open-cockpit aircraft then in use. I confess that every year when physical time came around I knew I had a devil sitting on my shoulder until I walked out of the doctor's office with an okay to fly, but only for the next 365 days.

In my career I experienced many emergency landings with dead engines, fires, and large parts of the aircraft torn off during flight and never had a single problem with my eyes. These were the very eyes that Dr. Morris had so firmly and fatalistically predicted would only serve my flying hopes and dreams in a coffin.

As the reader will have realized, my mother, father, Craig Isbell, and many others like Charlie Scott both disciplined and encouraged my flying affliction all the way. In hindsight, I can now see why my doctor father's strong "HELL NO" was understandable. He wanted me to be a professional aeronautical engineer. In 1937, in the depths of the Great Depression, there were absolutely no professional flying jobs in the minuscule aviation industry. Only the arrival of World War II provided an opening for me in a now massively increased world of aviation opportunities. Without the war my dad would have been absolutely correct in his fatherly beliefs.

Chapter 3

# A Stranger on a Train

## 10 and 11 November 1942

Some great writers have begun their epic prose with the foreboding: "It was a dark and stormy night," and if I had only known then what I know now I would never have gone up to Murgatroyd Manor to visit Darlene. Ominous worked for them; therefore, I shall speak forebodingly while raising my curtain.

10 November 1942 was a very hot day in several ways. First, it was warm for that time of year, it was Indian summer exactly as Sitting Bull would have liked it: 80 degrees, cloudless, and windless. To compound the heat, I was wearing my only Sunday-go-to-meeting, winter herringbone suit made of heavy wool. I had walked over two miles to the pay phone outside the Republic Aircraft factory on Long Island, New York, and two miles back to the Long Island Railroad station at Farmingdale. If I were to interview for a job as a test pilot I thought that I should at least appear as a gentleman of sorts. I even had a tie on, but it had become loosened shortly after my curt discussion with Joe Parker, chief test pilot for Republic. It had taken him only one question to shoot down my trip to the phone booth. He had asked if I had military aviation experience and when I said no he hung up instantly.

It was hot because the train was constructed long before air conditioning had been invented and the steam engine was puffing and raining soot down on the car I was sweating in. The windows were mercifully closed to keep out most of the ashes.

The real heat was internal. I had essentially thumbed my nose at Captain Mike LaPorte, my interviewer at Pan American Airways, when he had sarcastically suggested to me that I should get a test pilot job after I had asked him if there was any possibility of using my three-and-a-half years of MIT engineering education were I to join Pan American. And now I was going to have to eat a large portion of crow because Republic had just exhausted my total list of corporations to get a test-pilot job.

I had received the same turndown that Joe Parker had given me from all of the seven companies I had visited. All of them wanted only military-trained pilots. Fred Chamberlain, the Chief Test Pilot at Curtiss-Wright, had first suggested to his boss that they should hire me. Since I had no military flight experience his boss had turned thumbs down. Lockheed and Curtiss-Wright hadn't bothered to answer my telegrams. Lyman Bullard, the Chief Test Pilot of Chance Vought, had interviewed me twice. Twice his boss Paul Baker had said no. Brewster Aeronautical in Long Island City had said that they had no requirements at that time but they would "keep my name on file." I had struck out everywhere and I hadn't even been up to bat.

As I sweltered in my seat, the train started to fill up with passengers going back to New York City. An older fellow sat down next to me and seemed to take great satisfaction in sitting down. My fidgeting and disconsolate countenance must have attracted his attention. Or, I could have just started blurting out my plight just to have someone sympathize with me. My usual high spirits were now down in the deepest of dumps. As I began talking the train started with a great lurch, as steam trains were wont to do, and I felt a little better now that I was putting Republic miles behind me.

I hadn't related much of my sad story when the older fellow interrupted and asked me which side of the train I had sat on while coming from New York. I thought it a strange question, but as he continued he said that I had missed a very large aircraft factory by sitting in the left-hand seat coming out to Farmingdale. He said that he didn't know the name of the factory but that it was a big one. As I was again sitting on the wrong side of the train to see this new factory, he suggested that we both move over to the left side of the coach. It was only three miles from Farmingdale to Grumman station, so almost immediately we were passing a factory and airport that had hundreds of light-blue fighters lined up on the runways and taking off and landing.

Needless to say, I got out at the Grumman station and went to the nearest phone to call the chief test pilot. But this

*Vice President of Flight Operations Bud Gillies, who hired me at Grumman on 11 November 1942, about to fly a Curtiss F6C-3 in the early 1930s before he came to Grumman in 1933. He was a great mentor from his experience as an experimental test pilot. He helped and disciplined me on many proper occasions until he retired in 1944. We stayed close friends until his death in September 1990. (Northrop Grumman History Center)*

time I had decided to say that I did indeed have government training, which I did, if the question of military training came up. I was asked the bad question and when I said that I had completed all seven courses of the government-sponsored Civilian Pilot Training Program, and that I had Commercial, Instrument, Instructor, and Multi-Engine Ratings, I was told to wait for the crash truck to come out to pick me up. It was amazing how fast one's emotions can go from dismal to cloud nine.

Only a few minutes later a crash truck, driven by an elderly gentleman named Dave, arrived and I was carried to Flight Operations in a style that I had not been accustomed to since my wandering began two weeks earlier. I was escorted to the

*Connie Converse, in flight gear, was the first person I talked to at Grumman and is shown here talking to Bob Hall, the assistant chief engineer for experimental engineering, at the time I came to Grumman. Bob was a fabulous test pilot and would be my mentor in test flying for the next 20 years. (Northrop Grumman History Center)*

*Twelve F4F-3 Wildcats and TBF-1 Avenger torpedo aircraft on the Plant 4 production area about the time I came to Grumman in 1942. This second-floor view was what I saw while Bud Gillies was interviewing me. It was most difficult for me to take my eyes off of these light-blue Navy carrier combat aircraft that I was to begin flying the next day. (Northrop Grumman History Center)*

second floor of the tower to meet Connie Converse, the Grumman chief test pilot. After a few cursory questions about my hours and ratings he called Bud Gillies, the vice president of Flight Operations, to come over and interview me further.

While I was waiting I saw and heard more fighter aircraft within 200 yards of the tower than I had seen in my entire lifetime. The glass panels of Connie's office were like a vision into the biggest aircraft candy store in the world.

Bud Gillies arrived shortly and asked me the same questions that Connie had asked me. Then he said that Grumman paid $80 a week straight time for pilots. I multiplied that by four and it came to $320 a month; $120 more than I would have earned as fourth officer at

Pan American. Bud continued to say that they paid 50 percent overtime, which I mentally figured to be $480 per month to fly those lovely aircraft that I was trying so hard not to look at over his shoulder. I also told him that I had three-and-a-half years at MIT and the University of Illinois. He proudly said that he graduated from MIT in 1926, and then asked me why I hadn't stayed to graduate. Having all the pilot ratings possible, I said that I just couldn't remain a bored student while every other 22-year-old man had been taking actions against a foul enemy who had stabbed us in the back. After almost a year into the war, you cannot imagine what critical looks a young man not in uniform received in public.

He then looked me straight in the eye and asked if I would like to come to work for Grumman. The abrupt change in interest in me by the aviation community, the fantastic salary, and those beautiful Avengers and Wildcats that I would be flying had me speechless. I just couldn't get the word "yes" out fast enough. It seemed to me that it took half an hour to nod my head, say "yes," and shake his hand. He brought me back to the land of the living by asking me if I would like to ride back to New York with him, as he was going in there for a meeting.

Just before I got out of his car in New York he said that when I returned tomorrow morning he would have a special setup for me to bypass the usual details of the hiring procedure so that I could start flying as soon as possible. When I got out of his car I had to review the details of the last hour and a half so that I could really believe what had happened. I was hired to be a real live supplemental test pilot starting tomorrow!

I was living with three of the other pilots that I had trained with in Burlington, Vermont. All of us were then to work for Pan American. They thought that I had really fallen into fat-cat heaven because they had arrived a month earlier and complained that, as fourth officers in the Boeing 314s, they weren't allowed to fly the aircraft yet. They were still navigators and I was going to fly fighters.

My father called that evening from Springfield, Illinois, and said that Captain LaPorte had called several times wanting to know where the hell I was and why I hadn't enrolled in Pan American two weeks ago. He also added that if I didn't show up the next day Captain LaPorte was going to have me drafted into the walking army.

The next morning fear became top priority over a dash to Grumman. I went to see the CAA (now the FAA) at LaGuardia to suggest to them that I thought I would be using my training and education much better at Grumman than at Pan American. Mr. Frank Andrews, a retired Air Corps general, who was the head of the CPTP government program that trained me, agreed heartily and said that he would do the necessary calls and paperwork with Captain LaPorte. This cleared my way to hop the next train to Grumman. I went through the hiring process in about an hour and then checked out in a 400-hp Grumman J4F Widgeon amphibian that same afternoon.

The reader might think that this was a once-in-a-million good-luck event. It was and it wasn't. Several years later I was to learn that Chief Test Pilot Connie Converse had told Grumman management that he needed to bow out of experimental flight-testing, which he had been performing for the last nine years. Bob Hall, who was the assistant chief engineer and an excellent test pilot, had been doing the more critical half of the experimental flight-testing since he came to Grumman in 1937. Grumman management had informed him they wanted him to act full time as Director of Engineering. He knew his future test-flying career would soon have to end. At all levels in Grumman, the need for another engineering test pilot was clearly recognized.

I have often wondered what my entire life and profession would have been if I had not sat next to an unknown person who prompted me to move across the aisle to look at "another aircraft factory." He changed my life forever.

Chapter 4

# Grumman Environment – 1942

## The Big Picture – Management

Grumman had an innate asset that gave the test and military pilots a real shot in the arm. When I arrived at Grumman, four of its top management were practicing part-time test pilots. LeRoy Randle Grumman was naval pilot #1216 in World War I and a naval test pilot for several years thereafter. He then managed Loening Aircraft Corporation, a Navy corporation, and flew its commercial and military amphibians until 1930, when he organized his own company on Long Island. He took with him 16 top Loening leaders who did not want to move with Loening to Philadelphia. He flew all Grumman aircraft, including the Hellcat fighter, until the end of World War II.

B. A. "Bud" Gillies was a graduate of MIT, a naval fighter pilot since 1926, and flew many first flights in Grumman experimental aircraft during his career at Grumman from 1933 until he retired in 1947. He hired me.

Vice President for Experimental Engineering Robert H. "Bob" Hall was a famous test pilot who designed, tested, and raced several Thompson Trophy winners that he himself had designed. He was an engineering test pilot at Stinson for three years, and then moved to Grumman as an engineering test pilot in 1937.

Roy Grumman, B. A. "Bud" Gillies, Bob Hall, and Connie Converse made themselves easily accessible to test and military pilots in order to utilize their knowledge and background. These four pilots also had a great influence in making Grumman a "pilot's aircraft" organization from top to bottom. Grumman was the only company in the United States that I know of that had such a test pilot-friendly team at top management.

I heard Mr. Grumman give his design philosophy regarding Grumman fighters many times: "Grumman will only deliver aircraft that a 200-hour wartime-trained pilot can fly from a carrier, fight in aerial combat, return to the carrier, and land safely at night to fly again the next day." It was clear to everybody in the company that making a pilot-oriented aircraft came first. Everything else was second. Most presidents of aircraft companies gave first priority to the financial aspects of the corporation and left the quality of the product to subordinates.

Former Navy pilot Seldon A. "Connie" Converse was Grumman's chief test pilot from 1938 until he retired after 32 years of production and experimental test flying.

Grumman was a non-union operation from the day it opened its doors in 1930 to the day it was sold some 60 years later to

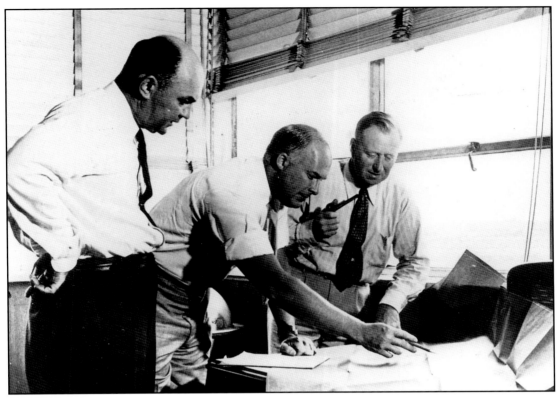

*The three Grumman founders (left to right): Vice President Jake Swirbul, Vice President Bill Schwendler, and President LeRoy Grumman showing their close working relationship. Jake and Roy had their desks in one office facing each other for making decisions much faster than having separate offices. (Corwin H. Meyer Collection)*

Northrop, another non-union company. Mr. Grumman's philosophy, therefore, could easily permeate all Grumman personnel with his strong dedication to make only the best carrier aircraft.

President Leon A. "Jake" Swirbul received his first aeronautical experience as an Air Corps inspector in the Thomas Morse Aircraft Company during World War I. He then went to the Loening Aircraft Company and rose from chief inspector to shop superintendent. That is where he learned his basic manufacturing conviction that the shop workers were the most important group to keep satisfied. He knew that the quantity and quality of their work was what made the corporation profitable. With Jake's Navy background, his ease with people from shop sweepers

to admirals, and his manufacturing accomplishments, it was natural that he and Roy Grumman became the real sales department of the corporation to the Navy.

An example of Jake's understanding of people's needs was that in order to recruit the large number of women needed at the beginning of World War II, when men were all going into the military services, Jake set up a huge nursery for workers' children to be cared for while their mothers were occupied in all departments and in both shifts at Grumman. This was a first in the industry, and it was a great help in delivering Hellcats ahead of schedule throughout the war.

The third person of the Grumman triumvirate was William T. "Bill" Schwendler, who was chief engineer and who also came from Loening in 1930. Bill was a dedicated structural analyst who would rather have the aircraft a little overweight than under strength. He always added "the Schwendler 10 percent" to every design structure before it was finalized. Very early in their history, Grumman fighters were able to exist under more extreme carrier operations than other manufacturers' aircraft could tolerate. That meant that Grumman aircraft could fly without the additional maintenance required on other aircraft. Not only did the mechanics like that asset, but also the pilots soon named Grumman aircraft as being made by "The Grumman Ironworks." Pilots could overstress a Grumman fighter in many ways in combat operations and carrier landings and sleep very well back on the carrier that night. You will see many examples of the Grumman Ironworks during my flight-testing. I became a Schwendler advocate very early in my career during my first Navy demonstration in the F6F-3 Hellcat. And the fact that I am now 85 years of age shows that Bill had a great influence on my career.

We all remember Jake, Roy, and Bill giving out big, fat turkeys at Christmas time to every single employee. Jake knew most Grumman employees by their first names.

When I was Senior Vice President of the 23,000 people in Manufacturing Operations, Jake gave me a lesson, in one sentence, which I never forgot. He said, "Corky, if you don't personally make all of the 23,000 people who work in your departments feel part of a great team, they can easily find another manager called 'the Union' who will." Like Jake, I made weekly walks to have conversations throughout the many plants of my organization. I answered all questions asked and rewarded suggestions that were made. I'm proud to say that Grumman was still strongly non-union when I retired after 14 years as the manager of Product Operations: Manufacturing, Flight Test, Quality Control, and Procurement Departments.

Grumman and its associate-contractors Columbia Aircraft and General Motors lost only seven test pilots while delivering 46,971 commercial and military aircraft of 121 different designs and models. No other aircraft company ever came close to that fantastic safety record. Navy pilots set the highest kill-to-loss records of enemy aircraft in the 18,677 Grumman Wildcat and Hellcat fighters delivered during World War II.

Between Jake's production knowledge and communication skills, Roy Grumman's design and naval test pilot experience, and Bill Schwendler's structural talents, these three had all the necessary qualities to be successful. As a start-up corporation they became financially profitable only two years after they started in 1930, and they remained so throughout the entire 10 years of the Depression.

## The Small Picture – Flight-Test 1942

Let's get some flight-test definitions from the original test pilots. Orville Wright compared test flying to riding a spirited horse. "If you are looking for perfect safety you will do well to sit on a fence and watch the birds fly, but if you really wish to learn to fly you must mount the machine and become acquainted with its tricks by actual trial."

Wilbur Wright described the hazards even better. "The balance of the gliding or flying machine is simple in theory. It merely consists in causing the center of pressure (wing lift) to coincide with the center of gravity (aircraft weight). But in actual practice there seems to be an almost boundless incompatibility of temper which prevents their remaining peaceably together for a single instant, so the operator, who is in this case peacemaker, often suffers injury to himself while attempting to bring them together."

## Test-Pilot Hiring Requirements

Twenty-first century requirements for hiring an engineering test pilot are: passing a military physical, a minimum of 2,000 hours in your logbook, a previous flying career in the Army, Navy, Marines, or Air Force, a technical college degree, a graduate of a military test pilot's school, and combat training. It is preferable to be single, and after all the above time-consuming requirements are met, to be as young as possible.

When I was hired at Grumman as an experimental test pilot, my assets were very limited compared to today's requirements. My eyes could not pass the CAA physical's important eye exam test legally. I only had 423 commercial hours in my logbook, not even minimum flight experience, no military flight experience, no college degree, no test pilot school, and no combat knowledge. I was, however, single and 22 years of age. The only reasons I could find for Grumman to hire me were: the pressures of wartime, scarcity of all pilots, and the fact that the military and the airlines were grabbing every single pilot they could get their hands on. These six "no" and "not" demons in the list above would haunt me during my entire 36-year career at Grumman, especially after the end of World War II when veteran pilots came home. It only took 53 years before I was finally declared a "real" naval test pilot. In 1995 I was inducted into the Carrier Test Pilots Hall of Honor on the USS *Yorktown* Museum at Charleston, South Carolina.

There are two more assets a test pilot absolutely must have that are impossible to determine during the physical tests. They can only be found in his mind. He must have an unquenchable desire to make his total career as a test pilot. He needs to have a great curiosity and a desire to be the part of the team to find the secrets that the engineers, mechanics, and inspectors haven't been able to determine from their imaginations, calculations, wind tunnel, and ground tests. Many test pilots believe that they are the only ones in the company who put their lives on the line each time they climb into the cockpit and, therefore, are above the rest of the crowd. Fortunately, I was hired to be part of engineering. I worked with mechanics and inspectors from the beginning of my career. Most of them also had an excellent working relationship with engineering and Grumman's top test pilots in management.

The other requirement is judgment. Most test pilots, blocked with male egos, don't discover judgment early enough in their careers. They are unmoved by all of the messages from their previous flights in which the aircraft, the weather, and peer pressure can provide valuable lessons. They don't ask enough questions from experienced test pilots, mechanics, and engineers, which could provide them with missing pieces of the experimental flight-testing jigsaw puzzle.

If a test pilot does not react to strange noises and vibrations in flight and cannot determine what is wrong in his aircraft while it is still flyable, the only way to uncover the problem is to land ASAP and get the whole team working on it. I can remember several persistent test pilots who continued looking for answers in the air far too long and lost not only their lives but an irreplaceable test aircraft as well. You will soon read about the several times at the beginning of my career that I was almost one of those pilots.

There is a myth that all laypersons intuitively believe that a test pilot must have exceedingly rapid reflexes. This is only half right. They must additionally have the mental agility to think precisely under the emotions of emergency flight conditions. A wise test pilot once said, "A superior test pilot is one who uses his experience and planning to avoid situations that could be caused by his all-too-rapid reflex responses." In World War II many air forces had a strict cockpit test that blindfolded pilots had to pass. This required them to locate and actuate all the instruments and switches in the cockpit as fast as possible at the instructor's command. Passing this test made all too many pilots overconfident. They would actuate the wrong switch or handle under the pressures of actual emergency conditions. Actuating the wrong switch or handle was, and still is, the cause of many accidents.

I learned about this gospel just before I came to Grumman when I was practicing for my Multi-Engine Rating in a Lockheed 10A Electra. We had just attained 500 feet after takeoff and I was checking traffic when the instructor sneakily shut off the fuel from the left engine to simulate an engine failure. I zipped through my previously practiced single-engine procedure very precisely, or so I thought. When I finished I looked to my right to receive my instructor's praise. At that very instant the right engine quit to a resounding silence, shortly broken by laughter from the rear cabin's several pilot-observers. In my ego-driven haste I had rapidly but mistakenly turned the fuel selector valve from the "both" engines position to the "left" engine position that the instructor had just killed.

Because of the many necessary qualities that I didn't possess and the mistakes I made in training, the reader well might ask, "Where then did Corky get his specific test pilot education?" I started test fly-ing in 1942, four years before any military test pilot schools had opened in the United States. I received my schooling from on-the-job training in new and untested aircraft coupled with mentoring from several interested professional test pilots at Grumman. In hindsight it was a much more impressive learning process than a repetitive by-rote test pilot school using only proven aircraft and ground-bound instructors. Trust me, the many not-in-the-book lessons I encountered in my aerial school of very hard knocks will be clearly described in the following chapters.

Grumman test pilots had two other singular advantages. They could request that a fighter chase plane join them to observe maneuvers and check the aircraft externally in case of an emergency. For more critical flights, a test pilot could also request an amphibian aircraft to stand by in case of a bailout or the need to ditch the aircraft. Grumman test areas were either over the Long Island Sound or the Atlantic Ocean. Republic Aviation test pilots did not have this advantage, but they could, and did, call on our amphibians for several saves. When helicopters came into vogue, Grumman added one of them to the amphibian inventory for even faster pilot recovery. Grumman standby aircraft really gave Grumman test pilots a genuinely warm feeling that few other companies offered to their pilots.

The second advantage was their pioneering in structural flight-testing. I only had to perform two complete new aircraft structural demonstrations in the Hellcat with no stress instrumentation onboard. To do this I could make only one pullout and then had to land for a careful aircraft inspection between flights to be sure that I had not overstressed the aircraft. On the next flight I could then, with some hope, push the envelope to the next higher G-load increase.

To get more hangar space after receiving the XFF-1 contract they moved to the Curtiss airport in Valley Stream, Long Island, where they produced the Model A and B float and started the FF-1 production contracts. After their one-year contract expired they moved again to the Farmingdale plant to get more production space for their expanding fighter contracts. (Corwin H. Meyer Collection)

Grumman was first to have six-channel oscillograph stress instrumentation. This could tell the exact stress that had been put on various points of the aircraft but still only allowed one maximum stress point per flight. The final data had to be developed and printed on the ground before it was known that the next point could be safely performed. Soon, 12-, 32-channel and more oscillograph channels did a much better job. But only after Grumman became the first to telemeter finalized data to the ground station from the aircraft were we able to do more pullouts per flight. The engineer on the ground could instantly read out the stress of the last pullout and check it with previous ground tests. This took only seconds. Pullouts could follow as long as the pilot could tolerate the Gs. Anti-G suits, which became available in late 1944, made the pilot's physical tolerance much greater. Grumman was also first in obtaining these suits from the Navy for their pilots.

## The Real Meaning of Extra-Hazard

Before leaving Wilbur and Orville's simple definitions of flight-testing, I have a story which may better explain this subject to the reader. For extra-hazard flight-tests like first flights, spins, Navy-required flight envelope structural expansion, and carrier landing maximum structural flight-tests, selected pilots were offered an extra-hazard bonus to perform them.

After completing my first difficult Navy demonstration in the Hellcat, I asked Bob Hall for an increase in my bonus. I reasoned that I had to perform twice as many dives and pullouts than originally planned; therefore, I should receive double the original bonus. The more I pleaded my case the more he smiled at me. He then ended the discussion by slowly saying, "I don't think you were under any more extra-hazard, Corky. You're standing right here in front of me now." That was the end of the discussion, with laughter emanating from both of us.

Many years later he confessed he had tried the same ploy on Mr. Grumman and received the same answer. Several years later as Director of Flight Test I took pleasure in answering the same question from several other hopeful test pilots with his same words.

## Summary

I'm thankful for all of the above and for many other reasons that my short but torturous and wandering path led me to Grumman for a 36-year career as a crazy test pilot.

Chapter 5

# The Longest Five Minutes of My Life!

## 10 October 1943

The Grumman TBF Avenger received the nickname "Turkey" by its squadron pilots very early in its operational history. Some have said that it looked like a turkey when approaching for landing because of its gangly long-span wing, flaps, and landing gear. It surely did look the part. Others have said that it received that derogatory nickname because of its unfortunate combat record during its first operational year. The first torpedo runs were made without fighter cover, with torpedoes that had such high failure rates that very few hits were successful until service-reworked torpedoes became available in 1943. After it began to

*Two beautiful restorations of the Grumman/General Motors TBM-3Es flying over Midland, Texas, in October 1999. Number 309 is owned by the Rocky Mountain Wing of the Commemorative Air Force (formerly the Confederate Air Force) and flown by pilot Bob Thompson. Number 54 in the background is from the Cavanaugh Museum and flown by pilot Doug Jeanes. Note that the number 54 has three 5-inch HVAR rockets under its wing. (Paul Koselka of the Commemorative Air Force)*

show its mettle the nickname "Turkey" took on a much more affectionate tone. Whatever it was, the name stuck with all pilots that flew it because it again demonstrated the Grumman Ironworks' reliability and strength in combat known by Navy pilots throughout World War II. Until the U.S. Navy retired the Avenger in 1956, it had the longest continuous use of any combat aircraft in Navy inventory up to that time.

## The U.S. Navy Torpedo Disaster

The many major torpedo problems at the beginning of World War II deserve relating because of the unbelievably large and unnecessary loss of life and material that they caused. The lack of fighter cover for torpedo aircraft was bad enough but the problems with the torpedoes for the first two years of World War II deserve

relating. Starting in 1933 the Japanese admirals diligently studied aerial, submarine, and surface ship torpedo launch tactic developments from the Americans, English, French, German, and Italian navies in order to learn from the experiences of others. They also purchased torpedoes and torpedo-carrying aircraft from these countries to gain the latest first-hand practical experience as rapidly as possible.

They had little to learn from the U.S. Navy because the Bureau of Naval Ordnance had stopped torpedo research and development programs in 1926 when the money from World War I ran out. The arrogant U.S.N. Ordnance personnel continued to blame the operational Navy for their low rate of hits until late 1943, when technicians in Hawaii performed detailed tests, which proved that all torpedoes delivered so far had three basic problems that were causing their abysmal lack of

*Torpedo launches by three Avengers. The first two have completed their launches and are departing the area as quickly as possible. With the advent of the Ring-Tailed torpedoes, launches could be made from 800-feet altitudes and speeds of up to 280 knots. This was a very great evasive action improvement over the early torpedoes that could not be launched over 100-feet altitudes and 100 knots. (Northrop Grumman History Center)*

hits. These tests were performed with 100 torpedoes against an undersea rock formation in Hawaii. They determined that torpedoes were running between 11 to 20 feet deeper than the depth they were set for, smashed 85 percent of the detonators against the target without exploding the torpedo charge, and that their proximity fuses were not working at all. These problems had previously caused the submarine, surface, and air launches to be made closer and closer to the targets to try to get hits. In doing so they became easier targets for the Japanese gunners. After the Hawaiian report got back to the Commander of Naval Operations a fabulous house cleaning was performed and torpedo hits soon increased from 20 to 85 percent.

In mid-1939 the Japanese Navy had determined that a large wooden stabilizer attached to the normal water fins of the torpedo would not only allow higher aerial launch altitudes and speeds but would also greatly reduce the excessive depths that torpedoes usually descended below the surface before they ascended to their proper cruise depth of approximately 15 feet. These fins would break off after the torpedo hit the water. Further improved Mod II oxygen-fueled, 24-inch Japanese torpedoes not only had twice the performance of U.S. torpedoes but they achieved 82 percent hits using 180-mph launch speeds from 33-feet altitudes. Kagoshima Bay had been selected for training because it was exactly the depth of Pearl Harbor at 40 feet. The final batch of Mod II torpedoes was delivered to the Japanese Pearl Harbor Task Force just 13 days prior to leaving for the infamous attack.

At the beginning of the war, only 100 of the U.S. Navy's 1935-design Douglas TBD torpedo bombers were available. They had to release torpedoes below 80-feet altitude, no faster than 100 mph or further than 1,000 yards from the target. This presented an awesome target for Japanese gunners. Sixty-one of the 100 TBD Devastators in Navy inventory were lost in the battles of the Coral Sea and Midway. The Avenger made its combat debut at Midway in June 1942. It had more than twice the horsepower, bomb load, range, and speed of the Devastator. Very few torpedo aircraft or dive-bombers were lost to enemy aircraft after the debut of the Grumman Hellcat fighter for protection in 1943.

To make matters even worse, training for torpedo pilots was almost non-existent. Bill Bedel, an Avenger pilot who later became a Grumman test pilot, trained during 1943 and told me that he dropped only two un-powered cement-filled torpedoes and one powered, but inert, practice torpedo to complete his training. None of these drops was checked against an aiming point. He also said that the torpedo sight in the cockpit was so complex and thus misunderstood by the pilots that it was seldom used for aiming.

Just before the attack on Pearl Harbor, the Commander of Naval Operations, Admiral Ingersoll, wrote a memorandum from Washington to all naval districts stating that a minimum depth of 75 feet was still required for a successful aerial torpedo launch. This 75-foot depth was required because it was necessary to complete the first steep plunge into the water from the 150-mph speeds and the 100-foot altitudes of an aerial torpedo launch. The torpedo then rose to a run-in depth of 10 to 15 feet so that it would not go under the target ship. Prior to World War II, torpedoes of all nations had been used only in open-ocean battles between ships.

After reading the memorandum, Admiral Kimmel, the Commander of the Pacific Fleet at Pearl Harbor, also stated, "Aerial torpedo attacks could not be used in Pearl Harbor. Its 40-foot depth was too shallow." If we couldn't launch torpedoes in Pearl Harbor, nobody could!

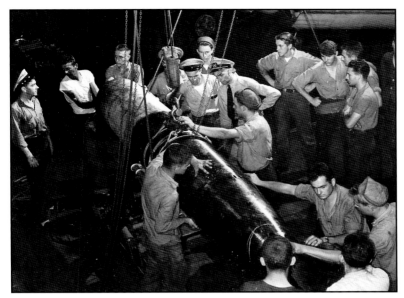

An instruction course in the checkout, handling, and installation of 1,300-lb Mark III torpedoes on the carrier hangar deck early in the war. The crew is just about to lower the torpedo onto the dolly to be run under the bomb bay of the Avenger in the foreground. It will then be hoisted up and secured into the torpedo racks in the bomb bay. (Corwin H. Meyer via Northrop Grumman History Center)

It was not until the middle of 1944 that Caltech came up with many of the same fixes to our Navy torpedoes that the Japanese had used in training for about a year prior to Pearl Harbor.

Specifically, Caltech's Ring-Tailed torpedo modified a Mark 13-1A by wrapping and welding a 10-inch band around the fins. This stabilized it both in flight and under water and prevented damage to the controls, which allowed it to hit the water safely at much higher speeds. On 4 August 1944, 16 VT-13 Avengers, using this torpedo modification for the first time, sank a group of six destroyer-protected Japanese transports without losing an aircraft. This was a great ending for a sad unpreparedness story.

## Gestation of the Grumman TBF-1 Avenger

Grumman's TBF-1 proposal won the March 1939 Navy competition over 13 contenders for a new torpedo bomber to supplant the few Douglas TBD Devastators, which had been the mainstay of Navy torpedo squadrons since 1937. Newer production engines with twice the horsepower of the Devastator would soon make the TBD obsolete. As an insurance policy, and with possible war on the horizon, the Navy also awarded a "just-in-case" second contract to Chance Vought's TBU-1 proposal, which had a predicted 30-mph higher speed than the Avenger.

The XTBF-1 had two major innovations, which were not in Grumman's previous experience. It was their first aircraft with a hydraulic system that operated the landing gear, flaps, wing fold, bomb bay doors, cowl, and oil cooler flaps. It also had an industry-first, electric-powered rear gun turret. The Navy was not concerned, however, probably because of Grumman's prior 10-year on-schedule delivery reputation.

Besides those problems, all of Grumman's plants were working at full capacity producing Wildcats, Widgeons, and Goose aircraft for the Navy. For further insurance, Grumman had asked for and was granted two experimental prototypes so that the financial fiasco caused by their single Army Air Corps XP-50 prototype crash just a year before would not present a similar cancellation.

## A Very Contrary Bird Appears for Its First Flight

The XTBF-1 prototype was rolled out for its first flight on 7 August 1941, a record one year after the receipt of the contract. Bob Hall, the assistant chief engineer for experimental aircraft and also the chief experimental test pilot, looked forward to a reasonably normal first flight. He always made one short liftoff and immediate landing prior to a first flight to check that the aircraft's center of gravity was in the correct position to insure that satisfactory takeoff and landing characteristics would be achievable before flying to altitude.

He was greatly surprised to note on his first and only liftoff that he required full forward stick immediately after leaving the ground in order not to stall and crash. Fifty pounds of ballast was removed from the as-yet undelivered Emmerson Electric aft .50-caliber gun turret position. The next day his first liftoff showed that the aircraft was still far too tail heavy, so it was decided that the engine mount needed a 4-inch extension to further compensate for the newer weight estimate of the turret. Its first real flight came late the next day on 9 August 1941. This flight showed even more serious engineering miscalculations, which needed immediate redesigns. The oil cooling system indicated temperatures near the limit at cruising power with the oil cooler doors fully open. Directional stability showed a strong, rapid, negative force reversal when full rudder was applied in either direction. The rudder forces were much too light, making them disproportionate to the proper ratio with the elevator and aileron forces. It was a real back-to-the-drawing-board first flight. He told me that this was probably the most technically embarrassing first flight he had ever made.

A large dorsal fin was installed on the rear fuselage just ahead of the fin. The fin height was increased eight inches to attain the needed directional stability. A negative-balance tab was designed into the rudder to increase its pedal forces, and a much bigger oil cooler was installed. The fixes for these problems were not only needed for the prototype but also for the many production TBFs now in Grumman's Plant 2 Avenger assembly line. After a few more flights to make further flight adjustments, Bob turned his test flying duties over to test pilot Hobert "Bill" Cook and flight test engineer Gordon Isreal, who recorded flight data.

Detailed stability, control, engine cooling, performance, and handling tests continued at full speed. During a full-power climb on 18 November 1941, Bill Cook noted smoke increasing rapidly into the cockpit. It was later determined to be an electrical fire in the bomb bay area. He promptly commanded Gordon Isreal to bail out and immediately followed him. The aircraft crashed and burned in a non-populated scrub-pine area near Brentwood, New York, only 18 miles east of the Grumman plant. The Turkey was telling us something about full-power climbs.

Coincidentally, Grumman had picked a fateful date for an open house for all Grumman families to show off the new Plant 2 and the TBF's rapidly expanding production line on 7 December 1941. When Grumman management heard the Pearl Harbor news on the radio, the party was cancelled without telling the thousands of employees the reason. With the Japanese attack of such epic proportions management feared that, had they been told, pandemonium might well have followed while the crowd was driving home.

The construction of the second prototype was well along and it made its first flight on 19 December 1941, only three weeks after the crash.

To meet the Navy's Avenger contract commitment, the first production TBF-1 flew on 30 December 1941, and by the end of 1942 Plant 2 had delivered 646 Avengers to meet the rapid carrier operational squadron build-up schedule. Grumman was also delivering Hellcats, Wildcats, JRF Gooses, and J2F Widgeon amphibians. In contrast, and after many troublesome design problems from two production facilities working at full blast, only 180 of the Navy's second choice Vought TBU aircraft had been delivered, but none saw combat. Because of massive schedule delays the Navy soon cancelled the contract.

Avenger production at Grumman ended in 1943 after delivering 2,293 Avengers in just two years. In order to make room for priority Hellcat production in Plant 2, all Avenger production was transferred to the General Motors automobile plant in Trenton, New Jersey, by December 1943. General Motors geared up much more rapidly than either Grumman or the Navy believed possible, and together with Grumman they both delivered a total of 9,839 Avengers before the war ended.

On 18 November, only eight days after I came to Grumman, I made my first TBF-1 flight in BuNo 00379, the seventh production "Dog Ship" aircraft. It was so named because it remained at the plant for testing the many equipment and military load changes requested by the Navy. This was a much more interesting task for me than flying routine production-line test aircraft. I also began my on-the-job test pilot training with engineering, trying to solve the many challenges the Navy and we found during the first year of TBF-1 deliveries.

In late 1942 the operational gross weight of the TBF-1 was rapidly increasing and more power was sorely needed to shorten its takeoff distance on carriers. Catapults had yet to be installed on many carriers, thus free-deck launch take-offs required almost half of the deck length. To solve this problem the Navy asked Grumman to install the experimental 1,900-hp Curtiss-Wright R-2600-20 engine in the XTBF-3E prototype. This required a complete Navy re-demonstration by Grumman prior to its introduction into the General Motors production line. Every new engine has problems, but this engine

*Number seven production Grumman TBF-1 (BuNo 00379) after delivery to the Navy. I flew this specific aircraft over 20 hours, evaluating many performance and cooling changes to try to get more speed prior to its delivery. None of the changes were big enough to improve the performance as much as 200 horsepower increase did in the engine change to the XTBF-3. It was a great training program for me both in working with the engineering department and also in learning the many elusive vagaries of flight-testing. (Northrop Grumman History Center)*

*The first of two experimental XTBF-3s (BuNo 124141) photographed between the first and second engine failures. You can see that Grumman engineering finally decided to cure the hot engine and oil temperature problem. There are now engine cooling flaps 270 degrees around the cowling in place of the two small ones on the upper cowl of the TBF-1 series. There is also a separate larger oil cooler duct on the lower cowl. In spite of the engine running considerably cooler in these two departments, it managed to destroy itself for me in three different ways during full-power climbs. (Northrop Grumman History Center)*

was to demonstrate whoppers! The author had been selected by Bob Hall to make this demonstration to determine exactly what the problems were. The fun soon began.

On my first test flight I was making a full-power climb when I heard one exceptionally loud BANG from the engine while climbing through to 8,100 feet. The engine immediately lost all power. After getting over that great disturbance, I turned back to the airport for an exciting glider-type landing. I didn't realize at the time that I was soon to become quite proficient at this maneuver.

Inspection determined that the entire supercharger rotor had sheared from the engine drive shaft and the trash from this damage had completely plugged up the engine air-intake duct. With no air, the engine quit, thus providing me the gift of my first Curtiss-Wright dead-stick landing. Inspection also found that the abrupt stoppage of the engine had twisted the engine mount. It and much of the firewall

structure had to be replaced. My logbook shows that it took 46 days to receive another engine from Curtiss-Wright.

During my second flight in a full-power climb, the engine power became erratic, making small power changes without any motion of the throttle. As they were only small changes, I decided to continue. The engine began running rougher and rougher. Reducing power and checking magnetos and all gauges did not eliminate these disturbing events. I then fully retarded the throttle and started my letdown from over 18,000 feet to return ASAP to Grumman. At 4,200 feet the engine completely gave up the ghost. A second successful Curtiss-Wright-sponsored dead-engine landing now graced my logbook.

This engine was found to have the wrong carburetor, which caused that rapid incompatibility as the climb progressed. I began to think that Curtiss-Wright was becoming user-unfriendly. The best was yet to come.

A test pilot learns early in his career that an aircraft talks to him. If he didn't listen most attentively, as I didn't, it could soon get quite unfriendly. He also learned that the safest place to test a recalcitrant engine is on the ground.

Fifty-two days later a new and supposedly flight-tested Curtiss-Wright engine was installed on the XTBF-3 prototype. My mechanic had been bugging me for days to take him for a ride on the next test flight. I never liked to do this, as I didn't want the responsibility for another person in an experimental aircraft to panic along with me if anything went wrong. After the first two engine failures I really didn't want anyone aboard, but I stupidly gave in to his persistence. This was the first and the last time I made that mistake.

Bennie strapped himself in the bombardier's seat in the rear of the aircraft and we took off for a third try to, hopefully, complete a full-power climb. Just after the wheels had retracted and as we cleared the boundary of the runway, another Curtiss-Wright-furnished "boom!" jolted the aircraft and engine power deteriorated immediately from 1,900 horsepower to less than 300 (I was told later), still at full throttle. This is what a test pilot fears more than anything else, especially when the village of Bethpage is located directly ahead. The time-proven maxim after a very low altitude power failure immediately after takeoff is to go straight ahead and land, trees notwithstanding, but *not* into homes.

I didn't have to make up my mind that the shortest way to bypass Bethpage was to make a left turn and hope that the engine didn't quit entirely. I thought that turn I made was the most gentle and shallow turn I had ever performed in order to prevent a possible stall-spin accident. Because my airspeed was only 11 mph over the 77-mph stall speed for my takeoff weight, I was most thankful for the lower drag of my now fully retracted landing gear. The increased drag of my left turn dropped my airspeed a few MPH so I decreased my angle of bank ever so slightly. The intuitively powerful but fatal urge with a disabled engine is to turn as fast as possible to get to a safe crash landing area. But that is only a path leading to a stall-spin fatality.

Smoke was now beginning to appear over the wing right next to the cockpit. Also seeing this, Bennie shouted on the interphone that I should quit playing around and get the aircraft on the ground ASAP! I told him to shut up so loudly that people on the ground could have heard me without a radio. I would have killed him if I could have gotten to him.

I still have this stark mental, slow-motion image of the many small white homes, tree-lined streets, and several flag-poles of Bethpage all too slowly dragging by, practically scraping the belly of my aircraft. It seemed like I was in a bad dream slowly flying over the entire five boroughs of New York City at only 25 feet above their roofs.

I then called the tower to ask if they saw any smoke. They said that I was behind trees and they couldn't see me. I really needed to know. I decided to climb a few feet very, very slowly to lose as little airspeed as possible and hope to provide them a clear view of my abysmal situation. After slowly climbing, the tower said that they saw a little smoke under the belly. My worries now had something else to ponder.

The engine was running very rough but still holding its very meager power. By this time I noted that I had completed the 180-degree turn and was approaching the Bethpage State Park golf course. I began to feel a little better about the future because I could now see several long fairways ahead. Although the ground was hilly and there were lines of tall trees between each of the very narrow links, they looked great to me.

Bennie started to babble again, so I used some very strong four-letter words, which finally shut him up for good. By this time the smoke was getting quite dense and oil had completely smeared my windshield, with much of it coming into my open canopy and smearing my goggles. Navy procedure was to make all takeoffs and landings with the canopy open for quick exits for cases just like this. The smoke fortunately stayed outside the cockpit. The tower now reported that much more smoke was coming from the engine but was passing under the wing. Bennie later told me that he couldn't see out of his windows and smoke was pouring into the rear cabin. I'm sure I, too, would have used his plaintive, beseeching shouts if I had been in his smoking dungeon of futility.

Since the engine was still running, albeit disobediently, and I was maintaining the airspeed barely above the stalling speed, I elected to continue another careful 180-degree turn for a very short landing approach back at Grumman. The tower then happily reported that although the smoke was getting thicker, they had not noted any fire yet. In the last 90 degrees of our turn, they called "fire." As I was only 25 seconds or so away from touchdown, I continued the approach hopefully but without moving a muscle to retard the throttle. At this point I didn't want to irritate *anything* in the aircraft.

During the flaps-up landing rollout at about 60 mph, Bennie decided that his ride was over. He bailed out of the rear door onto the runway totally unbeknownst to me. The fire truck soon put out the fire. I stopped shaking about two hours later. Bennie was bruised and scraped plenty but came back to work about a week later. He never asked me for another ride. I think that he received my several lucid messages loud and clear. In

hindsight I realized that my angry bout with Bennie provided me with a sorely needed life-saving rush of adrenaline that kept me able to hold this sick aircraft in the air for as long as my strength, talents, and luck allowed.

Inspection showed that a very small part, an exhaust valve lock ring, had broken and the engine had swallowed the valve. This pushed the number 11 cylinder head completely off and punched it through the cowling. This opened the carburetor intake manifold pressure to the atmosphere and allowed very little of the gas mixture into the engine, thus greatly reducing the power available. The escaping exhaust gases also finally burned completely through a fuel line during final approach, which caused the fire. Although I had no more engine failures that close to the ground during my 36-year test piloting career, I purposely went way out of my way to avoid untried Curtiss-Wright products.

After he had inspected the engine, the Curtiss-Wright service representative figured that I shouldn't have had enough power to taxi the aircraft, let alone to fly it. By that time I had zero interest in their opinions. An old flight-test pilot axiom states clearly; the altitude above you, the runway behind you, fuel in the tank truck, and "what might have happened" may be ardent dreams but are useless for any pilot.

We belatedly learned that all of the engines Curtiss-Wright had previously sent us were experimental engines and none had yet performed the Navy-required 100-hour full-throttle ground demonstrations, or had been flight-tested. This consisted of a 100-hour full-power test from the ground to the service ceiling in an altitude chamber and then repeated in their flight-test aircraft. I was working for them without receiving their test pilot bonus. Three days later we received the first production engine that had completed

Manpower winch-loading of a 500-lb bomb into the bomb bay of the TBF-1 on shipboard. Because of the many problems with torpedoes until August 1944, the TBF-1 was used as a glide bomber in all theaters of the Pacific. It could not only carry a somewhat greater poundage of bombs than the Dauntless, but it could also carry a much larger variety of ordnance in the many bomb shackle variations possible in its bomb bay as well as 5-inch HVAR rockets on its six wing racks. (Northrop Grumman History Center)

its 100-hour full-power tests. After its installation I checked its logbooks and completed a 15-minute, full-power test run on this "new" engine. The XTBF-3 and I then concluded all the Navy contractor flight demonstrations: performance, structural, and handling qualities without any further loud noises or regurgitations. I then delivered the XTBF-3 to the General Motors test-site at Trenton, New Jersey, for a much smoother introduction to the Curtiss-Wright R-2600-20 power plants. The R-2600-20

In service with the French Aeronautique Navale flotilla 4F, 6F, and 9F, this pair of TBM-3E and TBM-3W Avengers flew as submarine Hunter-Killer teams from 1951 to 1961. They also participated in the French Suez conflict from October to November 1956 from the three French carriers Arromanches, Bois Belleau, and Lafayette. (French Army of the Air)

proved to be a very reliable engine in 7,546 TBM-3Es and in two other variants that GM finally delivered to the Navy prior to the end of hostilities.

The U.S. Navy, Grumman, and General Motors were a fabulous team. Together we made 9,871 Avengers and 7,904 Wildcats totaling 17,775 fighting combat aircraft that were used both by the U.S. Navy and Marine Corps from the very beginning of the war to many years beyond V-J Day.

Call it "Turkey" or Avenger... its perverse gestation was soon forgotten by the thousands of pilots in several hundred squadrons who flew Grumman Ironworks "Turkeys" very successfully for seven nations in glide bombing, anti-shipping, mine-laying, early warning, shore patrol, and anti-submarine missions in worldwide combat. The last one was finally retired in 1968. The Avenger was credited with having the longest continuous military life of any Navy combat aircraft up to that time. After the war the new Japanese Air Force's first combat aircraft request was for the "Turkey."

Chapter 6

# Up Is Not Always Easier

## 12 to 23 October 1943

A very good test pilot friend of mine wrote a book of his experiences entitled, *Living It Up*. If I were to write another book, I think I might entitle it, *Living It Down*. Although fuel in the tanks is limited, gravity is forever.

On 27 February 1943, after flying with Grumman for only four-and-a-half months, I had graduated from doing production test flying in Wildcats, Avengers, Widgeons, and Goose amphibians. I had made a few flights in the XF6F-3 Hellcat doing some modest but not very exciting experimental tests. My leaders were pleased enough so that I was taken out of the production phase of test flying for the rest of my career. I would only go back to production to fly special aircraft that had new items on them or those that were having trouble meeting the production criteria. I was now a full-time experimental test pilot.

One of the many new areas of the Hellcat performance envelope that had not been tested before was a climb to service ceiling, which was calculated to be about 39,000 feet. Previously we had done our entire test flying on the Hellcat below 30,000 feet to determine the altitude of its best high-speed level flight performance, which proved to be 25,800 feet. But no test pilot had flown over 30,000 feet altitude because of the special ground preparation necessary to eliminate the possibility of

very painful "bends" caused by excessive nitrogen bubbles expanding in arm and leg joints above that altitude.

## Pre-Oxygenation Begins With Hard Work

I had gone to the Navy low-pressure chamber for simulated high-altitude pressure-breathing oxygen training for flights above 40,000 feet. I had learned much about the problems that compounded oxygen failure at various altitudes up to 35,000 feet. I knew very well that one had only five to ten seconds of consciousness if the oxygen system failed above 35,000 feet and that one couldn't remain above 37,000 feet for more than a few minutes without pressure breathing masks, which Grumman did not have at that time. So I knew some of the gremlins that lurked in the cockpit waiting for me if I were not exceedingly diligent in my use and attention to the oxygen system above altitudes that I had previously flown to.

In order to get as much of the nitrogen as possible out of the leg and arm joints prior to a test flight, pilots were supposed to pedal a stationary exercise bicycle for a half hour breathing 100-percent pure oxygen and then get into the aircraft without missing a beat of continuous oxygen. I was assisted by others in helping me dress for the high-altitude flight, walking into the aircraft, which had the engine running, strap in, and after being transferred to the aircraft oxygen system, make the flight. Normally, on an altitude flight under 25,000 feet, we would strap on the mask in flight and start oxygen breathing at about 10,000 to 15,000 feet. Grumman did not educate me as well on the bicycle act, as you will soon see.

Meanwhile I got on the bicycle and enthusiastically started "riding" it by turning the rear wheel at about a 15-mph rate with the rear wheel off the ground. It seemed to me that the bicycle was going up a hill with a load that seemed to be dragging on the pedaling system considerably but if that was the way it was ordained... so be it. After I was on the bicycle for a few minutes my assistant went about his other jobs and I was left alone for the next 25 minutes. I started sweating a little at the beginning and then profusely at the end. Again, I had faith that this was a totally necessary aspect for this horrendous first climb to service ceiling in the newest fighter in Grumman's stable. Also, as the pedaling progressed, I began to feel quite a euphoria, which seemed as if I had been given a very dry martini or two through the oxygen tube. But, if that was the way all experimental test pilots did it, who was I to question their sagacity?

My assistant came back to dress me while I was still breathing 100 percent oxygen. He commented on my unusual amount of sweating but seemed to take it in stride. He then followed me with the portable oxygen system like a knight's personal lance bearer and lifted me into the running aircraft, strapped me in, and re-connected my mask to the aircraft's oxygen system. By this time I felt that we had a great cocktail party going on and I wondered just why they paid experimental test pilots to have this much fun. It was nasty work but some slob had to do it!

## The Happy-Hour Flight Begins

For a service ceiling attempt and to really test the oil cooling system over 30,000 feet, it was necessary to start the takeoff with oil at a much higher temperature than normal. It should then normalize in the climb. Rags were stuffed in the duct behind the oil cooler for this purpose and were removed by a mechanic just before I took off with the oil temperature at the limit. I was now cleared to go into the service ceiling battle with a much-too-happy rider on a soon-to-be balky steed.

The takeoff was normal and as I had to manually dial a selector switch and read out 32 engine temperatures continuously during the climb, I went to work concentrating on that chore immediately after leaving the

*Forty-four F6F-5s waiting for delivery during the peak month of Hellcat deliveries in March 1944 when 640 Hellcats and 85 other aircraft including F7F-1s were also delivered. This broke the record of 610 P-51s delivered by North American Aviation in February 1944 and set an all-time U.S. record of aircraft deliveries for World War II. The picture shows only two days' worth of Hellcats produced! (Northrop Grumman History Center via Corwin H. Meyer)*

ground. The oil temperature came back dutifully to its normal reading shortly after takeoff. I read off a stream of numbers in a very precise manner without taking my hand off of the mike button until the Hellcat's climb rate began to slow noticeably at about 18,000 feet. At 19,000 feet, still with full power, my 2,000-hp Hellcat stopped climbing. I looked around the cockpit at other gauges that I had not taken into consideration in the pandemonium of reading the engine instrumentation and sheepishly noted that I had not retracted the landing gear after takeoff! That observation sobered me to the point of distress knowing that I had really goofed on an important flight that had required so much preparation by so many people. It wasn't a taxi accident but it was much too close to

that kind of pilot error ignominy. I tried to salve my conscience by thinking that at least we now knew the service ceiling with the landing gear extended. No one, however, seemed to be vitally interested in the data of my newly set record.

With my tail between my legs, I so notified the engineering tower people that had been transcribing the data and came home to a meal of crow that was most hard to digest for a 22-year-old newly created experimental test pilot who had just blown his first important flight. The tower chided me that they saw the landing gear down but couldn't get a word in edgewise on the radio because I was spewing out data continuously on the flight-test channel from the time the wheels left the ground until I had disappeared in the climb.

The author flying the second production F6F-3 BuNo 04776 in February 1943, just before the climb to service ceiling fiasco with Pratt & Whitney began with my three partial glider flights because of engine failures. This aircraft was painted light blue on the topside and gray on the underside. They were only painted this way for a short time when they were then painted dark blue on the topsides. This aircraft has the original gun fairings, which were only on the first very few aircraft because they prevented gun gasses from leaving the ammunition compartment causing a possibility of explosion. (Northrop Grumman History Center via Corwin H. Meyer)

After the shards of shattered ego had been swept aside I asked the chief test pilot, who had done such pre-oxygenation before in service ceiling climbs of the Wildcat, just why I was on a simulated drunken binge during the first part of the flight after sweating so profusely. He said that I shouldn't have sweated at all because there was a motor that was supposed to drive the pedaled wheel of the bicycle and I wasn't supposed to do any work during my half hour of "riding" the bicycle. The electric motor was supposed to rotate my legs on the pedals! Everybody assumed that I knew to switch the motor on. I learned then and there the word "assume" really does make an "ass out of U and me." Because of my pedaling efforts I had used about 10 times the oxygen I should have consumed and thus had a real hyper-oxygenation drunk going on during the process. It is a wonder that I got anything right on that flight.

The next day, with the motor of the bicycle electrically operating and running my legs instead of vice-versa, all went soberingly well and the wheels of the Hellcat were duly retracted at the proper time. The flight went smoothly through 28,000 feet altitude where I had been many times. But as the aircraft continued to climb I became a little nervous because I was venturing into the same unknown that taxpayers do when walking through the IRS doors for an audit. I noticed the oxygen pressure to be where it should be, the oxygen blinker winking on my every breath, and my fingernails maintaining their pink color, so I continued spouting cylinder head temperatures to report the engine parameter data. The aircraft went through 30,000 feet and progressed towards the stratosphere, which was then known to be exactly at 34,762 feet on a standard day. I was not to invade the stratosphere as easily as Caesar crossed the Rubicon. I passed 31,000 feet still reeling out the engine data. Thirty-two thousand feet came and went. I was breathing less easily. However, as the sky was not turning black as it was supposed to do, I did take a short glimpse outside the cockpit to see if I could see the horizon and prove to myself that the world really was round. It was flat, sad to say, so I went back to the desultory work of continuous data transmissions to the ground crew. The engine and all the parameters were in their proper order and I was feeling that this stratosphere thing was grossly overdone. My flight in this terrific Grumman Hellcat was to be a piece of cake; however, my dream didn't last long.

## I Wasn't Finished Yet, But the Engine Was

At exactly 32,640 feet altitude the engine quit, as though someone turned the ignition switch off, without one belch, backfire, or even a bit of smoke to clue me of its imminent demise. That beautiful noise of the 2,000 horses in the front became startlingly quiet and the aircraft turned into an inexorably heavy glider descending as surely as a barn-bound horse. When I finally came to my senses from my recent decapitated reverie I informed the ground station of my plight and began working to get the engine running any way I could. ASAP was not going to be fast enough for this unhappy pilot.

The reason for my sense of haste was because of the engine-out fiasco I had performed weeks before in a Wildcat landing on our icy runway. The subsequent vertical ground loop coming to a stop with the aircraft upside-down had not quite left my mind. Ice in a carburetor combined with an icy runway is not as palatable as ice in a drink. The Avenger's three engine failures were also still on my mind.

I quickly checked the three fuel tanks for quantity and found fuel feeding from a full tank and the fuel flow at the correct pressure and amount. I looked outside of the aircraft to see if there was any smoke, fire, or oil visible, which there wasn't, so I then started to assemble my wits about me as this quiet engine occurrence was now getting all too repetitive.

## A Very Recalcitrant Engine

Fortunately, the person at the ground radio station was a former test pilot, and he knew that I was way too busy to converse with anyone while trying to sort out another engine stoppage.

I tried cycling the magneto switch—nothing happened. I tried to put the engine into a lower supercharger selection to take the load from the now defunct internal combustion of the fuel and nothing happened. By this time I was down to 29,000 feet and pointing towards the Grumman airport just in case an engine-off landing was to be my fate again. As my altitude decreased, my frigid anguish increased, as noisy results were not forthcoming. I then reduced the throttle with no restart of the engine. By this time I was down to 24,000 feet and starting to get a little upset with Pratt & Whitney and their well-known "Reliability and Dependability" logo attached to the oil sump on the front of the engine. Yesterday's sweating on the bicycle was penny-ante stuff now. I then reduced the propeller revolutions from the full power setting to a much lower cruise setting and still quiet reigned supreme. Next I started calling out my altitude, heading, and estimated distance back to Grumman and described what little effect I was having on the inexplicably speechless and uncooperative engine. The only thing that I could still think of was to reduce the mixture control from

*Seven four-plane divisions of F6F-3 Hellcats flying combat air patrol off one of the Phillipine islands in December 1943. To get a more extended range of time on station 150-gallon tanks became standard eqipment. Because of its vulnerability to gunfire it was dropped before entering combat. (Northrop Grumman History Center via Corwin H. Meyer)*

auto rich to auto lean. That only continued the silence.

Without any assistance from me, a soothing loud noise occurred at 17,000 feet and informed me that the engine had come to life. The cylinder head temperatures soon came back up the scale to normal readings with their newly found combustion. I could not have been happier if I had been given half of the king's realm and his svelte princess's hand in marriage. I then cautiously moved the throttle and propeller controls to increased power settings and the engine ran very rough, but it ran! I was then at about 15,000 feet and, although the engine was doing rough duty, I was totally out of steam. As I continued descending the engine became smoother, but the magneto check for spark plug operations showed the RPM drop was still over 300 per side but should have been less than a 100-rpm drop. Suffice it to say, I was surely much happier with the new lifestyle my engine had taken on.

I decided that I would get on the ground as soon as possible to solve this perplexing problem with the P&W engine experts. With the engine now running, the ephemeral excitement of going to service ceiling had abruptly changed places with a new interest—to find out just why the engine had so unceremoniously quit.

## The "Experts" Are All Too Quiet

Once on the ground I went over the salient points of the flight many times, especially to tell them how the engine finally started by itself. I was met with an ominous quietude that made me feel that such problems as I had gone through were as perplexing to them as they were to me. It was most disconcerting. The Pratt & Whitney service-engineering representative said that he would inspect the engine, change the spark plugs, replace the "knocklulator" pins, etc., and everything

would be back in its normal order. He was no more convincing than the Curtiss-Wright representative had been and I was now an unbeliever, too.

Prior to flight the next day I was told that there was basically nothing wrong with the engine but that they had put new spark plugs in it, adjusted the carburetor, and had done several other things that didn't sound too much like they had found the culprit. It's like the doctor who, after giving you a zillion very costly tests, says, "Take two aspirin and call me in the morning if you don't feel better."

## My Second Glider Flight

The next day I did the pre-oxygenation procedure now like a veteran and started the climb to service ceiling with some hopes but greater doubts. Although the engine again quit at 32,640 feet altitude, exactly like the preceding day, it was not quite the shock to my sensibilities as it had been. I called the ground station and proceeded to lower the pressures inside of the cylinders by at once moving all the handles on the throttle quadrant to the rear like I did the day before but much, much faster. I had the engine heatedly combusting again slightly above 30,000 feet altitude. I was most pleased with my new skill at making a quiet engine come back to life sooner and I decided that I could get no further enlightenment by trying to climb above 32,640 feet again.

The meeting after the flight was all too reminiscent of the previous day, and I felt that the experts were still at zero visibility for solving the problem. I again found that 32,640 feet had a firm clutch on my engine's desire to function correctly.

The third time I tried to go to service ceiling the same inexplicable event happened to the engine at the exact same altitude and I was getting most disheartened with the "assistance" we were getting from

Pratt & Whitney. Our Grumman engine experts admitted that they were completely out of ideas and looked to P&W for the answers, which were not forthcoming. Fortunately for me I was learning to be much more familiar and somewhat calmer in investigating engine stoppages in the air.

Sometime that afternoon I recalled that Republic Aviation's P-47 Thunderbolt pilots three miles to the east of Grumman were climbing P-47s daily to 40,000 feet altitudes and they had the same R-2800 model Pratt & Whitney engines installed as the Hellcat. I wondered if they had had the same problem as I had experienced. I was soon to find out that all P&W engines that fly in the Long Island Sound area had the same problem with air density.

Over the phone I introduced myself to Republic's Chief Test Pilot Carl Bellinger, who quickly became a long-time friend when he immediately said, "Hell, Corky, you will never go over 32,600 feet until you install a pressurized ignition harness on the engine. The electrical energy to the spark plugs is shorting out because of the much lower atmospheric pressure at and above those altitudes." He further told me that the engines in the P-47 did the exact same thing at 32,000 feet before they obtained the pressurized harnesses. (I later found out the same P&W engine in the Vought F4U-1 Corsair still had the problem at Guadalcanal when operating above 32,000 feet and a famous Marine fighter pilot ended up in the ocean because he was unable to get his engine to come back to life as I had.) What an eye opener. That made much more sense than all of the piddling "fixes" that the Pratt people had supposedly been doing to our engine for the past three days.

Carl Bellinger then said that the Army Air Corps had a very high priority and had requisitioned all of the pressurized harnesses that Pratt & Whitney could

*The Republic Aviation Corporation P-47 production chief test pilot, Carl Bellinger, to whom the author made a blind phone call in 1943 to find out why my Hellcat engine was quitting on a regular basis at 32,600 feet. He not only told me of the same problem he had but how to solve it by making a phone call to the President of Pratt & Whitney Engine Corporation like they had to do shortly before my call to him. We became great friends for the rest of the many years of our test piloting careers. (Northrop Grumman History Center via Corwin H. Meyer)*

produce for the Republic P-47 because it was soon going into high-altitude combat in Europe. Pratt & Whitney reps at Grumman knew all the time that the unpressurized harness that we had on our engines would indeed quit at an altitude of 32,000 feet. They had been put in an untenable position by their management. I did feel sorry for them when I heard that, but someone in Pratt management should have taken us to one side when they knew that we were going for service ceiling tests in the Hellcat. Trust me, this event was to serve me well for motivating P&W many times in the future.

Needless to say, we got the Navy brass in Washington to get us one of the pressurized harnesses for our Hellcat and I made a most anti-climactic climb to an altitude of 39,455 feet, which was just what we had predicted for the Hellcat's service ceiling. I had it made again... or so I thought. All new production Hellcats had the new harnesses installed immediately.

## Pressurized Ignition Harness Explanation

The ignition harness on aircraft engines prior to 1942 was generally similar to ignition systems in automobiles. They were wires that transferred the spark energy from an electrical source, the magneto on an airplane engine or the generator on an automobile engine, via wires to the spark plugs in the engine cylinders. The wires had normal rubber-type insulation, which when combined with the earth's normal, sea-level atmospheric pressure kept the electricity from short-circuiting outside of the system before getting to the spark plugs. These systems had been satisfactory for fighters whose service ceilings were not much above 30,000 feet altitude.

As P-38, P-47, Hellcat, and Corsair fighter operating altitudes increased well above 35,000 feet, the atmospheric pressure "insulation" of the wires had decreased so much from sea level at these altitudes that it allowed spark energy to easily jump the normal rubber-type insulation of the ignition wires to any metal of the engine nearby and short out prior to reaching the spark plugs. When this happened the engine would instantly quit as though the ignition switch had been turned "off."

Sealing each of the spark plug wires into flexible tubes from the magnetos to the spark plugs and then pressurizing the tubes, wires, magnetos, and spark plugs by an air pressure source from the engine developed the pressurized harness. This additional pressure maintained the entire ignition system operating environment to below 10,000 feet altitude thus the electrical energy to the spark plugs could be kept intact to the highest altitude attainable (40,000 to 45,000 feet) by piston-powered fighters.

Jet-powered fighters did not require ignition sources to sustain their continuous burning combustion cycles after starting and thus could operate at well over 70,000-feet altitudes.

## Lessons Learned

The following axioms learned from these flights proved to be most useful to my flight safety and have never left the back corners of my mind:

If you are sweating too much before the flight, you haven't asked enough questions.

If you are not sweating just a little during the flight, you are not attentive enough.

And, if you are not sweating-out your remaining questions with all the experts that you can think of after the flight, you may never find that beautiful pearl in the pig-litter!

# Chapter 7

# Claws of the "Obsolete" Wildcat

## 7 December 1942 to V-J Day

In the late 1930s and early 1940s I well remember reading articles in *Aero Digest*, the top U.S. aviation magazine at the time, regarding new U.S. fighter technology. *Aero Digest*'s pundits could always be counted on to pompously describe each new military aircraft as being "obsolete before it left the drawing board." Their statements of absolute fact informed the reader of the journalist's flawless knowledge of worldwide aerial warfare. It was a death knell from the high executioner to that fighter and all persons who had designed it in such a thoughtless manner. The Grumman F4F-3 Wildcat, Brewster F2A-1 Buffalo, Curtiss P-40 Warhawk, Douglas SBD Dauntless, and Bell P-39 Airacobra all inherited that same condemnation until 7 December 1941. After that date opinions about military aircraft were not permitted in print.

Considering the struggling aviation war efforts in progress to catch up with the enemy, it was fortunate for America that those fighters couldn't read previous *Aero Digest* issues.

Each day that I climbed into an Avenger I would enviously watch the other Grumman test pilots flying the small and feisty-looking Wildcat. By December 1942 it had become a fabled fighter that had finally managed to best the notorious Japanese Zero in the battles of Wake Island, Midway, Guadalcanal, and the Coral Sea.

It never occurred to me that my avid "coveting" of a flight in the Wildcat was breaking one of the "Thou-Shalt-Nots" of the Ten Commandments. As it was, I didn't have long to wait. On the first anniversary of Pearl Harbor Day, and only 26 days after I arrived at Grumman, I was

*The final F4F-4 configuration. After losing the competition with the Brewster Buffalo in 1938, Grumman management developed their XF4F-2 into an XF4F-3 and received a large contract from the Navy. They then installed the folding wing and the two-stage supercharger engine-which provided a much higher ceiling-making it an F4F-4. Between Grumman and General Motors they delivered a total of 7,905 of these "obsolete fighters" throughout the war. (Northrop Grumman History Center)*

scheduled to fly an F4F-4 Wildcat for a production check flight.

I now realize why I was pushed into the Wildcat so fast. It was not my talent. Flight Operations was under awesome pressure to deliver as many Wildcats as fast as possible to the waiting Navy delivery pilots to fill depleted squadron ranks caused by the combat losses and training accidents.

## The Simple Wildcat Had Four Built-In Bear Traps

The Wildcat's cockpit was well designed. It had a 31-turn manual hand-crank to raise and lower the landing gear, a hand crank to open or close the cowl flaps, a vacuum landing flap system, and a manually operated arresting hook and canopy. Its standard engine controls were generally similar to the Avenger and all were handily located. The fuel system had a manual tank selector valve for its 97-gallon main and 27-gallon auxiliary tank. Although it was sparsely outfitted, its cockpit was comfortable and roomy enough for a six-foot-three fellow like me.

There were, however, four hidden pilot snares inherent to the Wildcat design. They were explained to the new pilot in both specific and anecdotal detail for his safety. As you will soon understand, they were easy to meet but not easily managed.

The high torque of its 1,200-hp Pratt & Whitney R-1830-76 engine required the pilot to preset the rudder trim tab to three marks nose right (almost full right tab) prior to every takeoff. If the pilot failed to preset the trim tab and not attend to the rudder properly, the aircraft would veer strongly to the left during a takeoff run, requiring an abnormal amount of right rudder force to counter the problem. I witnessed many Wildcats veer to the far left side of the Grumman runway when delivery pilots forgot to preset their rudder trim

tabs. Once a pilot forgot to preset his tab, however, he *never* forgot it again! A later-model Wildcat, the more powerful FM-2, had a 10-inch taller fin and rudder installed but only after 3,147 small fin and rudder Wildcats had been delivered. However, it still mandated two marks of nose right rudder tab preset prior to takeoff.

The least of the bear traps was the manual landing gear retraction system, which had been used in every one of the 746 carrier aircraft that Grumman had built since 1930. It was simple in design, but its operation left a lot to be desired. The crank handle was located on the right side of the cockpit. Thus the pilot had to remove his left hand from the throttle (and sincerely hope that he had tightened the throttle friction knob before takeoff), grab the control stick, and use his now free right hand to actuate the landing gear lever to the "retract" position and then complete the strenuous cranking task of 31 turns to raise the gear. He then had to reverse the cycle to put his hands back to their normal positions after the arduous retraction cycle was completed. This swap-hands operation was required right after the aircraft had left the ground. It's no wonder that many pilots felt the flight was almost completed after the landing gear was finally retracted.

Ground observers could easily judge a new pilot's proficiency by the porpoising observed while the Wildcat's landing gear was being retracted just after takeoff.

In early Grumman aircraft, the manual retraction and extension cycle had led to several fatal accidents. The radio cable from the pilot's helmet drooped close to the landing gear handle on its trip from the pilot's helmet to the radio jack. Several times it became caught in the cranking cycle and pulled the pilots head down below the cockpit rail thus causing several fatal crashes. The Navy soon had a fix to this problem by installing an automatic simple quick-disconnect at the pilot's helmet. My helmet cable got caught in the retraction cycle once early on and I thanked the Navy profusely for that retrofit.

The Curtiss Electric propeller was the third bear trap, which carried a lot of mythology with its checkout. Early Curtiss Electric propellers had several areas where water could leak into the hub mechanism and short out its total operation during takeoff. Stories made the rounds of several pilots who had the propeller mechanism short out and run away to full low pitch, which tore the engine off of the aircraft. I was, therefore, warned that during takeoff (when I was also winding the landing gear up) I should keep my left hand (the one on the stick) ready to reset the four-way propeller control switch. The control was located on the lower left-hand instrument panel. To stop a runaway condition it was necessary to move the switch to the "neutral" position. Fortunately, this problem proved to be an old wives' tale without teeth at Grumman. Grumman's hangared care of the Wildcat before delivery prevented such antics. But having outside maintenance operations with constant wind, sand, rain, heat, and high humidity at combat airports like Guadalcanal, caused these evils of the Curtiss Electric propeller to be brought to the surface where the Wildcat was most needed.

The fourth and very embarrassing bear trap in the Wildcat was the narrow landing gear with its spongy oleos with very poor wheel brakes that would fade with seemingly little use. These weak oleos made a crosswind takeoff or landing even more difficult to control the aircraft laterally. A Navy adage bespoke of two classes of Wildcat pilots: those who had ground looped it and those who were about to. The Wildcat did have an inordinate number of ground loops in service, even though pilots were routinely warned to lock the tail wheel and make the rudder

tab preset prior to every takeoff and landing. I was soon to be in the "those who were about to" class.

## Why Didn't the Navy Insist That Grumman Fix These Problems?

You may wonder why the Navy didn't demand that these well known short comings be addressed back in 1941. With war on the near horizon, production considerations took priority over everything else. An exception was the incorporation of the F4F-4 folding-wing Wildcat. This innovation allowed each carrier to accommodate 54-percent more fighters than before. This, in addition to the great numbers of new carriers coming on line, would instantly require many more Wildcats than Grumman and General Motors would be able to produce even without any of the massive production and retrofit change delays these items would require.

Navy planning also knew that the Wildcat's replacement fighters, the Hellcat and the Corsair, were not scheduled to enter combat until mid 1943.

The Navy, therefore, mandated that no Wildcat changes be permitted.

## Flying the Wildcat

Checkout time in the Wildcat consisted of scanning a 6 x 10-inch, 40-page (printed on one side only) Pilot's Handbook. This knowledge could be absorbed in a half hour. It was immediately followed by a cockpit introduction by another test pilot who talked you around its very simple cockpit. After a few check flights, you would be allowed to perform more complex first flights... not quite like my five-day check flight for an F/A-18 Hornet 55 years later.

After my checkout pilot had watched the cartridge-started engine come to life on the first attempt and rechecked my rudder trim tab position for the third time, he rapidly departed to fly another aircraft. At that time Grumman was short of production test pilots. Grumman was delivering over 360 aircraft per month of four different Navy aircraft. Monthly schedule delivery completions were the priority.

Taxiing seemed easy because of the Wildcat's wide-angle view, especially forward. You could see the runway 50 yards beyond the nose. Therefore, standard S-turn taxiing was unnecessary. Even with the canopy open, the engine seemed to purr quietly. The takeoff checklist was quite similar to the Avenger; magneto check, prop check, tail wheel lock check, and fuel check. A last nervous look at the rudder trim tab setting completed the checklist.

Although the wheel brakes would allow a full-power takeoff start, I conserved them for the possible crosswind landing rollout needs. The tail wheel lock kept the aircraft straight until the tail was lifted at about 45 mph, when the rudder became effective. The long runway at Grumman was always crosswind and gusty because of the four large assembly plants located less than 100 feet from it. The Wildcat rudder, if used promptly, could satisfactorily handle most of these turbulence problems. Liftoff was easy at 85 mph after about a 500-foot run. Climbing began immediately after the 31-turn "exercise" with the landing gear retract hand crank. It was duly noted that I was watched critically for any roll oscillations by "Buzzard's Row" test pilots who were always enjoying a new pilot's takeoff. Being the youngest test pilot by 11 years, I soon joined these sidewalk superintendents.

Climbing to altitude at over 3,000 feet per minute for the first time in my life was certainly exhilarating. After completing all but the high-speed re-check item on my check sheet, I decided to have a closer look at specific Wildcat characteristics. I investigated spins up to 10 turns and found them to be very docile with only 4,000 feet of altitude loss and instant half-turn recoveries in spins to the left. The right spin recovery took two turns. All spins were exactly as described in the Pilot's Handbook. To foresee the Wildcat's low-speed handling characteristics, I performed stalls and accelerated stalls in the clean and landing conditions with both power "on" and power "off." I found the Wildcat to have excellent stall warning with little wing dropping and fast recovery upon the release of back-stick pressure.

I then climbed to 20,000 feet by shifting the supercharger blower from main stage to low blower at 12,000 feet and then to high blower at 18,000 feet. With these power increases the rate of climb continued to be over 3,000 feet per minute. I had no guns or ammo and less than half fuel remaining in the tanks. Now I was going to have some fun!

My last check was to assure that the wing-fold "feathers" (thin metal plates covering the wing fold joint) remained flush with the top of the wing surface up to 350 mph. After successfully completing that check I decided to try to exceed 500 mph so that I could say I had flown as fast as test pilot H. Lloyd Childs. He had been widely claimed to attain that speed while demonstrating the Curtiss Hawk 75 in November 1939. I climbed to 25,000 feet and with full power rolled over and pulled through to a vertical dive and watched the speed build up. The acceleration was fantastic! I couldn't keep up with the needle on the airspeed indicator and also watch the upcoming ground, so I made a last airspeed notation and a 5G pullout just below 7,000 feet. After recording the air temperature I later calculated that my corrected true airspeed had been 510 mph just before the pullout. I had now flown as fast as Childs! He was no longer "the fastest man alive." I kept that deed quiet. I was sure that I would have been severely chastised for taking such liberties on my first flight. It was a great feeling even if I couldn't brag about it.

With an approach speed of 80 mph, my first crosswind landing on the long runway was accomplished without ground looping or brake fading. It surely appeared that a 250-hour Navy-trained pilot would have no trouble at all with this docile aircraft. Fighters were surely more exciting to fly than torpedo bombers. And, Grumman was paying me, too!

## My Second Flight Was Not Quite So Much Fun

The next morning I flew another check flight with only a few crabbed items that were fixed since the Wildcat's first flight. They were accomplished rather quickly in weather that was now much worse than the CAVU (Ceiling and Visibility Unlimited) the day before. It was cloudy with more snow predicted and very high humidity, so after only 31 min-

utes of flight time I returned to the Grumman airport. I made a descent through the overcast at low power to the downwind leg of the landing pattern. After extending my wheels and flaps I nudged the throttle forward to add power for level flight. There was zero response from the engine. I then hastily moved the throttle full forward. Still no response! I scanned the fuel gauges. There was plenty of fuel. I switched the fuel boost pump on. The engine was dead.

Now gliding rapidly through 500 feet altitude it was abundantly clear that I did not have the speed or altitude to complete my approach and landing on the main 5,000-foot runway. I immediately made a steep left turn to a short final approach on the short runway (2,300 feet) in my rapidly descending lead sled. My concentration was now on the end of an empty but icy runway with high piles of removed snow on both sides of it. I was fortunate, as it was usually lined with aircraft awaiting delivery. Barely clearing the wires at the end of the runway, I plunked down on the

The famous Navy Commander "Butch" O'Hare and his wingman flying Grumman Wildcats during the early part of World War II over the Pacific. Commander O'Hare shot down five twin-engine Japanese Betty bombers in one flight while flying combat air patrol in his Wildcat, and received the Medal of Honor for his deed. He was later killed in a flying accident. The Chicago O'Hare airport is named after him. (Northrop Grumman History Center)

This is a view of the cockpit of my second Wildcat landing with a dead engine on an icy runway in a strong crosswind after it overturned vertically. With my seat up to the highest position it is amazing that my head wasn't fractured when the canopy was ripped off in front of me. I have always wondered just how I got out of this 9 x 15-inch hole so fast with my seat parachute still strapped on. My guardian angel was flying this aircraft right up to the end of its unique landing. (Northrop Grumman History Center)

*The rather violent end to the author's second Wildcat flight on 8 December 1942. Note the one prop blade that was not damaged and the very small dent in the cowling from the aircraft's cartwheel. This aircraft was repaired and deployed in just over a week after the crash. (Northrop Grumman History Center)*

end of the runway fully stalled at a high rate of descent. I then breathed a wonderful but premature sigh of relief, completely forgetting that I was also being pushed by a 25-mph quartering tailwind from the left.

With full right rudder, the nose of the Wildcat finally turned parallel to the runway. But the strong crosswind skidded me directly into the two-foot snowbank at the edge of the runway. This made my brakes useless. The tail of the Wildcat immediately rose off the ground and I could see clearly where I was about to go. It actually happened quickly, but I seemed to be rotating upwards in slow motion. The nose hit the runway, the propeller stopped, but the strong tailwind kept the fuselage rapidly rotating over the top. As it was coming down on the other side of its cartwheel I kept wondering just when this uncontrolled landing would ever stop. It crashed on its back and slid backwards for about 50 feet, stripping the windshield, and sliding the canopy off the fuselage. I must have had my eyes closed because I never saw them disappear. The aircraft finally came to a halt. I was amazed my cloth-helmeted head did not become bald during this fias-

co. Fortunately for me, I had locked my shoulder harness prior to crashing.

For the next few seconds I wished I could say that I was in full control of my senses, but I wasn't. First, I wasn't in control because of the shock of the unexpected emergency landing and second, because it was now very dark in the cockpit, my head was in the snow, and I wanted to exit this dungeon ASAP. My next clear memory was that I was outside of the aircraft looking at my broken Wildcat lying flat on its back in the snow with several people in the background running towards the wreckage. Concerned about a possible fire, I dashed back to look up into the cockpit to see if I had turned the battery and magneto switches "off." Being on my back and squinting into a darkened, upside-down cockpit made the effort futile. There was no fire.

One of the first technicians to arrive at the wreck asked me how I felt. Being in the wildest daze of my life I mumbled stupidly that I was all right. The crash truck had now arrived so I was rushed back to Flight Operations to be fully checked out by the plant doctor. He found nothing wrong with me but recommended that a shot of medicinal vodka would be proper therapy. I found his diagnosis to be splendid. My continuing therapy followed the Grumman philosophy, which was to get the test pilot back into the air as soon as practical after an accident. I flew two TBF Avenger first flights that afternoon, and quickly forgot the morning's incident.

## A Wartime Conclusion to My Fancy Landing

Besides the damage to my wounded ego, there was amazingly little damage noted to the Wildcat after it was back on its landing gear. Although a great amount of snow had been rammed into the carburetor duct, inspection could find no positive indication of carburetor ice. Regardless, the carburetor was changed, two new propeller blades were installed on the same propeller hub, a new canopy and windshield were fitted, and a new right outer wing replaced the damaged one in order to deliver my Wildcat back to service immediately. (The damaged wing panel was repaired and re-installed on a production Wildcat coming out several days later.) A dent was hammered out of the cowling ring and the bent fin and rudder were replaced. After a thorough ground checkout, my Wildcat was test flown (by another test pilot who didn't know its recent history) and delivered to the Navy two days later.

The cause of my engine failure was never determined. Its carburetor had been designed to be impervious to icing. But that afternoon Connie Converse, the head of Flight Operations, put up a notice requiring all test pilots making low power let-downs in Wildcats to switch from the main blower to the low blower in order to raise the carburetor air temperature well above freezing, just in case.

I have never figured out just how my six-foot-three-inch frame exited the upside down, narrow, triangular hole of the cockpit so rapidly. I did it with my large seat-pack parachute still strapped firmly onto my over-sized behind. A large dose of adrenalin must have helped.

## "The Grumman Ironworks" Slogan Began With a Wildcat

Grumman test pilot Carl Alber and the author were hired on 11 November 1942 to be the first full-time engineering test pilots hired at Grumman. Carl had more flight hours and was five years older than I, so he was selected for the first extra-hazard bonus Navy demonstration. His task was to perform a single, vertical, terminal-velocity dive with an 8G pullout on the

XF4F-8 Wildcat with the new 1,350-hp Wright R-1820-56 engine. This engine had 150 more horsepower than engines installed in all previous Wildcats. Carl had never performed a terminal velocity 8G-pullout dive and his chase pilot had never seen one performed. A Navy V-G instrument, which recorded airspeed and Gs during the entire flight, was installed for this one-flight demonstration. It was located forward of the cockpit so it couldn't be tampered with during the flight. Word had it that such an incident had happened at another aircraft plant.

Carl climbed the Wildcat to 25,000 feet, rolled over on his back, pulled to a vertical dive, and held it to 8,000 feet where he pulled the stick aft slowly to make an accurate 8G pullout. He blacked out at 7Gs but continued pulling to what he thought was 8Gs. (The G-suit that prevented pilot blackouts had not yet been invented.) After he recovered to level flight he found that his cockpit accelerometer had only recorded 7.2Gs. So he climbed back to 25,000 feet and repeated the dive over again pulling harder this time during the recovery but noting the same 7.2Gs on the accelerometer when he came out of his visual blackout condition. On his third attempt he decided to pull as hard and as fast as he could to attain the required 8Gs. He got the same 7.2G result after being blacked out for over 30 seconds while the aircraft was rolling all over the sky with its temporarily blinded pilot. All this time his chase pilot thought that such antics were normal for this difficult dive.

Carl then decided that there must be something that he didn't understand about terminal velocity dives, and so, after he landed, he asked Chief Test Pilot Connie Converse about his problem. Connie was amazed with Carl's story, but he wasn't to be for long. After Carl parked the aircraft the plane captain tried to fold the wings but was unable to. Further inspection noted that the wings had been so deformed that quite a few rivets had popped out of the main spar of both wings.

The Navy V-G recorder was removed and checked. It showed that the aircraft had indeed reached its maximum terminal velocity speed but had recorded 9.5Gs, 11.5Gs, and 12.5Gs for Carl's three dives! The cockpit accelerometer, still indicating 7.2Gs, was then removed. During the subsequent ground calibration it was also noted that it wouldn't record over 7.2Gs. Opening it revealed a bent cog on one of its gears, which completely prevented it from recording over 7.2Gs.

Twelve Gs was the Wildcat design's ultimate or breaking load. It should have totally disintegrated during the last two pullouts of that flight. Fortunately for Carl, its structure and his were somewhat over-designed. Inspection also discovered that the engine mount was bent beyond repair. In spite of these problems the Navy accepted the demonstration flight as valid. New wing-fold outer panels were installed, and with a new engine mount the Navy accepted the aircraft for delivery three days later. It was then delivered to the General Motors Wildcat plant in Linden, New Jersey. It would be used for the life of this model, evaluating Navy changes or new equipment installations before putting them on the production line. General Motors then delivered 4,437 of these extremely rugged Wildcats to the Navy before the end of World War II.

The wildness of that flight, however, convinced Carl that he had enough engineering flight-testing to last him a lifetime. He subsequently asked to be transferred to production test flying. I was now the only full-time engineering test pilot.

## Another Wildcat Evens the Score With Corky

Five years later the Navy added a new rolling pullout maneuver to the Grumman F9F-2 Panther jet's structural demonstration maneuvers. Grumman also was the first Navy contractor to perform this maneuver. Thus no other aircraft company had any prior experience to assist with our rolling-pullout education.

The Grumman structural engineering department rightly suggested that the Wildcat, because of its combat and Carl Alber-proven unlimited structural strength, would be the best aircraft to investigate this maneuver prior to attempting it in the Panther. There was one very small difference in the Wildcat's design that I was to remember vividly every day for the rest of my life.

Unfortunately I attacked the rolling-pullout investigation with more than my usual vigor. This maneuver required a specified 500-mph airspeed, at which point the test pilot would slam the stick to full deflection to the right or to the left in less than one second to attain maximum rolling velocity. He would then pull the stick aft to impose the required 5Gs on the structure and then recover. In one seemingly easy single practice flight in the Wildcat, I planned to perform this complex gyration in build-up steps of from 1 to 5Gs both to the right and to the left at 10,000 feet altitude at 300 mph.

I performed all of the right stick rolling pullouts up to 5Gs at 300 mph sitting vertically with no twisting necessary. I then performed the same maneuvers to the left with my right arm. I had determined that the stick forces were too high for my left arm strength. This decision necessitated using my right arm, requiring me to twist my body almost 90 degrees to the left in order to perform the full pitch stick in less than one second. Further body twisting was then required to pull the stick aft enough to apply the 5Gs after hitting the left aileron stop. It was becoming more difficult to perform as the Gs increased. After the 4G left rolling pull-up I was quite tired and I should have stopped for a breather, but I felt the job was almost complete so I continued with an old college try for the final 5G point. This time vigor outpaced good sense. When I twisted my torso even further to attain the full left stick plus the 5Gs aft stick pull, I felt a massive shock of pain in my lower spine, which quelled my enthusiasm for the day. Once I was back to an untwisted, level cruise flight condition I was still in exquisite pain from the bottom of my spine to my neck. The pain was overwhelming.

I let the aircraft fly itself around for 15 minutes or so hoping that the pain would diminish. It finally did decrease a bit, so with great effort I went through the landing checklist. I knew I had done some first-class damage to myself when I performed the 31 turns to extend the landing gear. The sharpness of the pain returned with every motion of the handle. After parking the Wildcat I found that I was totally unable to lift myself out of the seat. Two strong mechanics gently grabbed the shoulder straps of my parachute and lifted this moaning test pilot out of the cockpit. The company sent me immediately to a physical therapist for an infrared heat treatment, plus several hours of massage. This procedure managed to return me to a semblance of health. I did not know it at the time, but heat treatment would need to be repeated many times for the rest of my life.

## A Simple Explanation for My Back Disaster

During the debrief the next day one of the structural engineers discovered a previously unremembered stick/aileron dimensional difference between the Wildcat and all later Grumman aircraft. It had an 11-inch travel from stick center to the full aileron deflection stop. All other Grumman aircraft designed since the Wildcat had only a 7-inch full deflection

requirement. I was delighted to find that I could perform a full stick deflection for rolling pullouts in the Panther without any torso twisting necessary because of its 4-inch shorter stick motion and its hydraulic power-boosted ailerons providing very low stick forces.

My back has given me trouble off and on since that time. It was so bad that Grumman sent me to the Mayo Clinic in 1978 for one of their first laminectomy operations (the repair of a smashed spinal disc), which gave me almost total relief. As I have aged the Wildcat still claws at the arthritis in my lower back above and below that fracture, and in my neck every time that I forget and try to pick up anything without first bending my knees. I am thankful, however, because doctors have stated that with such a major distress of my back in 1947 I should have had my massive arthritis well before I was 40 years of age. The arthritis didn't hit me until I had attained 82 years of age.

## The Wildcat Continued Clawing Corky

On V-J Day I was flying the same engineering "Dog Ship" (BuNo 12249) F4F-3 Wildcat on its 32-minute final check flight prior to its delivery to a Navy storage center in Arizona. I had remained close to Grumman Bethpage airport, thoroughly enjoying the remembrances of all the interesting flights I had made in this bird. While taxiing back to the flight-test hangar in Plant 5, the tower called me with this terse message, "Bud Gillies wants you to report to his office immediately!" I sagged in my seat and thought, "What the hell did I do wrong today?" I was soon to find out.

When I entered his office the first thing I noticed was that his left cheek was twitching. I prepared for the worst. He shouted, "What the hell were you doing in the last half hour flying down Fifth

Avenue at third floor level with another Wildcat?" He could easily be heard all over the 20 or more adjacent low partitioned offices. I was aghast! So, I blurted out, "I was flying on a local check flight on our Dog Ship and hadn't been within 20 miles of Fifth Avenue. Who gave you that report?" He answered, "The Civil Aeronautics Authority called our tower 20 minutes ago when those Wildcats were still buzzing New York City. You were the only pilot we had flying a Wildcat." When I gathered my wits a few minutes later I suggested that he call Floyd Bennet at Navy Operations to see if they had any Wildcats flying. He found out (much to my thankful relief) that two lieutenants, junior grade, who had been on their last flights before separation from the Navy, had just confessed to the deed. We both laughed... he much more heartily than I.

In spite of his gruffness he taught me a lot more excellent real-life test piloting lessons until he left Grumman after the war. He visited our home many times whenever he came to New York on business until he passed away in 1991.

## Meanwhile, Back to the Prewar Pundits' Prophecies

The "obsolete" Grumman Wildcat was the only carrier-based fighter available in squadron numbers for the first 21 months of the war. Pacific Theater Wildcats attained a 9-to-1 kill-to-loss ratio. The Wildcat's better diving speed, armor plating, and six .50-caliber guns, in combination with the hard-earned fighter tactics learned in the first months of the war, proved that it wasn't "obsolete" by any standards.

The more powerful Hellcat and Corsair were to show a great improvement in fighter capability. The Corsair was not acceptable for carrier operations until December 1944 because of its high carrier operation accident rate. It did, however, show splendid prowess in Marine Corps land-based fighter-bomber operations. The Grumman Hellcat entered the fray in August 1943 during the Marcus Island raid.

On 16 April 1942 the Assistant Secretary of the Navy for Air, the Honorable Artemus L. Gates, came to Grumman and presented the "E for Excellence" flag for: "Greatly exceeding scheduled contract deliveries of the Wildcat and Avenger." This was the first such flag given to a U.S. aircraft manufacturer.

The "obsolete" Wildcat spawned a lot of famous warriors. The following Wildcat pilots not only earned the nation's highest award, the Medal of Honor, but this team shot down a grand total of 119 Japanese aircraft with many more probables; Commander Butch O'Hare USN, Brigadier General Joseph Foss USMC, Colonel Jefferson de Blanc USMC, Brigadier General Robert Galer USMC, Colonel James Swett USMC, Major General Marion E. Carl USMC, Colonel John L. Smith USMC, and Lieutenant Colonel Harold Bauer USMC.

Official statistics below show the Wildcat's standing with two of its other "obsolete" American compatriots* in the Pacific Theater of Operations.

| Fighter Types | Victories | Aces |
|---|---|---|
| F6F Hellcat | 5,156 | 306 |
| F4U Corsair | 2,140 | 93 |
| P-38 Lightning | 1,700 | 90 |
| *F4/FM Wildcat | 1,006 | 58 |
| *P-40 series | 706 | 27 |
| P-47 Thunderbolt | 697 | 32 |
| P-51 Mustang | 296 | 5 |
| *P-39 Airacobra | 243 | 1 |
| P-61 Black Widow | 63 | 1 |

Hundreds of Grumman and General Motors-built Avengers and Wildcats flying from Jeep carriers as Hunter-Killer teams were utilized in the difficult but complete destruction of the German submarine menace in the Atlantic Theater of Operations from 1943 to the end of hostilities.

Eleven hundred twenty-three Lend-Lease Wildcats were flown from British carriers for the entire duration of the war. Two Royal Navy Wildcats from Squadron 804 were the first American-built aircraft to score victories during the war. On 25 December 1940 Lt. L. V. Carter and Sub Lt. A. Parker shot down a German Ju-88A bomber over the Royal Navy Scapa Flow Naval Base in the Orkney Islands.

Wildcats were also used in substantial numbers in the U.S. Naval Fighter Operational Training Command until the end of the conflict.

## Supporting Quotes

"Grumman Saved Guadalcanal," a quote from Under Secretary of the Navy, James Forrestal, in July 1943.

Vice Admiral John S. McCain, who later became Chief of Naval Operations and who is the grandfather of Senator John McCain from Arizona, stated in early 1943, "The name of Grumman on an aircraft or part, means the same as sterling on silver."

Mark Twain's famous quotation is equally succinct, "The rumors of my demise have been greatly exaggerated." It well described the prewar pundit predictions concerning the "drawing board obsolescence" of the F4F Wildcat, the Curtiss P-40, the Bell P-39, and the Douglas SBD Dauntless dive-bomber.

The hunter-killer team of the Grumman-designed, General Motors-built FM-2 Wildcat and TBM-3E Avenger that flew off to many American escort carriers in the Atlantic campaign to break the back of the German wolf-pack submarine menace that sank over 4,600 allied Merchant ships and also sunk 785 German submarines. Both aircraft have been restored and are flying with the Commerative Air Force (formerly the Confederate Air Force). Doug Thompson is flying number 309 Avenger and Jim McCabe is flying the Wildcat. (Paul Koselka via Northrop Grumman History Center)

Chapter 8

# Hellcat Versus the Corsair

## 9 September to 8 November 1943

Whenever Navy and Marine aviators who flew and fought in propeller-driven fighters gather, there will always be the argument about which was the better fighter, "Whistling Death" as the Japanese aptly named the Chance Vought Corsair, or the Grumman Hellcat. I am sure that many beers have been consumed and many loud, unemotional "Italian" discussions have evolved on this subject.

I was introduced to the Vought Corsair when the Navy delivered an F4U-1D Corsair (BuNo 17781) to Grumman on 10 September 1943. I had just returned from evaluating the P-47 Thunderbolt at Republic, so I was eager to try another renowned fighter that was a great competitor of the Hellcat.

In the desperate 1943 climate of World War II the Navy decided that the easiest, quickest, and least costly way to tweak the utmost performance out of its two carrier fighter producers would be to let rival manufacturers flight-test the latest versions of each others' products. It was in the summer of 1943 when the Navy delivered our competitor to Grumman. I was the project engineering test pilot for the F6F-3 Hellcat at the time, and was assigned to make the evaluation on the Corsair. I made 37 such flights in it during its two-month stay at Grumman.

Grumman's specific orders from the Navy were to improve the Hellcat's speed

*Number 2 production Hellcat (BuNo 04776) flown by B. A. "Bud" Gillies. This aircraft was the designated structural demonstration airplane and was used for the first investigations into the compressibility or transonic regime, which was unknown until test pilots of the time ran into it and found their controls frozen. I completed the final structural demonstration of the Hellcat in early 1944 after several bouts with compressibility that was quite impressive to a 24-year-old neophyte test pilot. (Corwin H. Meyer via the Northrop Grumman History Center)*

by 20 knots and to design better aileron controls on it so that it would compare favorably to the incomparable Corsair. We were motivated by the strongly implied "OR ELSE" between the lines.

We were also pleased to learn that we had not been singled out for harassment of our sterling product when we heard that Chance Vought, our friendly competitor from the other side of the Long Island Sound, was also sent an F6F-3 Hellcat and ordered to improve Corsair cockpit visibility, cockpit internal layout, stall characteristics, and to redesign the landing gear oleos. The Corsair bounced badly on carrier landings. In other words, they were ordered to make the Corsair land aboard carriers without bouncing like their friendly competitor, the Grumman Hellcat.

If this contest had been for beauty of design between the two aircraft, we would have given in immediately. Our baby, the Hellcat, was beautiful to us, but in comparison to the graceful lines of the Corsair, the Hellcat looked more like the box the Corsair came in rather than a new Navy

*Original XF4U-1 (BuNo 01443) in flight in 1940. This aircraft started with the fuel in the wing center section like the Hellcat and thus had fairly good visibility over the nose. When it was found that the complexity of the center section fuel tank construction made it almost impossible to manufacture and that the fuel was insufficient for the mission, a 3-foot 4-inch fuselage extension was added ahead of the cockpit for the fuel tank, moving the cockpit aft of its strong attachment to the wing and greatly limiting the pilot's forward visibility. (Corwin H. Meyer via the Northrop Grumman History Center)*

fighter. We always used the euphemism "functional," instead of "ugly," as a description of the Hellcat.

We were sure that Vought was going to have a difficult time solving their tasks. Most of their deficiencies would require major changes in configuration. We were also steeped in the tradition that Grummanites could always make better Navy fighters than Connecticut clam diggers; thus, our tasks would be accomplished in a trice. Our performance improvement challenge turned out to be much easier than we ever hoped for, but the aileron solution turned out to be nearly impossible.

## Corsair Development Program

It is necessary to discuss the Corsair's long and difficult development program because Vought had never constructed a production fighter before. The Corsair had to overcome a lot of learning problems prior to receiving full Navy carrier certification. In contrast, the Hellcat only took one year from contract signing on 7 January 1942 to the delivery of 12 aircraft at the end of that same year, and over 2,500 fighters in 1943.

The contract for the Corsair design was signed on 11 June 1938. Vought won more than four very competitive proposals. The V-166B proposal had the R-2800-4 engine of 1,804 hp for takeoff and 1,460 hp at 21,400 feet. It was projected to soon have 2,000 hp for takeoff.

Lyman Bullard made the first flight of the V-166B on 29 May 1940 at the Stratford, Connecticut, airport. Bullard experienced almost disastrous flutter, which tore off both of the elevator trim tabs. He was visibly shaken upon landing. Installation of aerodynamically balanced trim tabs corrected the situation completely.

On 11 July 1940, while performing low-altitude high-speed runs in very stormy weather, test pilot Boone Guyton had to make a forced landing caused by bad weather and had insufficient fuel to return to base. He was forced to land on a golf course. His brakes were useless because of the rain-slicked fairway and he ran off the end of it, flipped inverted, and hit a tree, which severed the fuselage and imprisoned him in the inverted cockpit. After coming to, he carefully opened his safety belt release and was able to crawl to safety.

With the factory working 24 hours a day, the XF4U-1 was flying by the last week in September 1940. It finally demonstrated a speed in level flight of 404 mph. It was the first Navy fighter aircraft to exceed 400 mph. Another engine failure occurred when Guyton experienced excessive propeller governor overspeed, which burned out his engine in a matter of seconds while demonstrating the 10,000-foot vertical dive requirement. He had to make another dead-stick landing, but this time on his home base at the Bridgeport, Connecticut, airport. The new R-2800 2,000-hp engine was having its own growing pains. I was very pleased to have had the R-2800 engine failure experience and fixes on the Republic XP-47, the Vought XF4U-1, and Grumman XF6F-1 Hellcat before I started test flying behind that great Pratt & Whitney engine.

The Corsair also had spin recovery problems after two turns of spin when trying to meet the Navy eight-turn spin recovery demand. After making several recoveries, one of which required the deployment of an anti-spin parachute, the Navy limited the Corsair spin requirement to two turns in both the clean and landing condition. The Pilot's Handbook, however, prohibited any intentional spins in service use. The Hellcat had no spin restrictions for up to an eight-turn spin.

The final Navy acceptance of the XF4U-1 Corsair structural demonstration occurred on 24 and 25 February 1941, and a contract for 584 production aircraft was

The Chance Vought Corsair production line on 23 December 1942. The Hellcat had approximately twice the number of aircraft on its production line on this date even though the Hellcat's first flight occurred two years and one month later than the first flight of the experimental Corsair. The Hellcat was a much more straightforward aircraft to produce than the Corsair. (Corwin H. Meyer via the Northrop Grumman History Center)

not signed until 3 March 1941. But its official carrier qualification was to take until December 1944 due to its high accident rate. Causes included poor visibility during approach, poor stall characteristics, insufficient directional control capability after applying high power required for a go-around from balked carrier landing, and uncontrollable bounce on landing (and sometimes bouncing over the barrier and crashing into the landed aircraft on the foredeck).

## Flying the Corsair

Having the same engine/propeller combination as the Hellcat, the Corsair cockpit checkout was quite simple. But, as we had heard and as was obvious, the cockpit was deficient from many standpoints. The most glaring deficiency was the lack of a cockpit floor. Behind the rudder pedals only two small heel panels offered any protection against dropping a pencil, chart, earphones, etc., into a three-foot-deep yawning black hole of Calcutta. Consider the havoc this could create if the pilot's relief tube or map dropped down there on a very, very long mission.

The bubble-type sliding canopy did give the Corsair great ground and air visibility except over the nose. After lineup with the runway for takeoff, the path ahead completely disappeared. I could only see a small portion of the runway to the side and ahead of the wing. This required lifting the tail as soon as possible to have adequate runway visibility during the takeoff. I soon discovered many months later in the program that the Corsair had the worst over-the-nose visibility of any aircraft I had ever flown, even with the decreased over-the-nose angle that was solved by extending the tail wheel oleo strut seven inches.

Takeoff was normal. The roar of the engine was much more subdued than the Hellcat by virtue of the 43-inch-long nose extension. This was the result of moving the wing center section fuel tanks into the forward fuselage ahead of the cockpit. The complicated curved wing center section structure made it impossible to install a reliable, leak-proof fuel tank system in that location similar to the Hellcat's straight-wing center-section tanks.

Once in the air, the Corsair's good points became quite obvious. It had lower levels of stabilities around all three axes compared to the Hellcat, excellent balance of the three control forces for maneuverability, and powerful ailerons, which were the best I had ever evaluated for both formation and combat maneuvers. This gave it the feel of a very agile fighter. Much less monitoring of the three trim controls was required during combat. Flying the Corsair was a fighter pilot's dream. It could out-roll any fighter except the latest Lockheed P-38J-25-LO Lightning after it had the hydraulic power-boost system added to the aileron system in 1944. We

then tested the Hellcat with ailerons made to exactly the same contour as the Corsair, but had no success. Grumman finally approached the Corsair's rolling performance with the NACA—designed spring-tab ailerons. These new ailerons provided much improved rolling performance with lower stick forces. They were soon retrofitted to over 3,000 earlier Model F6F-3 Hellcats previously deployed.

## Actual Performance Found to Be Almost Equal

All performance flights were flown in formation. Except for the Corsair having an 18-mph actual speed advantage over the Hellcat in the main sea-level supercharger stage, both fighters had almost exactly the same speed at both low and high blower from 5,000 feet altitude up to a service ceiling of over 35,000 feet. In essence they had the same combat performance. These flights showed that both aircraft (with similar power settings) were in closely stabilized formation at all altitudes tested above 5,000 feet. At some altitudes the Corsair would slowly gain a lead of about 100 to 200 feet after five minutes of stabilized power flight and sometimes the Hellcat would do the same. Considering that both aircraft had the same engine, propeller, gross weight, wingspan, etc., they should have had about the same performance. We did notice that during these runs the Corsair always had an 18-mph indicated airspeed advantage. We didn't realize just how embarrassing it would be to solve that dilemma.

The reason the Corsair was faster in the main stage blower was that its engine was provided with ram air coming in directly from the forward-facing wing duct into the carburetor, which provided the engine with a higher pressure supercharging effect. The Hellcat had the carburetor air coming in from the accessory compartment of the fuselage just behind the engine; therefore, it couldn't make use of the speed of the aircraft to ram the air into the carburetor for supercharging effect like the Corsair did. Our engineering department defended this arrangement because taking the warmer air for the main stage blower would prevent inadvertent carburetor icing engine failures in the takeoff and landing patterns. The Hellcat design had already been reviewed and approved by the Navy.

You might remember that I also had a carburetor icing accident on my second flight in a Wildcat a few months earlier on final approach. This resulted in my first dead-stick landing and vertical ground loop. I heartily agreed with the Grumman and Navy decision.

## Indicated Speed Performance Equalized – The Hard Way

After noting the 18-mph indicated air-speed difference that had caused the entire "lower performance" ruckus for our Hellcat, we eagerly decided to change the airspeed system so that it would read even-ly with the Corsair when they were in formation. We had taken a lot of flack from all who had flown both aircraft and, there-fore, everybody knew that the Hellcat was inferior in high-speed performance. We liked our simple and less complicated airspeed system with the static orifices on the airspeed head, but we decided to go whole hog and put a static orifice on the fuselage like that on the Corsair, and then tailor the Hellcat system to read 18 mph higher. We tried several orifice locations to get the required reading. After I did a thorough testing of the final system over the entire flight envelope, or so I thought, I proudly flew the aircraft to the Naval Air Test Center at Patuxent, Maryland, for their evaluation. We soon found out that we had not purloined the Corsair airspeed system design thoroughly enough.

We soon received the glowing Navy report of the new system. It said that the Patuxent flight test pilots had never tested an aircraft with such remarkable low-speed performance in their entire history. They found that in a left sideslip with the wheels and flaps extended the Hellcat could fly at zero airspeed. Wonder of wonders! Grumman led the industry again. Upon re-evaluation we found that the engineers, inexperienced with flush static airspeed systems, had designed ours with only one orifice on the left side of the aircraft and it was completely unbalanced during landing configuration in left sideslips. As the senior engineering test pilot I was in deep doo-doo for not testing the new system in both left and right sideslip conditions. A dual orifice system located way behind the low-ered flaps, similar to the Corsairs, finally provided a satisfactory means to give the Hellcat a cockpit indicated airspeed reading comparable to the vaunted Corsair. That was the last we heard of the Hellcat's performance gap with the Corsair. Performance case closed.

## Simulated Gunnery Runs

I made several simulated high-side gun-nery runs on some friendly Hellcat produc-tion test pilots and found that the long "hose-nose" of the Corsair considerably impaired lead visibility for gunnery when compared to the Hellcat's 43-inch shorter nose and 8-degree increased down angle over the fuselage nose for aiming the guns.

Except for the poor lead visibility over the nose, a 200-hour trained pilot could become acclimated to the aerial combat abilities of the Corsair very easily.

## An Unusual Benefit of Low Lateral Stability

On one flight during full-power per-formance testing at 25,000 feet altitude, I had the chance to see the practical benefits the low lateral stability in the Corsair would provide in an emergency. Pat Gallo, another experimental test pilot, was flying the Corsair and I was flying the Hellcat for a full-power speed comparison, heading over the water towards Bermuda. I noticed that Pat no longer answered my radio calls as I was trying to remind him to check his estimate of the differences in our speeds. When I finally passed his Corsair I found him peering at me very glassy eyed, in a real daze. I also noted that he was wearing one of the unsafe light gray Mine Safety oxygen masks that I thought we had destroyed many months before after I had an almost fatal problem with one of them at high altitude. He should have been wearing the dark green Navy-issued mask with the balloon bag under the pilot's chin that clearly showed the oxygen flow by the expansion and contraction of the balloon bag with each breath.

*An F6F-3 Hellcat being manhandled onto one of the two main elevators to lift the aircraft from the hangar deck to the flight deck. Crews could perform this operation in less than 10 seconds. Note that there is no retractable fence on the flight deck to protect the crewmen working near the edge. (Northrop Grumman History Center via Corwin H. Meyer)*

I immediately realized that I was faced with making one of the most critical decisions I would ever have to make for a fellow test pilot. I was unable to communicate with him. I knew that in another 10 minutes at full power he would be halfway to Bermuda and would run out of gas over a very cold and unwelcome winter Atlantic Ocean. It became quite clear what I had to do, but I worried that my actions could have dire results.

I slowed to formation speed on his left side and closed into him until my right wingtip was just under his left wing tip. I then gave a strong left push to my stick and rolled him into a 30-degree right bank. His Corsair started down in a long, slow spiral with me in trail. I did not know if my actions would lead to a steep dive to the water or not, but I knew I had to do something. With the help of God, the Corsair's very weak pitch and roll stability slowly took over and we leveled out heading back to Long Island at 19,000 feet. Much less hesitantly I then repeated the maneuver two more times. When we were at about 9,000 feet he started talking to me in a most querulous and angry tone, inquiring as to what damn maneuver were we going to do next. Using my most diplomatic tones I told him that we were very low on fuel, and that he should reduce his power from full throttle to cruise and return to base with me. His usual Irish nature seemed all too docile until he said that he wasn't feeling too well and suggested that I talk him through his landing. On the ground he confessed that he didn't remember anything about the flight from climbing through 10,000 feet to awaking at 9,000 feet before we landed. Needless to say I now had positive comments about the Corsair's weak lateral stability and many more foul ones about the Mine Safety masks still in our ready room lockers. The Mine Safety masks were all located and trashed that same day by me.

## A Very Jumpy Takeoff

Before measuring Corsair takeoff performance, I had performed the usual required evaluation stalls in the clean and landing configurations, but I did not put two and two together from my observations.

This model Corsair had the new 6-inch stall trigger wedge on the right wing leading edge to better balance wing-dropping tendencies during stalls and recoveries. The Hellcat was much more docile and controllable during and after stalls, especially in accidental turning stalls while making carrier approaches. The Corsair still had more abrupt wing dropping in the normal stalls and it took more time and altitude to un-stall than the Hellcat. Even worse, the Corsair did a totally unexpected, inadvertent double snap roll when I performed a 5G accelerated stall in the clean condition. I should have been more impressed with my next series of tests than I was. The Corsair really had talked clearly to me.

We had found that the Hellcat could shorten its takeoff roll by about 100 feet in a calm wind if the tail were raised to almost level flight position during the first part of the takeoff roll and then slammed down at minimum takeoff speed. We named this method a "jump takeoff" versus the normal three-point type. This became a way to make short take-offs in the Hellcat prior to having catapult-launching capability. Not so in the mighty Corsair.

After making 10 measured three-point take-offs, I told the engineers that I was going to begin jump take-offs. I pushed the stick forward and waited till the airspeed indicated 76 mph and lowered the tail wheel down on the runway as I had many, many times in the Hellcat. Lo and behold, as the tail wheel hit the runway I got a very strong wind into the left side of the cockpit as the aircraft prematurely left the ground. It instantly twisted 30 degrees

left, stalled, dropped the left wing, fell to the ground, and departed the runway promptly to the left without any help from me. We were headed at full power straight into a batch of Hellcats on the delivery line. Navy delivery pilots who have flown from Grumman's Bethpage airport know there isn't much empty space there and would understand the interesting but unplanned path the Corsair was grinding out for me.

The action of the Corsair was so precipitous that it seemed like it took me way too much time to begin taking prudent defensive actions. I yanked the throttle back, raised the tail of the aircraft so I could see what the near future held for me, and began a frantic braking on what happily proved to be hard-packed and dry ground. I finally stopped about 50 feet from the nearest Hellcat in the delivery line area. I sat there for a while until the earth stopped trembling, then slowly taxied back to our experimental flight line, and decided to call it a day for jump take-offs.

My Army doctor brother was visiting me at Grumman that day and was out on the runway to watch the proceedings. While we were having cocktails that evening, he hesitantly asked me if I did this for a living EVERY day.

## The Corsair Becomes an Excellent Fighter-Bomber

The early production F4U-1's armor was soon increased 150 pounds around the cockpit and oil tank. The aileron span was increased for greater combat rolling capability and the landing flap down angle was decreased to reduce drag in take-offs and landings. The number of guns was finally increased to six with a total of 2,350 rounds of ammunition. A frameless bubble-type canopy was installed on the 369th aircraft in mid 1943. This provided a huge improvement in visibility for the combat pilot.

Water injection was added to the 1,550th aircraft by the installation of the R-2800-8W engine, providing 2,250 hp for takeoff. This gave the aircraft greater bomb load capability and better combat performance. Two hundred F4U-1Cs were modified with four Hispano 20-mm M-2 cannons replacing the six .50-caliber guns, which increased its tank-busting and ground strafing capability by a large amount.

In April 1944 the F4U-1D model was equipped with a centerline store rack to carry a 150-gallon drop tank, extending sea-level range by 210 miles. Two center section bombs, 160-gallon tank racks, and pylons for eight under-wing 5-inch HVAR rockets were installed. Range with a 2,000-lb bomb load was increased to 510 miles.

With these modifications the Corsair was now equal in combat capability to the Hellcat and other Army Air Corps land-based fighter-bombers in the war. These aircraft did yeoman work supporting the ground-based troops during the island hopping fighting to Iwo Jima and were ready for the invasion of Japan scheduled for November 1945.

A Marine Corps F4U-1D Corsair carrying two napalm firebombs over a bomb-devastated Okinawa gets set for his run to the target. This extremely close air support was much appreciated by the Marine troops performing the fierce fighting on the ground. (Harold Andrews and the U.S. Marine Corps)

## Finally Curing the Corsair's Carrier Problems

After the Corsair had been removed three times from carrier trials, the Chief of Naval Operations Training in Jacksonville, Florida, sent a scathing statement to Washington, again stressing the Corsair's still-strong tendency to bounce dangerously over a carrier's flight deck barrier into the parked pack of aircraft on the forward deck, especially by inexperienced pilots. To keep this document from being spread around too much, Vought decided to form another team to cure the bounce by providing a much longer landing gear oleo stroke with low rebound ratios.

On 29 June 1943 F4U-1D (BuNo 57157) was delivered to Grumman with Vought's new landing gear strut and was put in the Plant 5 ground test hangar to help cure the bad bounce problem. After two weeks of testing and several modifications to the new Vought strut, it was pronounced comparable to the Hellcat and was given to flight-test. I made 15 Field Carrier Landing Practice landings and reported that it was indeed comparable to the Hellcat. After Navy Commander T. K. Wright and Marine Lt. Col. J. Dobbins performed 113 landings aboard the USS *Gambier Bay* it was officially pronounced fixed. Marine Squadron VMF-124 then went aboard the USS *Essex* on 21 December 1944, and its newly trained pilots verified that the Corsair was squadron carrier qualified, three long years after its first squadron deployment.

## The Royal Navy Received 2,102 Corsairs Under Lend-Lease

I have been asked many times just why the British Royal Navy was able to carrier-qualify their Corsairs two years earlier than the U.S. Navy. Many articles

*Number six production F6F-3 Hellcat camouflage paint job in early 1943. It was a very plain but effective paint job to give the pilot his greatest protection from enemy detection. (Grumman History Center)*

on carrier aviation have also had this question unanswered, so I decided to call Captain Eric Brown, the Royal Navy's most decorated World War II test pilot, for the answer. He had been a friend since he was my Panther chase pilot in 1947 as an exchange Royal Navy test pilot to NATC Patuxent River, Maryland. I called him on 23 July 2003 and put the question to him.

His answer: "We were quite desperate at that time with carriers being launched faster than we were able to equip them. As an example, the Royal Navy had 83 carriers deployed at the end of the war. The Corsairs gave us a bit of a hard time and we clearly understood why the Americans had so much trouble with them. The problem was the bad view over the nose. If one got slow on approach and added full power to go around again one could induce an uncontrollable torque roll. Because of the small fin and high power, the aircraft would yaw, roll, stall, and spin into the water. It also had a non-resilient land gear that would bounce the beast over the barrier, demolishing the already-landed aircraft parked on the foredeck.

"Its redeeming factor was its high kill rate, second only to the Hellcat. But the high accident rate cost a lot of allied pilots their lives. The Royal Navy considered the Seafire and Sea Hurricane aircraft trash because they were not designed from the ground up for carrier operations and had even more problems than the Corsairs." Question answered.

## Conclusions

Any objective analysis must acknowledge that the United States Navy and the British Royal Navy were fortunate indeed to have Grumman and Vought teams to produce the "firstest with the mostest" so soon after Pearl Harbor. Part of the heat in the discussion to decide whether the Hellcat or the Corsair was the better aircraft is generated because they both so well met the exacting demands for both carrier and land-based combat in large numbers during World War II. Although Grumman regularly sends me a pension check and Chance Vought doesn't, I still won't take sides; both of them were needed, timely, and excellent weapons.

Chapter 9

# A Test Pilot's Super Lady – Dorky

## October 1943 to 1984

I agree that the title of this chapter sounds like a melodrama from a television soap opera like *All My Children*. In spite of what you may think of the nickname similarity, this is the true tale of how we met.

In my younger days I was very shy of the opposite sex because I simply did not have time to study the pretty damsels of grade school, high school, and college. I spent all of my waking hours reading about aircraft and building lots of model aircraft. The few dates I did have were quite unremarkable.

At Grumman I worked in engineering and had to spend a lot of time in the adjoining experimental hangar in order to understand completely the twin-engine XF7F-1 Tigercat fighter that was under construction. The passageway to the hangar between the two buildings had been hastily roofed and then was used as an expanded drafting room. It was aptly named Siberia. The name came from its drafty construction, which left much to be desired in the heating and cooling systems year-round. One young lady draftsman worked next to the aisle that I used. Her colorful dresses, and especially a purple herringbone skirt and jacket, caught my eye every time that I found an unnecessary reason to walk through that area.

By asking around I was amazed to learn that her name was Dorky Fyfield. I

later heard that her real name was Dorothy but she had gotten the nickname from her brother who could only pronounce Dorothy as Dorky when he was very young. She had accepted that title and, to this day, she still uses it. She was a very beautiful, slim, blue-eyed blonde. I was immediately smitten with her, but didn't

*Dorky at the age of 21, seen here at the Lime Ridge, Connecticut, airport where Dorky was learning to fly. Although flying was restricted on the East Coast during World War II, this airport was on the western side of the eastern coastline "NO FLY Zone." (Meyer Family Picture Collection)*

have the courage to ask her for a date. Remembering my first disastrous date in high school, I was most apprehensive about dating beautiful, blue-eyed blondes again. After spending many days trying to plan a successful attack I can only remember blurting out my message. I was amazed to receive a very sweet "yes."

Trying to be a gentleman, I asked Dorky where she would like to have dinner. She suggested the Westbury Hotel, which was well known for its excellent food. Our dinner and drinks were great and we got to know each other during that delightful repast. I learned that she had an older brother who was flying fighters in the Navy and who had worked at Grumman for several years before entering the service. That was why she decided to leave her excellent job as a secretary with a top manager of Banker's Trust in New York City. When her brother joined the Navy she thought that becoming an engineer at Grumman would contribute more to the war effort than being a banker's secretary.

As we progressed, I got one of those hasty but brilliant ideas that are never really well thought out before taking action. Our route to her home was lonely, and I spied a water tower at the top of an oncoming hill. I said that I had never kissed a lady next to a water tower before, stopped the car, put my arms around her, and planted a kiss on her lovely lips. The kiss ended very shortly thereafter and she planted a very powerful right-handed slap on my left cheek. She then curtly suggested that I was to take her straight home, post haste. With my ardor long gone I made my apologies. They were proclaimed unanswered. At her door I finally realized that more words would only dig my hole deeper so I murmured goodbye in a very contrite but hopeless voice. Driving home I knew that I still had a lot to learn about blue-eyed blondes—they were puzzlement! I wondered if I should change to brunettes.

Dorky and Corky coming out of the First Presbyterian Church in Huntington, New York, on 7 April 1945 after our marriage ceremonies. We worked as a great team for 41 years thereafter. (Meyer Family Picture Collection)

A week or so later I hoped that she realized I now knew my exact position in her life, so I cautiously asked her for another dinner date. To my utter amazement she accepted and we began a much slower but normal courting process. Thankfully, in our long future together, I didn't shoot myself in the foot too many more times.

I need to describe two examples of Dorky's natural mechanical talents and her available wisdom for instant action to solve problems. One Sunday when I was visiting her at her home I told her that I needed to clean out my fuel pump bowl because of a strange grunting in my car engine. During the process of removing the fuel bowl it slipped out of my hand and shattered on the cement. Without laughing she immediately said, "I'll be back in a minute." She came back with six shot glasses and said in a matter-of-fact voice, "One of these will fit." A pot-bellied one with gold stripes fit. My car still had it installed when I sold it four years later.

We went skiing in Stowe, Vermont, in the winter of 1943 with another Grumman couple. While driving through a small Vermont village at midnight, my radiator started boiling, with visible steam coming out from under the hood. I was quite perplexed until Dorky said in an unemotional voice, "Let's find a garage and reverse-flush the radiator." I was aghast, thinking just where the hell we would find a garage open at midnight in this forgotten village and what she could possibly know about reverse-flushing a radiator? Dorky then remarked, "There's a light on in the building ahead and it looks as if it might be a garage." It was a garage. Again, I kept my mouth closed and thought that surely it would be closed tighter than hell at this hour. As we drew nearer she continued, "There is a house next door that has several lights on. Let's ask them where the owner lives." We did and, lo and behold, it was the owner's home. He opened the garage and said that I could use his tools but that he was going to bed. Most appreciatively I slipped him a five-dollar bill, and following Dorky's directions successfully reverse-flushed the recalcitrant radiator. In about a half hour we were back on the road without further need for Dorky's unbelievable and timely assistance. I realized that I really needed her, but the kissing would have to wait until I earned her approval. However, the skiing trip was not over. I got to take a chance at being a horse's butt once again.

The next day we all rented skis and attacked the beginner's slope. Having never been on skis before, I decided that it was too difficult to ski to the T-bar lift to go to the top of the hill so I walked over to the T-bar, put my skis on, went up the hill, took them off at the top, walked a short distance over to the starting place, put them on again, and started down the hill. As one might expect, I fell down three times on that trip but fortunately was not going very fast before the falls. I repeated the same

procedure and came down the second time, only falling once. I was improving. On the third trip I didn't fall and was almost at supersonic speed when I collided with a large mogul at the bottom of the hill. My crash was classic. When I took my left foot out of the tangle my ski rotated around several times before stopping. I immediately knew that I was done skiing for the day. I went to the ski slope doctor who pronounced that I had broken the fibula bone that keeps one's toes facing forward. He put a knee-length cast on it and told me to, "Take two aspirin and go to bed."

My friend Paul Anbro did almost the same thing a few minutes later and he was pronounced to have a badly sprained ankle, which also needed a cast. We both remained in bed for the weekend while the ladies, who found many other Grummanites there, wiled away their daily and evening hours partying. I drove us home without any further self-caused events. Dorky made no derogatory commentary on the trip home, so I bravely hoped that she now believed that my stupid skiing accident would not affect our future.

I did, however, worry about my flight status, as I was the only pilot checked out to fly the Tigercat. I taxied it on Monday morning and found that its novel hydraulic-boosted brakes required very little motion to activate and thus they caused me no undue problems. My flight status was intact.

I soon met Dorky's parents and we became "steadies." On Valentine's Day of 1945 I took her to Tiffany's in New York and bought her an engagement ring. When we arrived at her home I learned her mother was pleased that we had become engaged on her birth date. I did luck out every once in a while.

To show Dorky's absolute absence of nagging, I must tell you the story about her checkout on my greasy and ancient 1932 Harley 74 motorcycle. We went for a ride

At his mother's request, Johnny kisses his new brother Peter after the great New York snow of 1948. I doubt if he would do it today. (Meyer Family Picture Collection)

one Sunday and she asked if she could ride it herself. I told her about its workings but failed to give her a most important piece of information. She went about a half a mile down the road when she decided to make a U-turn. I forgot to tell her that she must take it out of gear and coast around the turn or keep the clutch depressed until the turn was completed. I saw it fall over on her and I started running down the road pell-mell to see if she was hurt. While I was running I saw a car stop to help her. Puffing hard when I got to the scene I noted she was uninjured. I silently thanked the Lord that I had a machine that had two sissy bars, which prevented her from injuring her legs in that type of accident. To my consternation I also heard the two young Good Samaritans sweet-talking her into getting into their car in order to permit them to take her safely home. She turned them down graciously and we mounted the machine for the ride home. When we arrived at my apartment she asked in a pleasant voice, "Are we getting married next Saturday at 4:00 PM?" I answered in the affirmative. She then added, "Do you think that you could sell this motorcycle by 3:00 PM on that date?" I did and I never missed it. We were married on 7 April 1945

and had a delightful honeymoon in the hills of Connecticut. Grumman President Jake Swirbul sent a sort of congratulation telegram to us. It stated, "I'm leaving all of my sleepless nights to Corky and Dorky from now on." We soon appreciated the hidden depth of his message.

I lived in an apartment before I was married and my roommate and I had an agreement that the first one who got married left the apartment to the unmarried one. So I had to find a house for Dorky and me immediately. Because it was still wartime, rental houses were very difficult to locate, but I finally found an ancient, former farmhouse in town that also had 60 hens as part of the deal. We became partial farmers upon returning from our honeymoon.

At one of our flight-test meetings I was told that pilots who flew at very high altitudes were unable to sire children. "It was a well-known fact," all the older pilots stated. Fortunately, my body didn't understand that verity, and John Fyfield Meyer appeared on the scene 13 May 1946, Peter Corwin Meyer arrived 21 July 1948, and Sandra Louise Meyer was born on 19 April 1950. Because they were each born two years apart I felt they were well-planned production programs.

When Dorky was carrying Johnny we decided that we needed a more substantial home, so we bought a 1920s home just outside of Huntington, which we both immediately agreed upon. Johnny and Peter were born there. Before Sandra arrived we decided the two-bedroom house was not big enough for three children, so Dorky went house hunting. She announced that she found a servant's quarter house on the Vanderbilt Estate a few miles away and that she had already set up a date for me to see it the coming Saturday. It was not the picture of what I had in mind—by a long shot.

The house turned out to be a beautiful four-bedroom estate with about 3,500 square feet of living space. It had a curving slate roof and three-foot-tall copper English lightning rod decorations on all the peaks of the roof. It was built of stone that we later found out was shipped from Quincy, Massachusetts, in 1917. It sat in the middle of three-and-a-third acres with large flower gardens surrounded by a nine-foot black iron fence. It had a very stately iron gateway with lions carved on the top of its two stone gateposts. It also had a very large pump house, which I converted into a two-car garage, and more than 150 espalier fruit trees-which are low horizontal trees that one had to bend over when picking the fruit-lining about 300 yards of gravel walkways. There were no other houses nearby except the main Vanderbilt home on the other side of the road. It was beautiful and had been vacant for two years. Dorky was in love with it and so was I. I had saved enough money before I met Dorky so that we could easily handle the down payment. Mortgage rates at the time were only one-and-a-half percent. We moved into the house in 1952. The former caretaker, Mr. Martin, told us that he had had five servants to care for it. Our weekend chores became quite clear shortly after hearing that welcoming statement. We quickly became the five servants.

Besides the full-time load of bringing up three children ranging in age from two to six years, Dorky did all the decorating, made the drapes, and helped me paint acres of walls and cabinets. She always pitched in with help or ideas no matter what her child-rearing load was. The dining room drapes hung over several very large windows with a 10-foot ceiling. Everybody who came to our home remarked on the beauty of the draped windows.

My first major task was to make two small bedrooms in the upstairs wing into one room for the two boys. It required taking down two walls, removing a stairway in between them, and removing the

Dorky with three-year-old Sandy and her two brothers at five and seven years of age. They were on the team that would always pitch in until our five home restoration jobs were completed. They each learned how to use every tool in my shop at a very early age. (Meyer Family Picture Collection)

second floor portion of a 10-foot-high chimney section whose external top portion would have to be supported by a platform above the second floor ceiling. I constructed the platform of eight two-by-ten beams; both glued and bolted into the two-by-ten eave beams. On this I put flooring made of 10 solid four-by-fours and before I completely severed the chimney I installed oak wedges all around the base of the attic chimney. When I took out the two remaining bricks supporting the top chimney it sank less than an eighth of an inch. Even after a mild earthquake it did not sink any further during the four years that we lived there.

We eventually sold this home for $46,500 to double our original investment. In 2002 it was sold back to the Vanderbilt Estate for $1.4 million. And the swimming pool that Dorky and I constructed was still in operation! A friend took some pictures of the home in 2003. What a great satisfaction for both Dorky and me. Maybe we should have stayed in it until 2002.

In 1952, Grumman's Bethpage airport and plant facilities could be expanded no further. Grumman built a new Final

Assembly Plant and Flight Delivery Center on a 7,000-acre Navy facility with a 10,000-foot runway at Peconic, New York, 40 miles east of Bethpage. I would be required to commute 30 miles to that facility, so Dorky and I decided that we would look for another home halfway between the two Grumman facilities. We located another servant's quarter estate home that had been on the market for over two years. This one was 4,000 square feet with another 1,000-square-foot home on the premises for additional servant's quarters. We had doubled the money from selling the Vanderbilt home so we had no financial problems purchasing this two-and-a-half acre, two-home site. It fronted on the wide-mouthed Nissequogue River and was about 200 yards from a small, little-used public beach on the Long Island Sound. It was an ideal place to bring up three children. We moved in and the work began again. We decided to have the small home, which for some reason had been located between the front of the large home and the river, moved behind the large home. We also erected a large two-car garage with a good-sized living area attached to our home. Dorky and I then went to work on both homes on weekends to make them livable and to make the small home rentable.

We (with three children who were always interested in helping) took out a total of 44 feet of walls, making the two dining rooms into one and two of the three first-floor bedrooms into a den. We removed the back stairway to make an alcove for Dorky to do her bookkeeping chores in. We then took out a wall in the upper floor staircase to make two very small and unusable closets into one big one. This was followed by removing a 26-foot non-supporting cement block wall in the basement to make it useful for a playroom for the children, a basement garden for Dorky, and a shop for me.

Again Dorky did the interior-decorating scheme, hanging brilliant patterned wallpaper and painting vivid colors in the rest of the house. One job that she asked me to do was to paint the brick exterior white. It was made of indented cement brick and was, therefore, going to be a long and painstaking job. I told her that I would buy a paint sprayer and soon get on with it. The "soon get on with it" was postponed many times by her reluctant husband until I came home one Friday night and found Dorky and her 70-year-old father painting a 3 x 15-foot area on the side of the house with small brushes—right where people driving by could see it. They said they had been at it all day long. I used a few manly expletives and said with a groan that I would buy a sprayer the next day and "get on with it." Dorky quietly said without turning around from her painting, "It's in the garage with all the white paint needed for the house and aqua paint for the shutters." Two long days later, when I went to work Monday morning, the house painting was finished. The 44 shutters, with their pristine aqua glow, were re-hung the next weekend.

Dorky's sense of humor was not confined to her husband. It could emerge under very unsuspecting circumstances. One day a friend of Dorky's reminded her of an old adage regarding money: "Dorky, remember, you can't take it with you." She looked him straight in the eye and quietly retorted, "Well, then I'm not going!"

One of her best-timed senses of repartee happened when she, our daughter, and I visited Athens, Greece. After taking the usual tours we decided to take a round-trip boat tour to the beautiful Greek island of Hydra. After we arrived at Hydra we were walking on the beach. We looked back to where our boat was docked and were very surprised to see that our boat had departed to Athens. We rushed back and the folks at the boat station said that the captain had told them that we were staying at Hydra, which was why he left without us. We took an express boat back and caught up with our captain, who stuck to his story that everybody said we were staying at Hydra. By this time we were very angry and decided to complain to the main office the next day.

The next morning we waited on the second floor of the un-air-conditioned, hot, and humid tour office for the owner who turned out to be a Greek Adonis. He smiled, told us that he had gone to college in the United States, and then asked us the reason for our visit. In a very heated state I began my story and was in the middle of it when he excused himself. A minute later he returned with a sheaf of letters in his hand. He told us the letters were from all of the captain's customers who had been delighted with his services on the boat tour. I was about to hit him when the always-perceptive Dorky suggested: "Would you please go back and get the stack of letters from all the people he left at Hydra who were pleased with the captain?" Now realizing who was the real leader in the Meyer family, the visibly shaken owner turned to Dorky and said, "Mrs. Meyer, it is too late today to take another tour, which will be gratis to you, but would you like to take one to Delphos tomorrow?" We received the tickets and left. On the morrow once the bus was full the driver announced, "Mr. Meyer, Mrs. Meyer, and Sandra Meyer please raise your hands," checking that we indeed were on the bus. The other people asked why we were getting such attention. We told them our previous day's problem, but we learned the driver was instructed not to drive the bus off without seeing our raised hands at every stop. Even in a heated discussion Dorky always knew exactly what to say with very few perceptive words.

Dorky had a fantastic imagination for design, interior decoration, inventiveness, management, and quiet but forceful

Johnny, Sandy, and Pete were not far from retiring at the time this picture was taken. Where does the time fly to? (Meyer Family Picture Collection)

motivation for me, her assistant. She did many other non-ladylike jobs without complaining, like pitching in and manually hauling hundreds of cement blocks up from the basement and carrying them 100 yards to the embankment of the Nissequogue River. She was also magnificent at her cooking talents, at bringing up children, and at being a caring wife—all of this with a quiet sense of humor that always cracked-up all who knew her. She has since been successful in real estate, has managed her own jewelry store, has had a career in interior decorating, and at 80 years of age is now the top boutique salesperson in the most posh hotel in Naples, Florida. Her father lived to be 90 years of age so chances are she still has a long career ahead of her.

In the house rebuilding we did together I gained an asset that was to be very necessary to me in my future. I had a very strong concern regarding how and where I would fit into Grumman if I flunked the yearly FAA medical, which would end my flying career. After we rebuilt four large estate homes, Dorky gave me the self-confidence to know that I could take on any other job in life as well as test piloting without batting an eye. It still causes me to smile with pleasure that she cared enough to slap me so hard on the left cheek while parked next to a water tower.

# Chapter 10

# The AF-2S and AF-2W, A Great Hunter-Killer Team

## June 1944 to June 1951

By mid 1944 the Navy knew that it would take much longer than they had planned for the Allies to win World War II. The Japanese were putting up very stiff resistance to the American efforts, and it was expected that an invasion of Japan would be required to attain an unconditional surrender.

The Grumman Avenger had taken quite a beating in the early years of the war when torpedo problems made pilots go in very close to enemy ships to obtain hits at slow launch speeds. Development efforts were now under way to make successful torpedoes that could be launched at up to 400 mph. The Navy knew that such a launch speed required at least twice the engine power of the Avenger. Grumman offered a twin-engine configuration called the XTB2F-1, which met all of the new Navy requirements. However, the aircraft was too large for Essex-class carriers being deployed. The XTB2F-1 was cancelled shortly after the Navy's full-scale mock-up inspection in June 1944. Grumman then submitted five single-engine prototypes. The basic design was the G-70 (Grumman design number) with the R-2800 Pratt & Whitney engine rated at 2,100 horsepower and a dorsal gun turret like the Avenger. The G-70A had a Curtiss-Wright R-3350 engine with 2,500 hp. The G-70B had a 3,000-hp Pratt & Whitney R-4360 engine

and a G.E. remote-controlled turret. The G-70C had an R-3350 engine and a G.E. I-20 turbojet but without the turret. The G-70D had the higher-thrust Westinghouse 24C jet engine as a replacement for the I-20 in the G-70C. With both engines running the G-70D had the calculated performance the Navy wanted: 394-mph top speed, 4,880-feet-per-minute rate of climb, and takeoff distance with a 25-mph wind over the deck of 204 feet. This was a fabulous increase in performance over the TBM-3E Avenger then in production.

Grumman and the Navy soon discovered that the production schedules of both the R-3350 and the I-20 engines would preclude making the Navy's deployment schedules. The Navy then asked Grumman in January 1945 to prepare a sixth design with the 2,300-hp Pratt & Whitney R-2800-34W (now with water injection power increase) and the Westinghouse 19XB turbojet. This model had slightly less performance than the G-70D. Its speed at sea level would be 367 mph and takeoff distance was only 330 feet. The Navy contracted with Grumman to build three XTB3F-1s in this design. The first flight was made on 23 December 1946. The Navy put a stop order on the program the next day.

The Navy had just given large contracts for the Douglas AD-1 Skyraider and the Martin AM-1 Mauler to take over the primary bombing and torpedo roles. The Cold War soon spurred an important requirement for a state-of-the-art, multi-seat anti-submarine warfare (ASW) aircraft to replace the aging Avenger Hunter-Killer teams. On 27 February 1947 the Navy instructed Grumman to complete the second and third XTB3F-1s, without the jet engines, to be prototypes for an improved ASW Hunter-Killer team. Removal of the jet engine provided space for three equipment operators that were needed for these missions. These two prototypes were flown in November and January 1949. The first production versions, now called AF-2W and AF-2S Guardians, flew one year later. A total of 386 aircraft were built and in service from November 1950 until November 1957.

I was never a project pilot for either of the XTB3F or AF programs. But after being advanced to Senior Engineering Test Pilot in November 1945, I was brought into the pro-

Corwin H. Meyer flying the XTB3F-1W (BuNo 90505) prototype during the fall of 1948 just before it went to Patuxent for its first carrier-suitable tests. During these tests it was determined during landing arrestments that the 13-foot-diameter propeller was damaged from pitch-over and its diameter needed to be reduced to 12 feet 2 inches for service use. This aircraft did not have the AN/APS-20A radar yet installed in the wooden radome mockup attached to the aircraft. The first aircraft to have radar installed was the first production AF-2W several years later after the aircraft designation was changed. (Northrop Grumman History Center)

gram many times to check development fixes and to fill in after the sad demise of three AF project test pilots. Pat Gallo had experienced a fatal low-altitude parachute jump from an F8F-2 Bearcat. Bill Cochran died in a USAF record-attempt takeoff in a KC-135 accident flying as a Federale Aeronautique Internationale (FAI) witness. Mike Ritchie was unable to fly after making a very high-speed, 200-foot altitude parachute exit when the first XTB3F-1 crashed on Long Island. He landed on top of the crash and was hospitalized for many months before returning to an engineering ground assignment. The Pratt & Whitney engineer in the aft fuselage, performing an in-flight propeller vibration survey, died in the crash. Because of these depressing events, I logged 218 flights in the AF program in between my regular job of fighter testing.

## Solving Some Interesting Guardian Flight Problems

After Pat Gallo's death I was asked to find out why the present project test pilot, who had just arrived at Grumman, had determined that the prototype was unstable in the roll axis and would not maintain its trimmed altitude flying hands off. This would make a long, low-altitude cruising flight in turbulent air intolerable to the pilot. When I was ready for flight I made my usual full deflection tests of the three controls and found that the stick motion fore and aft had an excessive amount of friction—11 pounds. Stability in the air was usually measured within the limits of that force, so I asked the aircraft captain what cable tension was set for the elevator control. He responded that it was 135 pounds. I decided that it would be pointless to make a flight with this much friction and asked him to re-tension the cables to 25 pounds. The new test pilot stated emphatically that the Navy's sacrosanct minimum

The production AF-2S Guardian carried three HVAR (High Velocity Airborne Rockets) rockets installed on each wing inboard of the searchlight and search radar. They cannot be seen in this picture. These rockets were lethal to submarines on the surface. It also carried four 500-lb bombs or four Mark 54 depth charges. For night work it carried a six-million-candlepower AN/AVQ-1 searchlight on its port wing and a short-range AN/APS-31 search radar on its starboard wing. To extend their search range from four to eight hours, both the AF-2W and AF-2S could carry two 150-gallon external fuel tanks. (Northrop Grumman History Center)

## AF Directional Stability Problems

A few months later I was asked to fly the AF-2W Hunter prototype to find out why pedal forces went to zero when the rudder was pushed to full deflection in flight. During my pre-flight walk-around I noticed that this prototype now had a very large dorsal fin attached to the main fin, which should have increased rudder pedal forces at full deflections. I also noticed that the rudder had a large balance tab that was usually installed to reduce pedal forces. I assumed at first that the balance tab was the problem. I found that it and the increase in fin area were both culprits. In flight the rudder forces went to zero at full deflection, so I landed and asked the mechanic to reduce the balance tab gear ratio with rudder deflection to half its present travel. On the next flight the rudder forces decreased much less at full deflection so I had the balance tab ratio reduced further to 25 percent motion, which cured the rudder-overbalance condition.

I was also concerned that such a large increase in total fin area would require very large pilot rudder deflection requirements for safe crosswind take-offs and landings. The excessive total fin area would also make the aircraft weathercock more easily into the wind and make it difficult to control on the ground during these maneuvers. I took off in a 10-mph, 90-degree crosswind. It took large rudder pedal deflections for satisfactory directional control. When I landed in the same crosswind I decided that I should ask why the big dorsal fin was installed. The project aerodynamicist said that they thought that such an addition was necessary to cure the rudder force reversal problem. After I had the big dorsal fin removed and the original quarter-sized dorsal fin reinstalled, the crosswind weathercocking problem disappeared and proper pedal forces at full deflection were retained.

cable tension requirement was 135 pounds and could not be reduced.

I suggested to him that the objective was for the test pilot to find ways to make an aircraft meet its requirements safely; then, if necessary, have the engineers obtain the needed changes in Navy requirements. I had experienced similar problems several times during my prior five years as an engineering test pilot.

With the cable tension now at 25 pounds, the measured friction was only a half-pound, so I took off for a 15-minute flight. I found that the AF prototype now had sufficient roll stability to make turbulent air cruising satisfactory. A similar stability condition is built into the steering of modern automobiles, which steer themselves in a straight line because directional stability angles are built into the alignment of the front wheels. When a car gets older and has hit a lot of bumps with its front wheels, causing improper steering angles, combined with friction in the steering mechanism from tire wear, steering becomes a chore.

*The first carrier qualification of the production AF duo was made in May 1951 on the USS Palau Jeep carrier. The author participated on this trial that brought out several more aircraft flight and handling problems, which were solved after this session without serious delays. (Northrop Grumman History Center)*

During my flights I also noted that two long, leading-edge spoilers had been installed on the wing. They caused a large amount of pre-stall buffeting during take-off and landing. The engineer told me that the spoilers were designed to correct excessive wing rolling in takeoff and landing condition stalls. I asked him if they had tested for any increase in stall speed since installing them. He answered "no," so on my next flight I measured stall speeds and asked the engineer to compare them before the strips were installed. He acknowledged that the stall speed had increased by 7 mph, which would cause longer takeoff distances and an unnecessary amount of energy that the arresting cables needed to stop the aircraft during an arrested landing. They would also give the pilot too much buffeting, causing him to increase his approach speed, thinking that his aircraft was flying much too close to the stall.

I suggested that because the right wing strip was 30 inches long and the left 36 inches long, that the right strip be eliminated and the left one shortened to 6 inches. My flight tests showed that the stall speed had gone down by 7 mph and the excessive buffeting had been reduced but

still provided satisfactory stall warning with no wing rolling at the stall.

## Patuxent Problems With the Prototype XTB3F-1

In February 1949 the XTB3F-1 Hunter prototype with the Westinghouse AN/APS-20 radome installed in place of the bomb bay was evaluated at the Patuxent NATC for carrier trials and general handling characteristics. During these arrestments it was found to have nose-over tendencies after catching the arresting wire. Its propeller diameter was reduced from 13 feet 6 inches to 12 feet 2 inches to give the propeller proper deck clearance during arrested landings. It also had the prototype hydraulic-powered flaperon spoilers inboard of the ailerons to increase its rolling power during carrier approaches. During this evaluation, however, Navy test pilots had also found it to have unacceptably low directional and lateral stability.

The project engineer had gone to Washington and told the brass that the aft fuselage structure wasn't strong enough to add the amount of fin and rudder necessary to cure the directional problem. He said it would require a total aft fuselage redesign. Washington replied the next day that if an increase in fin area couldn't be made on the present structure, they would be forced to cancel the program. It was interesting to see how rapidly this ego-centered engineer changed his mind that the aft fuselage, as designed, was indeed strong enough to add a 43-percent increase in vertical fin area. He had already known that answer before he went to Washington.

Grumman test pilots who had been rebuffed by the project engineer were not satisfied with the enlarged fin and rudder fix, so two vertical fins were added at the mid-stabilizer span. These finally made directional stability acceptable for evaluation by Navy test pilots.

Several other problems had been fixed before our emergency visit to Patuxent during the weekend of 24 to 28 June 1950. One was the elimination of fuselage leaks, which caused excessive carbon monoxide in the cockpit and aft cabin areas. Another required the relocation of the long wingtip airspeed boom system. It was relocated to a spot under the wing pitot head with dual static vents on the fuselage. (We did not make the same mistake as I had made on the Hellcat, having only a single static vent, however.) We also had the two increased directional stability fixes now on the first production AF-2W Guardian (BuNo 123097).

I was selected to be the test pilot of the new team that went to Patuxent to solve two remaining problems and to hopefully find acceptable fixes. The first problem was improving the Guardian's lack of pitch stability. I flew three flights a day for three days with several new engineering pitch stability fixes without solving the problem. After thinking about it during those flights I made a suggestion that we rig both ailerons 10 degrees down and install fixed tabs bent 25 degrees up to prevent air loads from pushing them back up. I was hoping that the down-deflected ailerons would act like the wing had a greater dihedral angle, which hopefully should increase the pitch stability. Lateral stability was now acceptable for reasons that are still unknown to the Grumman aerodynamics department and to me. Sometimes wild guesses do work.

The other problem was that the AF-2W pitched up with right rudder deflections and down with left rudder deflections. Herb Crawford, chief of flight test, noticed that the Douglas AD-1 Skyraider had one elevator control tab bent up 20 degrees and the other elevator tab bent down. He asked one of the Navy test pilots why they were installed that way. The pilot told Herb that it cured a problem similar to ours. We installed tabs bent accordingly and cured our problem (with many silent thanks to the Douglas Aerodynamics Department).

After these flights I called my wife Dorky on Saturday evening from a very hot phone booth and in a very sweaty flight suit. I learned that she was having cool drinks with the children in our swimming pool, totally unaware of my perspiration pleasures of summer weekend test flying at Patuxent. Some phone calls are just not as gratifying as others.

On Sunday morning Commander Joe Reese evaluated all of our new fixes and pronounced them acceptable. On that evening the team flew up to Washington with Commander Reese in our Grumman Goose amphibian. At the first opening of the Navy Bureau of Aeronautics Monday morning Commander Reese reported his acceptance of our fixes to the Guardian Project Desk and the program was not cancelled. What a weekend!

## Solving the AF's Weak Tail Wheel Problem

Early AF Guardian squadrons were having trouble breaking tail wheels during carrier landings when diving for the deck and flaring out to catch the arresting wire. During the fix program Grumman engineering had progressed from a stronger single tail wheel to a double tail wheel and then to a triple tail wheel. None of these fixes solved the problem. After I first noticed this amazing tail wheel configuration on our flight-test line, I asked Herb Crawford what the problem was. He told me the incredible tail wheel breakage story. I wanted to fly that configuration because I wondered if the AF program was having a problem similar to that which we had previously fixed on the XF9F-2 Panther. The Panther had smashed its tailpipe many times during its first carrier landings at Patuxent. It had been fixed by simply limiting its up-elevator travel from 30 to 11 degrees so it did not have so much excess elevator control power available during landing flare-outs.

I proposed some Guardian restricted up-elevator deflection landing tests with a nose-heavy center of gravity, which we had found to be critical to this problem in the Panther. I made 12 simulated carrier landings with incremental reductions of the up-elevator travel by a chain attached from the stick grip to a hook on the instrument panel. I determined that 11 degrees was sufficient up-elevator for a satisfactory flare-out during all carrier landings. The tail wheel would always hit the deck for proper hook snatching but now with significant stress reduction to the tail wheel.

Three Hunter-Killer teams from VS-30 over Norfolk, Virginia, at 8,000 feet in October 1952. The Guardian aircraft program made the transition from the ship-killer Avenger to the S2F Tracker during the continuous rush for better ASW equipment during the Cold War with Russia immediately after World War II ended. (National Archives)

Patuxent test pilots approved the 11-degree elevator up limit and it was put into production. The Navy had the change-information implementation duty for all service aircraft. They made a big omission in spreading this fix information, however. They did not send it to any of the three naval Overhaul and Repair (O&R) stations. Three months later Grant Hedrick, chief of structures, came to me and said that the Navy squadrons were again breaking tail wheels and my fix (which he hadn't approved of) was, therefore, no good.

I asked the Grumman Service Department to make inquiries throughout the Navy and we learned that only Guardians that had come out of one O&R station still had their elevators re-rigged to 30 degrees up. I was pleased to be out of Grant Hedrick's dog-house. All operational aircraft that had been through that O&R station now had their elevators re-rigged to 11 degrees and no more tail wheel bashing occurred.

Some of the other tasks I was given during this time were both enjoyable and thought provoking.

One of the inexperienced project pilots thought the rudder forces should have been much lower, so a powerful spring tab was substituted in place of the balance tab on the rudder. He had flown it and praised it highly. On my first flight takeoff the rudder pedal forces were so low that I was forced to take my feet off the pedals so I wouldn't over-control my flight path down the runway. In an hour's flight, trying to get used to them, I realized that a new Navy pilot on his first checkout flight would have a very difficult time getting used to these extremely low forces during a very important period of the flight. The ratio of the three control forces had been established years ago by NASA to be: elevator 1, ailerons 3, and rudder 10. Ten was the heaviest. With this rudder spring tab the ratio for the AF was now 1, 3, 2. I asked for another pilot's evaluation. He had better sense than I did and flew it around the field only once. He agreed with my recommendation to forget this "improvement." It was then cancelled.

Another new item for the Guardian's equipment list was night testing of a new 6,000,000-candlepower searchlight mounted under the wingtip. Submarines usually cruise on the surface at night for maximum range

The two fins on the horizontal stabilizer and the larger fin and rudder were easily adaptable to the original fuselage structure even after the project engineer had told the Navy that it couldn't be done without total fuselage redesign. The "Or Else" inference in the Navy's response helped to inspire this simple 100-percent increase in the directional stability of all of the Guardians produced. (Northrop Grumman History Center)

and battery recharging. Over the Atlantic Ocean it lit up every boat for 10 miles! A submarine would be a sitting duck for the killer AF-2S equipped with this powerful weapon. On landing it illuminated the entire airport to the pleasure of the pilot but to the displeasure of the surrounding neighbors.

One of the electronics engineers convinced Grumman management into funding his special autopilot, dubbed SALAD (Stability Augmented Landing Approach Device). It was promoted to make hands-off carrier landing approaches possible. This was right after the Korean War and commercial autopilots were not yet considered reliable enough to operate in the carrier landing approach mode.

It required many adjustments in the air before I was in the mood to try a complete hands-off landing. Even then, I kept my right hand very close to the control-stick grip. It was scary with its many inadequate and unpredictable motions in all three controls, especially during in-flight failures. The age of transistors had not yet arrived to supplant radio tubes. Fortunately, company management decided, with high approval from Grumman test pilots, to permit the pro-

fessional autopilot manufacturers to take on this easy job. It took 20 years for transistor autopilots to finally become reliable enough for this critical task.

A former Navy flight-test chore was given to Grumman in 1952. They were directed to test and evaluate all of the large variety of external stores and radars that the Guardian carried. With these items I flew many test flights to their structural flight envelope limits. This added much to my experience in understanding future aircraft external stores problems.

## Conclusions

The reader can easily see that being the Senior Engineering Test Pilot now made my job much more interesting. I was testing all Grumman aircraft, not just those that I was assigned to be project pilot on. With that in mind I now thought I would have enjoyed paying Grumman for my increased delight in flight-testing. Thank goodness they were unable to read my mind.

## Epilogue – Arrogance Ends the Grumman ASW Monopoly

After building 11,489 Anti-Submarine Warfare (ASW) TBF/TBM Avengers, AF-2W/AF-2S Guardians, and S2F-1 Trackers Grumman lost the next ASW carrier aircraft competition on 1 August 1969 to the Lockheed S-3A Viking. I went to Washington to try to understand why. I was shown the decision paperwork. It stated, "The Navy expected Grumman to win after their continuous 28 years of supplying the Navy with excellent ASW aircraft. Because of Grumman's pompous attitude expressed in their very skimpy proposal they were rated 25th in a five-company competition." I went home and read our proposal. It was a real dud. Engineering arrogance finally did us out of a very long-time, lucrative Navy ASW business forever.

# Chapter 11

# The Hellcat's Transonic Tribulations

## 21 March to 1 May 1944

"If you really wish to learn you must mount the machine and become acquainted with its tricks by actual trial." Wilbur Wright.

The flight of Chuck Yeager through the sound barrier in the Bell X-1 was a fabulous aviation milestone. Yeager flew this specially designed aircraft with all of the transonic knowledge known up to 1947, dedicated to do just that job: to see how far the totally unknown and uncharted transonic regime persisted. To this day many people in aviation think that Yeager's historic accomplishment was a one-time daring flight that conquered the mysterious sound barrier once and for all.

What I am about to relate has been buried in the wartime history of test flying. It is the story of military and civilian test pilots and engineers working in isolation against the completely unknown effects of an unexpected phenomenon, in steep dives, and in heavy-structured fighters. "Compressibility" was only a prelude to the transonic sound barrier. Unfortunately, too many service and test pilots lost their lives by unwittingly diving into this unknown and dangerous flight arena.

Just prior to World War II American aviation designers didn't understand what the newer and faster fighters then being tested were meeting in steep, high-speed dives. Very few aeronautical industry personnel outside of the government research facility called National Advisory Committee on Aeronautics (now known as NASA) had ever heard of Mach numbers or compressibility.

Research engineers who had tried to study this phenomenon in government wind tunnels in the 1920s and 1930s had run into the problem of shock waves developing on their models. These choked the test sections of the tunnels between Mach numbers .7 and 1.2 (Mach 1 being the speed of sound), completely scrambling all data being taken. Thus the engineers could only describe what they believed was happening in theoretical formulae that few could understand.

By December 1941 John Stack, head of the high-speed flight wind tunnel section at NACA, stated; "No one is about to solve this (wind tunnel choking) problem for some years to come—if ever". Thus many in NACA envisioned that there was only one alternative to boarding up the supersonic tunnels. It was to design a specially instrumented full-scale, transonic research aircraft. A meeting was held at Langley between NACA and service personnel on 15 March 1944 dealing with the possibility of such a machine. The pressures for combat aircraft production in World War II, however, greatly

*The F4F-4 Wildcat was Grumman's last fighter to evade the compressibility ogre because it didn't have the power or speed even in a full power vertical dive from the highest altitude it could attain. That was why it was selected for me to train in for the new Hellcat's dive demonstration. (Northrop Grumman History Center)*

outweighed the priority of this project until after the war.

## Orville Wright Introduces Me to Dr. Ernst Mach

My boss, Bud Gillies, vice president of Grumman flight operations, and I first heard the term "Mach number" while listening to Orville Wright give a lecture at the Institute of Aeronautical Sciences on 17 December 1943. He used the term as if everybody understood what he was talking about.

The next day when we both asked Charley Tilghner, the chief of Grumman aerodynamics, about Mach numbers, he said that he had heard of Mach numbers but didn't really know much about the man or his research work. Dr. Mach (1838-1916), a renowned Austrian physicist in ballistics, became the first expert in shock wave to determine the speed of sound. He timed the visible smoke of a cannon shot until he heard the sound wave at a long measured distance from the canyon. Thus Mach 1 (760 mph at sea level) is now the term for the speed of sound. Mach 2 is twice the speed of sound, etc. Without knowing it I was soon to further my education of Dr. Mach's numbers in the air.

## Training to Be a Structural Demonstration Test Pilot

Without knowing management's reasons, I was directed to stop the program for Hellcat speed improvements and begin a full dive training demonstration program in F4F-3 Wildcat (BuNo 12249). The Wildcat was selected because it had the capability of diving vertically from its service ceiling until it could gain no more speed (called terminal velocity) at 10,000 feet, and safely pull its designed load factor of 8Gs. Wildcats had also been in service squadrons for five years and had experienced hundreds of operational dives, many to over 8Gs without any structural difficulties.

Between 14 March 1944 and 3 April 1944 I flew 10 flights totaling 6.8 hours in a program of many build-up pullouts to 8Gs, at three different speeds, covering the Wildcat's complete flight envelope. It gave me practice in accurate G pulling in many dive angles and at several different altitudes. This aircraft had only a Navy installed V-G recorder for verification and proof the required amount of pullout Gs and speed had been attained.

I was delighted that the day after I completed my last dive in the Wildcat I was announced as the new F6F-3 Hellcat dive demonstration pilot. I was soon to learn the old axiom; "Many times Mother Nature gives us the final exam before presenting the lesson."

## The Hellcat and I Meet "Compressibility"

Connie Converse, who was the chief test pilot at Grumman, had performed initial lower G pullout build-up maneuvers required by the Navy demonstration. His greatly increased duties in the company became so onerous that he asked to be relieved of his flight demonstration tasks.

As the new Hellcat demonstration pilot I was instructed to perform my first high-speed dive point of 485 mph (580 mph true airspeed) combined with the two-and-a-half-G pull-up to start the Navy demonstration program, a seemingly easy conclusion to a straight forward dive.

On my first Hellcat demo flight in F6F-3 (BuNo 26101) on 7 April 1944, I pushed over from 28,000 feet to what I had estimated to be a 60-degree dive angle and concentrated totally on the buildup of airspeed versus the rapidly decreasing altitude. With full power the aircraft's descent rate soon built up to over 38,000 feet per minute! I estimated that I would attain 485 mph indicated airspeed just as I went through 10,000 feet and then make the easy two-and-a-half-G pullout. In order to maintain the 60-degree dive angle during the speed buildup I needed to continuously re-trim the elevator more nose down to overcome the aircraft's natural stability nose-up tendency with increasing speed.

Just before I was going to start the simple pullout I noticed with great alarm that the aircraft suddenly didn't require any more nose-down trim. The nose was now going down fast of its own volition, rapidly increasing the dive angle and speed without any re-trimming, push force, or desire on my part. I was no longer flying— I was a passenger!

To counter this frightening condition, I began to pull the stick aft by an amount that should have stopped the nose-down pitch to make the pullout. Nothing happened. So I pulled much harder. The nose was still dropping, further increasing the dive angle even with a maximum-effort two-handed pull force application now on the stick. The stick seemed to be solidly implanted in concrete. The nose-down dive angle continued to increase. With fear-caused adrenaline now flowing rapidly I was roaring through 6,000 feet altitude. It was abundantly clear that something way

beyond my comprehension and capabilities was directing the aircraft straight into the ground at over 600 feet per second. I had less than 10 seconds to live!

I instinctively yanked the throttle from full power to the idle position and then continued my forceful two-handed pull on the stick, praying for recovery.

A long second or two later all hell broke loose. The aircraft started buffeting violently and pitched up to 4Gs. My still frantic pull on the stick caused the Gs to continue to 7Gs with increasing buffeting before I could release my adrenaline-powered efforts. The 7G pullout finally bottomed below 2,500 feet altitude. The ground was now happily receding below me. As soon as I regained a little composure I gave the aircraft a check for damage and controllability. Having had enough excitement for the day, I slowly flew back to Grumman in a mental fog.

I was a confused young test pilot. Whatever happened was way beyond my comprehension. My mind was trying to assimilate the very strange and frightening high-speed flight characteristics that the Hellcat had exhibited. The first thought in my mind was that a mechanic had left a wrench or screwdriver in the aft fuselage section and it had temporarily jammed the controls. Loose and forgotten tools left in an aircraft were not frequent events at Grumman, but they had happened.

I landed, completely befuddled, and greatly shaken up. When I turned the engine off I was trembling so much that I told my airplane captain, Scottie McClain, that I was going to remain in the cockpit to write some notes while the flight was still fresh in my mind. I'm glad that he tactfully left me to tend to other aircraft needs because he would have seen a hand so shaky that it couldn't hold a pencil, let alone write with it. I knew that I would fall flat on my face if I tried to climb out of the aircraft. After I finally exited the cockpit I contacted the chief inspector and asked him to have a complete check made of the aft fuselage interior for tools or debris that might have jammed my controls. Nothing was ever found.

I immediately debriefed to some very wide-eyed engineers who could not believe my words as they tumbled out of my mouth. During this debrief a flight-test engineer had removed the smoked glass data plate from the V-G recorder in the aircraft and had put the definition grid on it to determine what speed and Gs I had attained. He was thunderstruck at what he saw. He had determined that I had drastically overshot my goal of 485 mph and had attained 512 mph. He also verified the 7Gs with strong buffeting during the pullout. The 7G buffeting stress on the aircraft should have overloaded the Hellcat's structure to destruction.

Examination revealed that I had bent both of the stabilizers at their mid-span, the right one up 15 degrees and the left one down 15 degrees. There was no question that the stabilizers had exceeded their permanent yield load strength, which was 15 percent greater than the operational limit load design strength.

Complete inspection of the entire aircraft amazingly showed nothing else bent nor rivets pulled, so I became an instant member of "The Grumman Ironworks," an unofficial fraternity of Navy pilots who had greatly over-stressed Grumman aircraft and returned to fly another day in the same aircraft.

## A Rational Explanation Is Happily Forthcoming

The confounding part of the entire post-flight episode was that nobody in engineering could explain the frozen controls and automatic and uncontrollable pitch down of my Hellcat just as I passed through 10,000 feet altitude or the auto-matic pitch-up and my subsequent regaining pullout control as I was passing through 5,000 feet. I was distressed because I knew that to satisfy the Navy I was going to have to repeat that dive after the stabilizers were replaced.

Grumman was very fortunate in having a research engineer named Dr. Leonard Michael Greene who, unknown to most Grumman engineers, had just completed a scientific treatise titled, "The Attenuation Theory of Compressible Flow." His tome described my predicament precisely, but because of the complex research theory of his investigation, few Grummanites were able to wade through his work. When he heard the details of my dive he said that he recognized the situation and described the problems of my flight in very simple English.

He stated that the Hellcat would generate Mach 1 supersonic shock waves over the full wingspan at .75 Mach number. (On my first dive Greene calculated that I had attained .77 Mach number! Cockpit Mach meter instrumentation had not been invented as of yet.) This was caused by the airflow speeding up to supersonic speeds in order to go around the wing's thick airfoil shape. Simultaneously with the formation of the shock wave, the wing center of lift would instantly move several feet back beyond its normal rear limit. These effects had given the aircraft its strong buffeting, stuck-in-concrete stick elevator forces, and pitch down in spite of my Herculean efforts. He continued by stating that my closing the throttle greatly increased the aircraft drag and that, coupled with the normal increase of the speed of sound with decreasing altitude, had reduced my Mach number sufficiently to back the aircraft out of its critical shock wave compressibility condition. With the center of lift again restored to its proper place, normal stick forces were instantly available, which over-assisted my frantic pullout to

7Gs just in the nick of time. He further calculated that had I attained only 5Gs I would have collided with the ground. Needless to say I began to take much greater interest in limiting my Hellcat demonstration efforts to conditions as far away from this "new" compressibility range as possible. The ground had come much too close for comfort.

The two stabilizers were replaced with a redesigned pair that was strengthened by the installation of full-span .040-inch-thick aluminum 10-inch-wide leading-edge cuffs to better withstand the violent buffeting incurred in my last dive. These cuffs essentially provided the stabilizer with another structural beam that hopefully improved its ability to withstand similar buffet loads.

## Necessity Is the Mother of a Dive Angle Indicator

Because the stabilizers had been redesigned, I was required to repeat the 485-mph 2.5G pullout. In order not to exceed the required speed again, I installed a series of Scotch tape angles at my eye level on the inside of the canopy so I could set up repeatable increasing dive angles to build up to the 485-mph demonstration point gradually and not wildly exceed it like I did on my first date with the "compressibility" demon.

Starting from a 40-degree angle on the next flight I performed short dives, increasing the dive angle by five degrees each time until I determined that a 55-degree angle would give me 485 mph at 10,000 feet altitude and hopefully preclude the possibility of overshooting into the frightening compressibility region again. I further determined that my estimated 60-degree dive angle of the almost tragic dive had actually been 75 degrees! The second flight was started with little peace of mind, but my second limit speed 485-mph dive was a "non-compressible" piece of cake.

Until Mach meters became available instrumentation in 1946, the canopy dive angle "protractor" was mandatory instrumentation for the many Navy dive demonstrations that I performed later in my 22-year career as a test pilot.

## More Transonic Trouble – The Buffet Boundary

To complete the Navy-required flight envelope of the F6F-3 Hellcat (BuNo 26101), I had to make 6.5G pullouts at 300 and 450 mph at 10,000 feet. Connie Converse had told me that he had pulled into the buffeting that started about 5.5Gs at these airspeeds and that he had experienced two stabilizer failures without reaching the required 6.5Gs. I prayed that my new leading-edge booted stabilizers would pass the increased buffet requirements needed to attain 6.5Gs. If the booted stabilizer structurally passed 6.5Gs, buffeting service change kits would be sent to all of the 4,000 previously delivered Hellcats for retrofits.

During the 6.5G pull-up into the buffeting at 300 mph, no stabilizer deformation occurred. During the 450-mph pull-up the intensity of the buffeting was so much stronger (the cockpit accelerometer hand was bouncing between 5.5 and 7.5Gs during this maneuver) that both reinforced stabilizers were again permanently bent. The stabilizer cuffs were then increased to .081 thicknesses, which satisfactorily withstood the 6.5G, 450-mph buffeting. The F6F-3 Navy structural demonstration was now finally completed. It had taken two-and-a-half years after the first Hellcat deliveries to the fighting squadrons.

The appearance of the previously unknown buffet boundary on the Hellcat was described by Dr. Greene as caused by its much heavier wing loading coupled with its ability to attain higher dive Mach numbers faster than the maximum .70 Mach number drag-limited capability of the Wildcat.

## Visible Shock Waves Noted During a Dive

While I was checking my dive angle protractor on one of the high-speed dives I saw two parallel black wavy lines on the surface of the wing from the fuselage to the wingtip. Because I was close to my dive speed and altitude requirements, I turned my attention back into the cockpit.

Later, when I proudly told my boss, Bob Hall, about the two lines I saw, he ignored my discovery and strongly admonished me to concentrate inside the cockpit until the pullout was completed. My observation was noted at approximately the same time as Major Barsodi's similar sighting while diving a P-51 at Wright Field. HIS boss congratulated HIM for HIS observation! (What we had seen were schlieren lines of the shock wave that had been previously noted in wind tunnels under certain lighting conditions.)

## My Second Look Outside the Cockpit

I performed another pull-up slowly into the buffet boundary dive at 300 mph in order to look into the rearview mirror and see the effect of the buffeting on the stabilizer and fin. I was amazed at the clearly visible torsional oscillations of the entire tail assembly during buffeting and the marked increase in violence of their motions as the Gs increased. The tips of the stabilizer were in a 6-inch amplitude blur. Bob Hall was right. I should keep my eyes focused inside the cockpit during dives!

When I described the buffeting stabilizer amplitude to engineering they said that I was exaggerating. They had not witnessed such torsional dimensions as I described while ground testing the tail assembly to its static torsional maximum breaking loads.

## The F6F-5 Demonstration Was a Walk in the Park

Because of the several guessed-at solutions for the F6F-3 demonstration, engineering had greatly stiffened the aft fuselage stations during the F6F-5 static test and designed an all-new stabilizer with thicker skins, and main beams of .081 aluminum sheets, which was considerably stronger than the second cuffed stabilizer on the F6F-3 demo Hellcat.

The F6F-5 prototype, F6F-3 (BuNo 42186) demonstration aircraft, was selected as the 1,000th F6F-3 aircraft from the planned end of the F6F-3 line. In 1944 that production rate was only two months lead-time for the changeover from the F6F-3 to the F6F-5 model. This was a very short time to get such a highly modified aircraft structure through its required additional increase of one G static proof tests to 7.5 limit load flight envelope and to incorporate and test all of the combat improvement changes. These were: The NACA-developed spring tab ailerons that greatly increased the high-speed rolling capability allowing the pilot to make much faster tracking and evasive combat maneuvers, a new clear-view windshield, a second 1,000-lb bomb rack on the starboard wing stub, three racks on each wing panel for the new 5-inch HVAR rockets, and installation of the improved Pratt & Whitney R-2800-10W engine with water injection for 250 additional combat horsepower.

This test aircraft also had Grumman's first in-flight-test photo-panel and oscillo-graph instrumentation installed in the aft fuselage section. The photo-panel recorded six important cockpit instruments and the oscillograph had six channels of strain gauges for in-flight checking of specific stress loads in the aft fuselage and horizontal stabilizer. Engineers could now find out for the first time exactly how close the aircraft was designed to its in-flight air load requirements at any G load. Fortunately for me the F6F-3 Hellcat was the last of the "by guess and by God" designed and flight-tested Grumman fighters. That pioneering era of dive testing was over.

The F6F-5 Navy structural flight demonstration was child's play after the exciting F6F-3 demonstration. I made nine build-up pullouts into the increased 7.5G buffet boundary requirement now with the ability to check the increasing loads between each flight. Even with the increased G loads and stronger buffeting, the new oscillograph instrumentation confirmed that the redesigned structure remained under the design operational limit load stresses. The F6F-5 demonstration was completed in eight days to the satisfaction of Navy witnesses. I was now a much more confident test pilot, having in-flight recorded stress instrumentation to check and verify design loads after each flight. Grumman was the first in the industry to use in-flight oscillograph load-recording instrumentation.

## Hellcat Compressibility Info Remained Buried at Grumman

I have always wondered why somebody in Grumman engineering, management, or the Navy, who had read my well-circulated flight reports, didn't insist that compressibility information be included in the Pilot's Handbook. Neither Grumman nor the Navy had put the compressibility word out to service squadrons. Many pilots, easily seduced in operational training by the F4F-4 Wildcat's docile dive qualities, assumed that the Hellcat

should have the same docile capabilities. After the Hellcat became operational, Grumman service reports related that all too many pilots who had performed steep dives from high altitude had continued straight into the ground. Almost every report concluded: "reasons unknown" or "heart attack."

I also saw several Navy photos of F6F-3 Hellcats that had exceeded the demonstrated buffet boundary G limits for combat maneuvers and lost the entire outer halves of both stabilizers and elevators. The fact that they had sufficient elevator power to land on the carrier is still almost unbelievable. Fortunately these breaks occurred just outboard of the middle stabilizer elevator hinge, similar to where the stabilizers bent on my demonstration flights. Thus, the remaining portions of the stabilizers and elevators still worked, however poorly, to land back aboard the carrier.

## The Navy Dives a Hellcat to Destruction

Naval development personnel at Chincoteague Naval Air Station, directed by Commander Gene Dare, retained the third production Hellcat, painted it all yellow for better visual reference, and installed radio control for pilot-less flight. They used ground-based theodolite tracking equipment to determine its flight trajectory speeds. During its last flight it crashed vertically into the ground from a planned 60-degree dive attempt starting at 30,000 feet. Their report stated that the crash was caused by radio-control failure. From my experience it was Grumman's opinion that nose-down pitching compressibility effects were more powerful than the radio control mechanism's ability to pull the Hellcat out of its dive when it exceeded its .75 critical compressibility Mach number.

*The number three production F6F-3 Hellcat that was used for the Navy radio controlled "Nolo" (no pilot) dive program managed by Commander Gene Dare. This program was designed to determine the Hellcat's limit dive speed without endangering a pilot. On the aircraft's last flight it went vertically into the ground at a theodolite measured speed of .79 Mach number. The Navy thought that their radio control had failed. We believed that because this aircraft had exceeded the Hellcat's critical .75 Mach number it would have been unable to be recovered by any available mechanical stick force. Unfortunately the meager data from this program provided nothing to increase our understanding of compressibility. (Northrop Grumman History Center)*

I was pleased that because of wartime production urgencies Grumman was never required to find out just what Mach number the Hellcat could attain in a vertical dive. Our engineers calculated that it would be about .80 Mach number because of its 16 percent airfoil wing thickness.

For me, the Hellcat was the first of a long line of Grumman subsonic and supersonic fighter cats to claw its way into and beyond the compressibility regime to supersonic flight.

## Epilogue

When they exceeded their critical Mach numbers, almost all of the allied fighters of the World War II era exhibited the same disastrous diving tendencies with buffeting and frozen stick characteristics like those the Hellcat had encountered. As an example, the Lockheed P-38 demonstration program lost Ralph Virden, and several other test pilots, which required the P-38's entire aft fuselage and tail structure to be redesigned to withstand compressibility effects.

To cure the symptoms of compressibility, NACA developed small dive recovery flaps to be installed on the underside of combat aircraft wings, which, when extended, immediately counteracted nose-down pitching and stick freezing. The extended flaps also added drag to decelerate the aircraft below its critical Mach number. These flaps, which had strong nose-up pitching characteristics when extended, also greatly assisted the pilot in making an immediate controlled pullout. They were installed on P-47s and P-38s in later production, but not until too many combat pilots had already lost their lives to this sometimes-fatal phenomenon. Sad to say, the Navy never required them to be installed on any of the 12,750 Hellcats they procured.

Before the end of the war I did a lot of flight-testing of these simple but wonderful devices on the Grumman Tigercat and Bearcat, easily probing deeply into and beyond their vertical dive compressibility Mach number limits with impunity. They were a godsend.

## A German Test Pilot Meets an Even More Violent Compressibility

Josef Hubert was one of the "impressed" German scientists who was coerced from Germany to Wright Field and then to Grumman in late 1945. He spoke excellent English and, being the chief aerodynamicist of the rocket-powered Messerschmitt Me-163 program, he taught me a lot about German swept-wing compressibility problems during our many one-hour car pool rides to and from Grumman. Through him I met Rudy Opitz, a German test pilot

This picture of the F7F-1 Tigercat shows that our original installation of the dive recovery brakes between the engine nacelles and fuselage did not take into consideration the many shock waves generated by the nacelle and fuselage, which caused violent reactions when these dive recovery flaps were extended at any speed. The final solution outboard of the nacelles provided a much smoother recovery when the Tigercat was flown beyond its limit Mach number of .72. (Northrop Grumman History Center)

who came with him to the U.S., but who worked for the Lycoming Engine Company.

When I saw the letter to the editor in the November 1999 *Air and Space* magazine in which aviation historian William Winter quoted that Rudy Opitz flew to Mach .99 in a 45-degree climb in an Me-163B, I phoned Opitz immediately to inquire about his near-supersonic ride. He soundly denied that it had ever happened and related the following details of his frenetic flight.

In June of 1943 he was scheduled to test the more powerful Me-163B to provide detailed engine data for the Walther Rocket Engine Company. Because of the complete lack of space in the instrument panel, Rudy had his mechanics remove the attitude gyro, the turn and bank indicator, and the gun sight so that they could be replaced with the needed engine instruments. He also installed a 35-mm camera on his helmet pointing towards the instrument panel so he could record data for the new engine during a high-performance climb.

During his almost vertical angle of climb at over 15,000 feet per minute, he soon noted that he had no horizon references. This was due to an unpredicted haze condition, which he had entered just after takeoff. He related that he then had to spend way too much time looking outside the cockpit for ground reference when he accidentally exceeded the .81 limit Mach number of the Me-163 and plunged into strong buffeting, violent nose-down pitch, and complete loss of his pitch control at .84 Mach number, which scared the living daylights out of him. He instantly yanked the throttle to idle. The drag of the aircraft finally brought him below the .81 limit critical Mach number where he could again use

his flight controls to recover from the ensuing steep dive.

Ground inspection showed that he had lost the rudder. Several of his big wing root fairings had almost pulled free from their attachments during his compressibility event.

Following Rudy's debrief he asked Josef Hubert to tell him more about compressibility. Josef retorted that Rudy now knew a lot more about compressibility than he did. The German wind tunnels had the same transonic choking problem that NACA tunnels experienced.

I also asked him what kind of cockpit Mach number instrumentation the Me-163B had installed. The production Me-163 aircraft had a big red light located next to the gun sight, set to come on at .81 Mach number so the pilot could easily see it when he was in combat and reduce his throttle immediately.

Rudy's vivid description of the violence and aircraft damage from the buffet and pitch down beyond the limit Mach number is understandable. The Me-163 had no stabilizer behind its wing to be a damping influence from the great change in downwash of the wing when the compressibility shock wave was entered.

An epilogue of this hair-raising flight was that the next day allied bombing raids demolished the V-1 and V-2 Penemunde Rocket Development Center, which was launching the V-1 and V-2 rocket missiles on London. This forced the Me-163B program to be moved to another airfield. To this day Rudy has never found out if his precious head camera data was ever received or used.

Opitz learned a lesson the hard way. The wise test pilot NEVER gives up his flight gauges required for a possible instrument flight condition happenstance!

# Chapter 12

# The Legendary Bob Hall – From Hire to Retire

Bob was born in 1905; just two years after Wilbur and Orville Wright had first flown at Kitty Hawk. During his youth, his father, a mechanical engineer, and his brothers instilled in Bob a skill for designing and building things mechanical. From an early age Bob was fascinated with both steam and the new internal combustion gasoline engines. While still in high school he built from scratch a steam engine, which successfully powered his high-speed model boat. He became an expert mechanic and had a well-earned reputation for repairing all sorts of auto, yacht, motorcycle, and aircraft engines. Bob spent two years at Harvard and completed his bachelor's degree in Mechanical Engineering at the University of Michigan in 1927.

## A Splendid Reason for Bob to Learn to Fly

Bob immediately went to work at the Fairchild Aircraft Manufacturing Company in Farmingdale, New York, as a general design stress engineer. The Chief Engineer, Roscoe Markey, soon noticed Bob's energy. One day Bob heard a heated argument between Markey and a Fairchild test pilot regarding a design change that the test pilot had determined was mandatory. Markey stated positively that he knew the change was not necessary. The pilot looked at him and said, "Have you ever flown an aircraft?" The engineer's flustered negative admission ended the argument. Bob decided then and there that to have a complete knowledge of aircraft design he must learn to fly.

It is a shame that the logbook containing his first 266 flight hours has disappeared, but it is almost certain that Bob learned to fly in an OX-5-powered surplus World War I Jenny or a Waco biplane while earning whatever license was required by the Feds. It had only been one year since flying licenses were required. His logbooks do not cite the date he received his commercial license, but I am sure that it was with the same order of high priority that he had worked at engineering and the rest of his exciting life.

## "Gee Bee" Speed Gets Into Bob's Blood

In late 1929, Bob Ayre, a good friend from Bob's Harvard days, convinced him to join the five Granville brothers in Boston. They were aircraft rebuilders, but really aspired to design fast sport aircraft for the wealthy. Bob Hall became Chief Engineer and Test Pilot (note his secondary position of importance) for Granville Brothers Aviation. The company soon moved to Springfield, Massachusetts, where they had found the Tait brothers who were interested in funding their new aeronautical ideas with their ice cream fortune.

Bob's first design was the Junior Sportster Model "X" in which he placed second in the American Cirrus Derby in Detroit. After designing and flight-testing Gee Bee Models A, Y, D, and E sport planes in 1929 and 1930, Bob convinced the Granvilles that the only way to make real money in the Depression was to win a high-stakes race. And the way to win big prize money was to enter an unlimited racing plane in the National Air Races.

Bob admits his entrance into the racing business was strictly mercenary. "That was back in the Depression days and the prize money was fantastic. You could build a plane for $5,000 and collect $10,000 for winning one race. Not bad."

Bob learned his next big, practical lesson of aeronautical engineering that was never taught at Michigan or Harvard. The mechanic-oriented Granville brothers were quite happy to go along with his premise, but with another fine-print condition. They said, "Bob, we'll build it and you will design it, but you must raise the money." Bob spent a great part of his "designing" days raising over $5,000, at $100 per share, in and around the Springfield area to fund the project. He spent his long evenings designing a short, stubby, high-powered racer.

This Model Z racer (probably named for the oldest brother, Zantford) was to be powered by the new Pratt & Whitney supercharged 535-hp Wasp Junior, the biggest engine available, intending to win the largest purse of the unlimited race at the 1931 Nationals in Cleveland.

It was built in an astonishing six weeks, painted bright yellow, gloss black, and trimmed in red. Appropriately named *City of Springfield*, Hall test flew it for the first time on his 26th birthday, 22 August 1931. He remarked that the rudder forces were so light that he never flew it again with his shoes on. He could much better feel possible idiosyncrasies from the very light rudder control forces in his stocking feet.

Shortly after the first flight he flew it to Cleveland with gas stops along the way. One stop was a highway landing where he fueled up at an automobile filling station, and then, using the same highway, he took off for Cleveland.

Although Bob designed and test flew the "Z," Lowell Bayles was a $500 sponsor for the aircraft and he was in the "driver's seat" to pilot it for the prestigious Thompson Race. The Gee Bee "Z" was undefeated in five races at Cleveland. It set a speed record in the Thompson Trophy Race at 236.239 mph.

It won the Goodyear Race at 206.001 mph, and Bayles won the Shell Speed Dash at a speed of 267.342 mph. Bob raced the "Z" model and won the "Mixed Free-For-All" and the General Tire and Rubber Trophy races, giving him a great deal of satisfaction and winnings of $2,750. The Gee Bee "Z" won a total of $17,000, bringing handsome returns to all the Springfield investors—Bayles, Hall, and the five Granville brothers. To this day aviation historians consider the stubby yellow and black Gee Bee Model "Z" the standard and epitome of air-racing aircraft.

## Stinson Gets Bob for Its Experimental Division

In March 1933 Hall once again followed his close friend Bob Ayre, who was chief engineer of the transport division of Stinson, to Wayne, Michigan, where he was put in charge of Stinson's experimental division. Soon after Bob arrived, Lowell Yerex, who owned eight Stinsons of TACA, a Central American airline, came to Stinson with $30,000 to purchase three counter-insurgency aircraft for the Honduran Air Forces. Bob designed the Stinson Model "O," a two-seat, high-wing aircraft using modified wings and tail surfaces of the Stinson Reliant. It had a .30-caliber machine gun on a swivel in its rear cockpit. He performed the first flight and did all of the necessary test flying for government approval. Although further sales were not too successful, three more were sold to China and two to Brazil.

Bob experienced his first bailout at Stinson on 12 July 1934 when a large amount of the wing fabric came off the float-equipped SR-5 Reliant during government-required spin tests. He described this flight to me many years later. After the first turn, the aircraft went "ass over teakettle" and no matter how diligently he applied anti-spin controls there was no recovery response from them. After all too many futile turns he bailed out. His logbook read, "I had to leave 'er." Thus he became a member of the Caterpillar Club. He impressed me with that horrendous event to illustrate a spin that I almost didn't recover from. My close-shave spin in a Grumman Bearcat should be buried in my embarrassment, but will be related in a future chapter.

Hall then collaborated with his old friend Bob Ayer on the classic Stinson Reliant SR-7, changing it from a straight wing to the gorgeous gull wing, which had obvious roots in the Springfield Bulldog. Its highly tapered wing, however, gave it some very nasty spin characteristics. It took Bob four weeks and 52 flight hours of spin testing in early 1936 to finally satisfy the Department of Commerce spin requirements. In those years 52 hours of spin testing strongly suggested that there were a lot of difficulties to solve in the SR-7's new wing planform.

Bob's last flight for Stinson was 26 August 1936. His logbook shows he accumulated 567 hours of flight-testing at Stinson, now making his total flight time 967:25 hours.

## Bob Becomes a Grumman Experimental Test Pilot

Up to 1937, when a fighter was ready for its first flight, Grumman would hire professional, military-trained test pilots on a contract basis to do the first flight and the Navy for final demonstration jobs. William Mc Avoy had done the XFF-1 and XS-1, Peter Hovegard the XF2F-1, Jimmy Collins the F2F-1 and

The first experimental XF8F-1 Bearcat on its second flight over Oyster Bay, New York, with Bob at the controls. It was before the dorsal fin was installed behind the canopy but only a flight after the stabilizer had been fully rebuilt with a 2-foot increase in its span. This 2-foot extension was the bare minimum necessary to attain the needed positive roll stability. Bob instinctively knew how to fine-tune fighter pilot's control systems. (Northrop Grumman History Center)

XF3F-1 and Navy demonstration. After Collins died in its crash, Lee Gehlbach did the first flight and Navy demonstration of the second XF3F-1.

On 2 October 1937 Bob performed the first flight in the XF4F-2, a monoplane fighter which he had helped design. This aircraft had severe engine cooling problems, which required many flights to solve. He also performed the 8G structural demonstrations to the Navy in vertical terminal velocity dives. He then repeated structural and spin demonstrations for the Navy at NAS Anacostia in February of 1938.

The XF4F-2 required such major engine and aerodynamic changes after Navy flight-testing at Anacostia that it failed to win a production order and was returned to Grumman. The aircraft that won the production competition was the lack-luster Brewster F2A Buffalo.

In order to maintain its position in the very lucrative carrier fighter business, Grumman redesigned the XF4F-2 at its own expense. It now had a 4-foot increase in wingspan, a 2-foot increase in fuselage length, redesigned tail surfaces, an engine with 150 more horsepower and armor plate, and was called the XF4F-3. As an engineer Bob contributed to the many major design changes and performed the first flight of the XF4F-3 Wildcat on 12 February 1939. In the following 14 months he flew 99 flights to complete all the testing necessary to satisfy the Navy requirements. Many of these flights took less than 15 minutes to find the critical answers needed by Grumman engineering to meet the more stringent war-anticipated Navy specifications.

In August 1939, after the XF4F-3 had demonstrated its performance, it was 45 mph faster than that previously demonstrated at Anacostia. After it had passed its carrier suitability tests at the Naval Aircraft Factory in Philadelphia, Grumman was awarded a contract for 54 aircraft. With great difficulty and dogged persistence they had now successfully launched from biplane to monoplane fighters.

## Bob Advances to Assistant Chief Engineer-Experimental

After his advancement in 1939 he was now able to put his analyses from his test piloting into actual fixes much faster than at any other aircraft manufacturer in the United States.

## Bob Tests the Navy's Largest Carrier-Based Aircraft

In December of 1940 the Navy awarded Grumman a contract for 285 Avenger torpedo bombers, the largest order Grumman had ever received. By the middle of 1941 it was clear to the Navy and Grumman management that much larger numbers of Grumman Avengers (and F4F-3 Wildcats) were going to be needed soon to fight World War II.

The Avenger was ready for its first flight under Bob's guidance on 7 August 1941. Forty-four days later Bob had flown it 26 times, with many major changes

*A picture of Bob Hall's "relaxed" goggles during a flight in the XP-50. Test flying to Bob was only a necessary means to become a fully knowledgeable aeronautical engineer. He was one of the very few, if any, in the industry since Wilbur and Orville Wright. (Northrop Grumman History Center)*

Bob flew the first flight of the XTBF-1 on 7 August 1941 after making major changes from his shocking impressions of it after just a few prior high-speed liftoffs at the Grumman airport. The big dorsal fin has not been added yet to give satisfactory directional stability at large yaw angles. The TBF/M series became the backbone of U.S. Navy, British, and New Zealand fleet air arms throughout the war in the Pacific. (Northrop Grumman History Center)

made between flights. The first prototype crashed. The second prototype XTBF-1 was ready to fly only three weeks later. Grumman was about to meet the challenge of producing more combat aircraft than they had ever dreamed of.

Between 3 and 9 February 1942 Bob completed the entire final Navy-required structural, spin, power plant, and flying qualities demonstrations of the first production Avenger (BuNo 00373). These demonstrations took place at NAS Anacostia in 19 flights averaging only 23 minutes per flight. Bob was never one to waste taxpayers' money.

After returning to full-time engineering duties on the XF6F-1 Hellcat fighter, Bob flew only 10 flights in various F4F Wildcat production aircraft in the next four-and-a-half months until the Hellcat was ready for the first flight.

On 6 June 1942 he made the first flight of the XF6F-1 Hellcat with the Avenger-proven 1,750-hp Wright R-2600-10 engine installed. Fourteen flights were made in this prototype before it was laid up to have the Wright engine exchanged for the new

Pratt & Whitney R-2800-10 two-stage supercharged engine. On 17 August 1942 during its fifth flight, while Bob was checking full-power performance above overcast, the engine froze from insufficient lubrication. After coming out of the clouds as a very heavy glider at 700 feet, Bob spotted a potato field ahead and dead sticked into it. He hit the ground quite hard and damaged his back but not permanently. The aircraft was badly bent, too, but was able to be rebuilt into another prototype Hellcat in less than two months. By this time Bob's total time was only 1,293 hours, considerably less flight-test time than is required to qualify for test pilot school entrance today.

## The Author Becomes Bob's Protégé

My first-year tasks were to fly all experimental and production Hellcat, Avenger, Wildcat, Goose, and Widgeon aircraft on their many detailed tests and to perform the final Navy demonstration of the Hellcat similar to the demonstrations

The XP-50 was the Grumman competitor to the Lockheed P-38 in the U.S. Army Air Corps competition. Bob first flew it on 18 February 1941. It was the fastest fighter in U.S. inventory with its 427-mph speed at 31,000 feet. Its career was cut short when Bob had to bail out of it on 14 May 1941 after one of its superchargers disintegrated and collateral damage kept the nose wheel from extending. (Northrop Grumman History Center)

Bob had performed on all previous Grumman fighters. I was a little kid with a big appetite and with unlimited credit in a well-stocked candy store.

As the XF7F-1 construction became more of a reality, Bob insisted that when I wasn't flying I had to sit on a wooden box squarely in the middle of the one-room experimental shop where the XF7F-1 was being fabricated, until it flew. This was the only action place to be where I could learn everything about this new fighter, not only from the personnel building the aircraft but also from the engineers working on it. I could ask any question of anybody and get a complete answer. I, therefore, pleasantly absorbed all aspects of its construction. The candy shop just got bigger.

## The Tigercat Flies

Bob flew the initial flight of the first Tigercat on 2 November 1943. It was powered with the same engine that was in the Hellcat—the tried and true Pratt & Whitney R-2800-10B. After only six flights he turned it over to me. He flew 11

times on and off for the next four months, but when the second XF7F flew on 2 March 1944 with the new Pratt & Whitney R-2800-22C engines, he suggested that I perform the first flight. I was delighted and I worked very closely with Bob from then on.

Bob continued to fly production Hellcats and Tigercats to check changes that were being put into them. Two years after the crash of the XF6F-1 his logbook shows an increase of only 42 hours. I had logged over 400 delightful hours in that same time period in the same aircraft.

## Bob Was a Very Terse Test Pilot

When he made the first flight in the XF8F-1 Bearcat on 31 August 1944, we all saw Bob at his test piloting best. He landed and with his Boston accent said, "Drag it into the barn immediately and add two feet to the stabilizer span!" I was amazed that he could command that change with absolutely no test data. I later asked him what data he had used to make his decision. He looked at me with some disdain and said, "That aircraft is totally unstable longitudinally." Enough said. It must have been very unstable because when I flew it after he had made the first six flights, it had only the bare minimum of longitudinal stability. A down spring and bob weight installed in the elevator control brought the longitudinal stability up to minimum Navy requirements. When interrogating Bob after his flights in the Tigercat or the Bearcat, I remember he didn't take down much data and took very few notes. He always seemed to know exactly what was needed to make a good fighter aircraft. I learned a lot from him on those two aircraft.

## I Am Finally Given All of Bob's Flight-Test Chores

Just before I flew Grumman's first jet, the Panther, on 21 November 1947, Bob made a high-speed taxi run, lifting the Panther a foot or so off the ground. He taxied back and returned it to me with a grin and the following terse statement, "It's all yours now, Corky." I was to perform all of the Grumman fighters' first

flights and Navy demonstrations until 1966 when I became director of the new airport at Calverton, New York, which included flight-test, instrumentation, final assembly, and production flight operations. My appetite was able to keep up with the candy store's enlargement for the next 10 years.

Except for a few more check flights in the Hellcat, Tigercat, Bearcat, and four flights in the post-war Mallard amphibian, Bob concluded his logbooks with 1,365 hours on 7 August 1947. This included 22 first flights, development flights thereafter, and much of the actual design engineering prior to and after these flights. I haven't heard of any pilot who has ever come close to his achievements. Not bad for a part-time test pilot.

Bob continued to head up Experimental Engineering through the Mallard, Panther jet, AF-2S and AF-2W Guardian anti-submarine warfare aircraft, and the JR2F-1 Albatross amphibian. During this period the Albatross made the transition to an international rescue aircraft used by our Navy, the U.S. Air Force, and Coast Guard, plus 20 other nations worldwide.

*The author assisting Bob to familiarize himself with the cockpit of the XF9F-2 Panther before Bob made a high-speed liftoff on the Grumman runway 21 November 1947, three days before the author made the first flight. It is a shame his engineering load of three new aircraft in design at this time probably accelerated his transition out of flight-testing his designs. He would have enjoyed flying jets. They were so much easier to fly than piston aircraft due to their pressurized cabins, great cockpit visibilities, quiet vibration-less engine operations, and fabulous thrust. (Northrop Grumman History Center)*

## Bob Becomes Chief Engineer

In 1950, with the retirement of Grumman founder William T. Schwendler, Bob became Chief Engineer. In 1954 he was appointed vice president of engineering. He was then responsible for the engineering of the following Grumman projects: the swept-wing F9F-6 Cougar, F11F-1 super-sonic Tiger, Mach 2 Super Tiger, XF10F-1 variable-sweep wing Jaguar, twin-engine S2F-1 anti-submarine tracker, carrier-on-board-delivery transport (COD TF-1 Trader), WF-2 (E-1B) early warning tracker, G-159 Gulfstream I, and many other programs. Bob Hall's 34 years of leadership in engineering and test flying played a great part in making and continuing Grumman's "sterling" reputation.

His personal legacy to the writer was that of a firm, constant, and kindly mentor who continuously applied his hard-earned knowledge and experience with a wry smile to a difficult young student. To this day, when I get excited I can still remember his admonishing me with his Boston accent as I entered his office after a flight: "Re-the-hell-lax Meyer and tell me the story."

## Lessons Learned From Bob Hall

When I first came to Grumman I heard from several reliable sources around the ready room that Connie Converse, who was the chief test pilot, was unable to make the F6F-3 Hellcat perform the four-turn inverted spins and recoveries required to complete the Navy demonstration.

Being educated beyond my intelligence in inverted spins during my Civilian Pilot Training Program training, I decided shortly thereafter that as an addendum to a Hellcat production test flight I would try my hand at making the Hellcat perform inverted spins. After many attempts I found out why Connie couldn't achieve an inverted spin. It was because of the very high dihedral (rolling) effect of the Hellcat's wing, which would naturally roll the aircraft to the left from propeller torque just prior to the inverted stall. The aircraft's nose would then fall through into a dive and the aircraft would un-stall immediately.

So I tried an entry by holding the wings level with aileron until I was near the inverted stall. Then I immediately pushed full forward on the stick and combined that with simultaneously applying full rudder deflection to make it spin. It spun and recovered beautifully. I found that by using that method I could easily perform the required four-turn right and left spins and recoveries on every attempt.

I immediately wrote up a flight-test report and sent it into Bob's office in hopes that I would gain his daughter's hand in marriage and half of his kingdom in gold for miraculously performing the "impossible" inverted spin requirement.

A day later I was sitting at my desk when I heard my name coming out of his office with FedEx dispatch. He came storming out of his office, shaking my report in his hand, and stating unequivocally for all of engineering to hear, "If you ever try to spin an aircraft with unknown spin qualities again without an anti-spin chute installed, tested, and rigged for use, I will kick your ass so far out of the test piloting business you will never find your way back!" There were some other strong words issued at the time but they have charitably been consigned to the dustbin of Grumman history. I soon became aware of all the facts about this unknown anti-spin chute installation.

Reading Bob's logbook notations, referred to previously, brings back another lesson learned. I remember being called into Bob's office one spring morning in 1948. Bob never beat around the bush. He said, "I understand that you have been working at Gyrodyne for Pete Papadakos and flying their experimental Bendix helicopter with absolutely no experience or knowledge of helicopters." After my embarrassment of being found out, I admitted his statement was correct and hastily added, "But it was on weekends and on my own time, Bob." He continued as if I had said nothing, "I looked up your pay records and they showed me that we paid you six times what we paid engineers last year. We feel that payment is enough to merit ALL of your time thinking about Grumman aircraft. Mr. Grumman spoke the same words to me shortly after I came to Grumman and I think his words fit your case. 'Which company would you like to work for?'" I had no more trouble answering that question than Bob did in 1937. And that was the last time I looked for greener pastures in aviation until my retirement many years later.

I later learned from Bob's logbook exploits what prompted Mr. Grumman's words to be spoken to Bob in 1937. During his first few months at Grumman, Bob did some ex-officio moonlighting by spin testing two Stinsons and a Howard DGA equipped with pontoons for two New York operators. Regarding these he had written in his logbook, "ATC tests at LaGuardia. Directionally unstable on first flight, seaplane fin added, directional stability okay, very bad in spins, however, seaplane fins added twice size regular fin, small spoilers added, spins were still unacceptable, returned to factory without completing tests." Previously at Stinson he had bailed out of a float-equipped Stinson during a spin and remarked, "Float plane spins, once burned, well learned." He had a good memory, too.

Another incident took place in 1949. We were having trouble reducing exceptionally high forces in the Panther jet's aileron system after failure of its hydraulic boost system. The Navy reported them as unacceptable during their first evaluation.

We had made several flight fixes to reduce the boost-off forces without any positive results. As I walked into the ready room in preparation for another boost-off fix flight I reflected to the pilot audience in a disgruntled voice, "I could fill out this idiot engineering data card without needing to start the engine."

I was shocked instantly thereafter when Bob came out of the shower room dripping wet with only a towel around his waist. He spoke very quietly but firmly in his Boston accent, "Cork, if I ever hear you getting into an experimental aircraft with your mind made up that you know all the answers for the flight beforehand, I'll kill you before your stupidity does!" He stood there several more long seconds looking me straight in the eye, thus clinching his argument. Then he turned around and went back to his shower. Nobody spoke for several minutes, but the entire audience learned a most important lesson under circumstances that test pilot schools can't teach.

A final lesson involved one of the many test flights in my career where his words came to mind. I had completed the spin tests of the F11F-1 Tiger several months before when one of the engineers said that I had to re-test spins because of a small change in the configuration in the rudder trailing edge. This required performing a few re-check spins in the new configuration. He further suggested that the change was so trivial that we didn't need to install the complex anti-spin parachute (whose deployment guaranteed spin recovery if the pilot determined that the normal anti-spin flight controls were not working). The engineer's comments made sense. From my previous experience of performing several hundred spins it seemed to me that a change in the rudder trailing edge from a sharp one to one inch of thickness should have little effect, if any, on the aircraft's spin characteristics. I

*Even at age 83 Bob still got a kick from being close to one of his early compatriots in aviation, the beautiful Stinson Reliant. I'm sure that his smile also reflects his thankfulness for parachutes on one test flight in an SR-5 Reliant on floats. (Eric Hall)*

almost agreed with him when a small Boston-accented voice in the back of my mind said quietly but firmly, "Don't have your mind made up before any flight." The anti-spin chute was installed.

After two turns of the first spin, and without any forewarning, the aircraft departed as I had never experienced before and went wild about all three of its flight axes. The recorded data later showed that it simultaneously pitched up and down 4Gs, rolled plus or minus 200 degrees per second, and yawed violently at one cycle per second! I was almost at the stage of blackout from the violence of these confusing maneuvers. I was barely able to see the actuation handle of the anti-spin chute and pull it. It came out and yanked the tail of the aircraft violently out of the spin as my vision departed.

After slowly coming to my senses I found the aircraft hanging vertically down, pointing directly into the center of the Long Island Sound. I released the anti-spin chute, recovered to level flight, and landed back at Grumman in one piece a very shaken up and thankful pilot. After making some additional flight-tests, which we should have done before the spins, we found that the increased thickness of the trailing edge had unpredictably increased the rudder effectiveness 100 percent, causing the unexpected abrupt change in spin characteristics. We reduced the rudder to half its normal angle and the Tiger exhibited normal spins and recoveries again.

These were only a few of the many more "interesting" examples of his mentoring during my all too few years of learning from Bob Hall. He and God are the only two reasons that I am still here. Fifty years later Bob's few quiet words still impress me in all things I attempt to do. He was a very wise and a most interested teacher of the wisdom he had learned the hard way.

# Chapter 13

# The Tigercat's Untold Story

## 10 November 1943 to 29 July 1947

### Was the F7F-1 Tigercat Designed in a Japanese Prison Camp?

In early 1944 Lt. (jg) Fred P. "Shorty" Turnbull was shot down by ground fire while fighting in his Hellcat near Formosa. He was dragged in from the surf by natives and turned over to a Japanese guard who threatened to decapitate him with a Samurai sword. Another guard shot

The author enjoying a flight in the first two-place F7F-3N (BuNo 80359) during the external stores structural demonstration with the 300-gallon belly tank installed. The engine oil cooler duct exits are on the top of the wing just ahead of the flaps with their shutters in the "closed" or "cruise" position. The two wing-mounted 20-mm cannon barrels can be seen next to the pilot's cockpit. They did not have the blast and flash deflectors installed for night gunnery. (Corwin H. Meyer Collection)

him, as he lay wounded on the ground. He was immediately incarcerated in a Japanese prison. His captors put him and his fellow prisoners through inhumanely harsh interrogations. They wanted to know everything that the pilots knew about any follow-on fighter that Grumman was planning to produce. The torture became so violent that Fred and his comrades decided that they would have to "invent" a design of a follow-on fighter to the Hellcat and describe it in detail to their Japanese interrogators.

They determined that this mythical fighter should have two Hellcat engines to provide superior speed and a range of over 1,000 miles, a tricycle landing gear like the P-38, which would ease its training problems, and it would have eight 20-mm cannons. They named it the F7F-1. The beatings lessened considerably with this information, and Fred and his compatriots were ultimately rescued from the camp in August 1945.

During their extensive debriefing at the Criminal Investigation Division of the Army in the U.S., a rather stern inquisitor asked Fred and his group who had been responsible for spilling the beans about the F7F-1 to the Japanese. They looked at each other in disbelief. The American debriefer went on to say that documents recently captured had a very accurate

*The first in-flight picture of the XF7F-1 with the rather proud author at the controls. The 3-inch ventral strake on the bottom, and the similar strake on the top aft fuselage were added in an attempt to reduce the minimum single-engine controllability speed during landing approach. It did reduce the speed about 10 mph, but we needed a much greater speed reduction to meet the Navy specification. In December 1943 Grumman redesigned the fin to increase the vertical fin and rudder area by 29.2 percent. (Corwin H. Meyer Collection)*

description of the F7F-1, which had come out of their prison camp! Fred and his fellow POWs broke up in laughter and told the debriefer about their mythical design. One of them added, "If you can imagine it, Grumman will design and build it."

## A Navy Twin-engine XF7F-1 Fighter Emerges

I was not privy to the XF7F-1's early months of construction because I was fully engaged in the Hellcat's final structural flight-tests. But in September 1943 Bob Hall told me that I was going be the project test pilot for the XF7F-1 after he made a few flights. Starting 23 October 1943 and subsequent I participated in engine runs, systems checkout, and high-speed taxi tests to burn-in the new hydraulic-boosted main wheel brakes. On 2 November Bob lifted it off for a few feet and landed it to evaluate its slow speed takeoff and landing handling characteristics. The next day he flew it 20 minutes for its official first flight. He flew it four more flights, all of which I flew as chase in a

Hellcat. During his de-briefs he related that it had excellent stall and flight handling characteristics up to 325 mph. He then turned it over to me as project pilot. It was beyond my imagination that this would happen so soon in such an imposing fighter design.

My first flight was 10 November 1943. At that time I had a total of 21 hours and 10 minutes of twin-engine pilot time in a Lockheed 10A whose total horsepower was less than 25 percent of the XF7F-1. Very heady stuff for a 37-hp Piper J-3 Cub trained test pilot.

The noise from the two 2,000-hp Pratt & Whitney R-2800-10 engines just outside the thin canopy was very impressive. I don't think that any other aircraft I ever flew, including jets, were as powerfully soul-stirring as my first several flights in the XF7F-1. All this took place just one day less than a year after coming to Grumman. To keep this eight-gun fighter in a 30-degree climb angle until it attained its service ceiling was mind-boggling. The soon-to-be-famous six-gun Hellcat fighter was now an elderly pussycat.

## The XF7F-1 Gets Named

The flight-test group had informally bestowed the name Tomcat to the XF7F-1 early in its flight-test program. The name seemed to fit a night-fighter, so Grumman proffered that name to the Navy Fighter Desk in Washington and was surprised when the name Tomcat was denied. The Navy letter stated, "The name Tomcat is unacceptable. It denotes feline promiscuity." Period, that was the end of the message. They did accept our second-choice name of Tigercat as being socially and politically acceptable. In a completely different cultural climate 25 years later, the F-14's Tomcat name went through the hurdles without a hitch. It may have been because the three top admirals in Naval Air at the time were all named Tom: Moore, Connelly, and Walker.

## Meyer's First Management Flight-Test

Bob's first flights had satisfied him that the handling characteristics of the Tigercat were basically satisfactory for a carrier-based aircraft. It had a very docile wings-level stall with power on or off and the visibility over the nose for landing was superb. Engine temperatures were all in the green, totally different from the massive cooling problems in the twin-engine XF5F-1 Skyrocket and its USAAC counterpart, the XP-50. The XF7F-1's only deficiency soon became quite obvious to him and to me after I flew it. The fin and rudder were of vastly insufficient area for satisfactory directional control after losing an engine during a carrier takeoff.

After I had made 10 flights and had determined that the XF7F-1 met its contract performance requirements, Bob told me to make a flight where I did nothing but qualitatively evaluate all of the good and bad flying qualities of the aircraft, without reference to any Navy specifications. I asked him what data he wanted and he said none. This request seemed so simple but so different from the tightly scripted flights that I had made from engineering flight cards that I was quite confused. But, he WAS the boss. I spent a very pleasant hour looking into every corner of the aircraft's flight envelope. My four-page flight report had the following summary:

"The deficiencies are: neutral longitudinal (roll) stability, capability of rolling with the rudder faster than with the ailerons, the sensitive rudder deflection from the hydraulic boost system, and the excessive minimum single-engine control speed in the takeoff condition. They were all items that a pilot could get easily used to. The excessive engine-out minimum control speed would be offset by both the enlarged fin and rudder that was already being developed for retrofit.

"The Tigercat's spacious and well laid out cockpit had excellent ground and flight visibility. Its fabulous twin-engine performance was 75 mph faster than the Hellcat. The tricycle landing gear was a vast improvement in ground handling and in take-offs and landings. The twin's well-developed Pratt & Whitney engines were reassuring. The eight centerline guns, with no convergence problems, made sighting simple. The wings-level power-on, power-off, and accelerated stall characteristics were excellent, not to be found in any other Grumman fighter."

I concluded that the Tigercat would make any fighter pilot feel that he could take on any fighter in the world on his first flight. Not hearing anything back from my report, I promptly forgot it.

Bob Hall told me two years later that Mr. Grumman and others in top management wanted to see if my report reflected Bob's comments so they could be sure that their new XF7F-1 project test pilot evaluated aircraft similarly to Bob's well-known insights. I am pleased I didn't realize the real purpose of the flight at the time or I would have failed miserably trying to outguess what the answers should be.

## XF7F-1 Goes Into Production

An illustration of the wartime priorities for aircraft production is that the XF6F-1 Hellcat and the XF7F-1 Tigercat were ordered by the Navy on the same day, 14 May 1941. By the date of the first flight of the XF7F-1 Grumman had delivered over 4,500 Hellcats to the combat zones.

The first experimental Tigercat had the 2,000-hp Pratt & Whitney R-2800-10B engine. This was the standard engine of the production Hellcat and continued Grumman's philosophy of not installing an untried engine in a new aircraft. Its performance met contract requirements but the second prototype with its 2,100-hp Pratt R-2800-22C showed it to be another 35 mph faster than the Hellcat with twice its rate of climb.

After the Tigercat's excellent performance and flight characteristics were demonstrated, the Navy decided that it

should go into production as soon as possible, this despite the fact that the fighter's minimum controllability engine failure takeoff speed was 40 mph over the Navy requirement. The reader must understand that in early 1944 the war in the Pacific was still a long way from looking successful: therefore, maximum production numbers were mandatory. We knew in November 1943 that the fin would have to be enlarged 29.2 percent to meet the single engine criterion but that that large a change could not be designed, ground tested, and implemented into the production line until the 106th F7F-3N Tigercat (BuNo 80365) was delivered in July 1945, two-and-a-half years after the problem was known.

## The Structural, Aerodynamic, Spin, and Power Plant Demos Begin

The structural demonstration of any fighter in wartime is first on the list in hopes that no major structure redesign changes will have to be retrofitted in a fast-moving production line. The structural program buildup to 7.5G limit load and 525-mph limit speed was initiated without

F7F-3 (BuNo 80503) showing the second cockpit for a radar man crewmember. These aircraft had AN/APS-6 radars installed. Although the Tigercat had a less than glorious combat record, it did pave the way for the information needed for the heavier, larger, tricycle-geared jet fighters and bombers for the many massive Midway-class carriers that were to be the Navy standard for the long Cold War which began immediately after World War II ended. (Phillip Makanna via Corwin H. Meyer)

troubles until I began the speed buildup from 460 mph to 525 mph. As speed increased during the dive, the aircraft began oscillating up and down in the pitch axis to plus or minus 1G with increasing frequency and amplitude as the speed increased. This had never happened before in any other Grumman fighter. It was tolerable but unnerving. The aerodynamic engineer said that it was probably Mach number effects and not to worry about it. I completed the 525-mph speed point with a "galloping" 2.5G pullout. I then flew the aircraft to Patuxent to repeat the full demonstration there for the Navy to witness. During the final 525-mph pullout my chase F7F-1, flown by Commander Don Runyon, said that he had no oscillations while flying close formation with me.

When I returned to Grumman I talked to the structural engineers and asked them to determine why my Tigercat oscillated and the Patuxent chase Tigercat didn't. They trammeled all of the aircraft's major dimensions and found that the tail of my Tigercat had been permanently twisted 2 degrees during the off-center carrier landing tests made at NAS Muslin Field a year earlier. It was twisted back into place and flew with no more oscillations. I learned a great lesson: not to consider all engineering answers as "found gold" in the future.

## The Tigercat Doesn't Enjoy Spinning

The normal Navy SR-38D spin demonstration requirement was five turns, both directions, and from both upright and inverted starts. All of our previous aircraft, except the very stubby F3F biplane fighter, had no trouble performing this requirement. A few aerodynamic additions to the aft fuselage and rudder of the F3F solved its spin problem.

I had spun and recovered the production F4F-4 Wildcat and the F6F-3 Hellcat upright and inverted 10-turn spins successfully as a buildup for the Tigercat demonstration. The powerful thrust available from an offset engine in a twin-engine aircraft was believed to be a satisfactory solution for an emergency spin recovery. And, an experimental anti-spin chute was considered to be unnecessary. I was to be the first test pilot in the United States to investigate twin-engine naval fighter spins. I should have balked at this engineering decision.

Bob Hall suggested that I proceed very slowly in building up the spin turns prior to recovery, only increasing a half turn at a time prior to recovery attempts. His wisdom was soon to be greatly appreciated. Let the spins begin.

The first half-turn spin attempt required a sluggish, half-turn recovery. After a one-turn spin it then took one whole turn to recover with full anti-spin controls. An alarm went off in my head. After one- to four-turn spins, the Hellcat and Wildcat recovered immediately upon release of the controls. After 10 turns those aircraft only took one turn for recovery.

In the Tigercat, the first one-and-a-half turns from either right or left spin entries, the nose showed tendencies to rise during the last portion of the spin and it took an all-too-long one-and-a-half turns for recovery with full anti-spin control deflections. An equal number of turns for recovery for the same number of spin turns should have raised a much louder alarm bell. I should have quit then and there, but I completed the two-turn spins. They required two slow turns for recovery and showed that the nose was definitely rising in the second turn before recovery controls were applied. This indicated that an unrecoverable flat-spin problem was very near. The two turns required for recovery seemed to take ages. I decided to return to base to talk to engineers and to

A beautiful view of the slim lines of the Tigercat showing its two large nacelles housing Pratt & Whitney 2,300-hp (with water injection power) engines. With 4,600 horsepower the Tigercat's 451-mph top speed made it the first carrier-based fighter to have better performance than USAF fighters. (Phillip Makanna via Corwin H. Meyer)

Bob Hall who had performed many experimental aircraft spins. I also wanted the center of gravity location to be checked for accuracy. I hoped that the engineers might find that it was accidentally too far aft, which would have caused such delayed spin recovery reactions.

The center of gravity was found to be in its proper location and the full control deflections were checked okay, too. The engineers suggested that maybe the large inertia mass of the engines was causing the spin to flatten and thus provide its slowness in recovery. One of the engineers suggested that we should check the Tigercat NACA spin-tunnel model report. I had never heard about any NACA spin tunnel or of such a report on the Tigercat's spinning tendencies. My education was expanding. That report showed that the spins did indeed show nose raising in the first few turns and go flat and unrecoverable after four turns. Bob Hall decreed that we stop at two turns. He then promptly discussed the problem with the Navy and got the Tigercat requirement limited to two-turn, upright spins only, to my great relief.

Because of the long and sluggish recovery cycle, the Navy also stated in the Pilot's Handbook, "All spins and snap rolls are prohibited maneuvers in F7F aircraft." I officially and successfully demonstrated these slow recovering two-turn spins at Patuxent in October 1944.

A few weeks later, a military test pilot at Patuxent decided that he would investigate spinning the Tigercat and, as predicted, it went flat at the fourth turn and continued spinning 20 more unrecoverable turns until he hit the ground flat as a pancake, killing him instantly. He evidently failed to read the latest Pilot's Handbook admonition, which clearly stated, "Snap rolls and spins are prohibited."

Every pilot who flew the Tigercat readily forgave its lesser handling qualities for its many outstanding flight characteristics and fabulous performance. The only major problem that stuck with it throughout its military life was carrier suitability structural deficiencies. This is why it was consigned early on to ground-based Marine aviation as a night-fighter where it just missed World War II but played a strong role in Korea.

## Tigercat's Continual Carrier Suitability Woes

The Tigercat carrier suitability problems started with the XF7F-1 and were only permanently cured in the last model, the F7F-4N. The problems were many, both in carrier arresting issues and even more so in its structural design deficiencies.

The Tigercat was designed for the large, 55,000-ton Midway CVB-class carriers. It required higher-capacity arresting gear than on 1944-45 World War II carriers. It also required a specially designed Davis Barrier for its tricycle landing gear in case of hook or arresting wire failure. This barrier was found to be cumbersome to set up and re-rig for the simultaneous operation of both conventional and tricycle landing gear aircraft. The Tigercat was too big for the hangar decks of the Essex-class carriers. It was difficult to move in both the hangar and on the flight decks. There is no question, however, that it did provide a lot of background to the Navy for handling all of the up-coming twin-engine, tricycle gear jet aircraft soon to be in inventory.

From the Grumman design aspect, engineering did not provide sufficient strength to the wing/fuselage attachment area. As a result the Tigercat's wide main landing gear caused such high loads that in two carrier landings the wing broke at that point.

Although several isolated carrier landing demonstrations did provide satisfactory results at the time, the Navy wisely decided that the Tigercat should be removed from carrier operations and given to the U.S. Marine Corps for land-based, day, and night-fighter operations.

Prior to the Tigercat, Grumman was not required to perform the high-sink, limit-load landing tests. Navy test pilots at Mustin Field, the Naval Air Development Center in Philadelphia, Pennsylvania, performed them.

Because of the F7F-1 and -2N Tigercat's continuous structural arrested-landing problems, the Bureau of Aeronautics directed Grumman in early 1946 to instrument the structurally redesigned F7F-3N (BuNo 80549) and demonstrate these very interesting 22-feet-per-second, high-sink, controlled crashes by Grumman test pilots. I soon added new and frightening experiences to my logbook. What I used to think was a "very, very hard landing" I found out was only patting the ground at a 7- to 10-feet-per-second rate of descent.

I began these tests on 18 September 1946. The beginning engine-cut-and-dive-for-the-deck altitude was 15 feet. Grumman engineer Bob Mullaney, who was a Navy pilot in World War II, was my

*The F7F-3N Tigercat of Marine Squadron VMF (N)-534 after a carrier landing on the USS Shangri-La during the February 1946 carrier qualification of that squadron's pilots. After touchdown and hooking a wire, the starboard wing failed between the engine nacelle and the fuselage which rotated the aircraft 180 degrees, causing it to roll over on its back. Lt. Chuck O'Mally, the pilot, was miraculously uninjured. (Corwin H. Meyer Collection)*

The Tigercat's folding wing height of 16 feet 4 inches required it to have a hangar deck ceiling 3 feet 3 inches higher than the F6F-5 Hellcat and, therefore, it was unable to operate in squadron numbers from the World War II Essex-class carriers. It was designed for the much larger USS Midway CV-class carriers with 20-foot hangar deck ceilings, which were ordered in 1942 but not deployed until after the war had ended. (Grumman via Corwin H. Meyer)

landing signal "paddles" officer. He would progressively slow me down so that the aircraft hit harder and harder, but never hard enough. So we raised the altitude up to 20 and then to 25 feet before the cut to finally get 22-feet-per-second landings. Twenty-five feet is a most unnatural altitude to start a landing flare out just above the aircraft's stall speed. Above 10 feet per second they all hit the ground so violently that I soon became numb to the seemingly very fast descent and violent thump when the 21,000 pounds of the Tigercat's wheels met the asphalt. The aircraft structure and its oscillograph structural instrumentation were very carefully inspected between each of the 18 landings; many of them were only 15-feet-per-second medium "crashes." The structure finally passed its 22-feet-per-second landing rate of descent for landplane landings without exceeding the limit load. The Tigercat and I were both glad. I had seen all too many slow-motion camera shots of my landings demonstrating large deflections of the landing gear and tires, engine nacelles, wings, and the horizontal and vertical tail surfaces that were too fast to be seen by bystanders. I delivered F7F-3N (BuNo 80549) to the Patuxent test pilots who

added many more arrested landings. F7F-3N (BuNo 80549) was then officially ready for carrier landings.

Shortly afterwards another F7F-3N crashed on the USS *Shangri-La* during the carrier qualifications of VMF (N)-534 after quite a few pilots had previously checked out in it. The starboard wing again broke at the fuselage; the aircraft rolled over on its back, slid up the deck, and trapped Chuck O'Malley in the cockpit. Fortunately O'Malley was unhurt. Carrier operations were suspended. Inspection of the other 11 aircraft showed damage to the wing spars, engine mounts, and landing gear struts. This led to further major landing structural redesign in the new F7F-4N model. Naval Technical Order 147 dated 21 May 1947 prohibited arrested landings of all operational F7F aircraft. It was back to the old drawing board.

## The F7F-4N Tigercat Finally Makes Carrier Qualification

The Navy sent a Letter of Intent to Grumman dated 25 May 1945 to purchase 1,250 structurally redesigned F7F-4Ns. At the war's end, however, the production was reduced to 12 F7F-4Ns (BuNos 80609 through 80620), which were delivered between 9 September and 7 November 1946. I had the dubious pleasure of again demonstrating 22-feet-per-second land-plane landings (without arresting gear loads) in the now highly instrumented F7F-4N (BuNo 80610) during six flights between 26 September and 11 October 1946. The Naval Air Test Center test pilots at Patuxent then took it aboard the USS *Franklin D. Roosevelt* in October of 1946 for carrier trials. The F7F-4N model Tigercat had finally passed all of its structural requirements even to 22-feet-per-second rate of descent maximum, off-center arrested engagements that provided the highest loads of all carrier landings. Whew!

## The Tigercat External Stores Programs

Prior to the Tigercat, flight-testing of external stores were relatively insignificant in Grumman flight-test programs. Grumman F4F Wildcats were limited to two wing-mounted 100-pounders. In the F6F-3 Hellcats, external tanks, 1,000-lb bombs, and 5-inch wing-mounted HVAR (High Velocity Airborne Rockets) rockets were installed and tested in the fleet squadrons and rushed directly into combat.

As external stores became more varied and much heavier towards the end of the war, the Navy requested that Grumman perform external stores structural and aerodynamic handling qualities tests as soon as possible to determine the safe flight limit envelope of the many new external weapons being deployed. I performed this program on the Tigercat with a single 300-gallon centerline drop tank, dual 150-gallon drop tanks on racks located between the engine nacelles and fuselage, with eight 5-inch HVAR rockets located on the outboard wing panels. I also tested a Mark 13 aerial torpedo and the 1,300-lb Tiny Tim missiles located on the fuselage centerline. The Navy Test Center at Patuxent then tested all external stores for release, gun firing, and drop-test accuracy.

Limit flight speeds of the centerline stores and tanks were usually determined by the greatly increased drag as the speed increased in dives. Wing-drop tanks, which were carried between the fuselage and nacelles, showed their distaste for speed by causing the aircraft to wallow and pitch sufficiently to inhibit any accurate aerial gunnery or ground-attack possibilities above 350 mph.

Marine Corps Col. Joe Renner performed a 2,324-mile flight from MCAS Cherry Point to San Diego against a

*F7F-3N (BuNo 80549) with a 300-gallon centerline fuel tank. The unsatisfactory flight characteristics of this large tank limited its satisfactory speed to 375 mph, which was less than its high speed in level flight. This tank would have been dropped when combat occurred. It did, however, extend the Tigercat's Combat Air Patrol flying time. (Grumman via Corwin H. Meyer)*

25- to 40-mph headwind with a special triple, 300-gallon tank arrangement on F7F-3 (BuNo 80382). He had 115 gallons of fuel remaining when he arrived; enough for an additional hour cruise. He came back with a 40-mph tailwind and set a new unofficial transcontinental speed record of 6 hours and 33 minutes. This was to demonstrate the F7F's ability to cross the Pacific for combat. In spite of this interesting test, Marine Tigercats rode on ships and arrived at Okinawa the day before World War II ended.

The F7F-3N and the F7F-4N with 2,000-lb bombs on the centerline, two 1,000-lb bombs on the inboard wing stations, eight 5-inch HVAR rockets on the outboard wing panels, four .50-caliber machine guns in the nose, and four 20-mm cannons in the wing roots would surely have made a lethal ground-attack aircraft for the invasion of Japan.

## The Tigercat Compressibility Tribulations

The Tigercat was a very slick, fast-accelerating aircraft. Its 525-mph full-power dive limit speed could be attained at 35- to 40-degree dive angles in less than 30 seconds. Its great weight and twin engines made it the slickest accelerating prop fighter that I ever flew in a dive, including our new single-engine F8F-1 Bearcat.

In October 1944 during the Joint Army/Navy Fighter Conference at the Naval Air Test Center at Patuxent, Maryland, many test pilots were introduced to the NACA-developed Dive Recovery Flaps on the P-47 Thunderbolt and the Lockheed P-38J Lightning. They also had the new cockpit Mach number instrument to tell the pilot just what percent of the speed of sound that aircraft was traveling. Previous to the Fighter Conference, all flight-tests into and beyond the critical Mach number of a

fighter had to be made "by guess and by God." The several compressibility dives that I performed in the Hellcat were really into the unknown. I didn't have a Mach meter to know when I was about to enter the unknown until I was riding (not flying) a totally uncontrollable aircraft in a steep dive. I took the opportunity to fly both the P-47 and the P-38 to evaluate these great life-saving additions when fighters were accidentally flown beyond their critical Mach numbers.

Shortly after the Fighter Conference the Navy requested that Grumman dive beyond the limit critical Mach number of the Tigercat to check its recovery characteristics with use of dive recovery flaps. With a Mach meter now in the cockpit, and dive recovery flaps, it sounded easy. Wrong!

Our dive recovery brake installation was located between the fuselage and the engine nacelles on the underside of the wing 30 percent behind the wing's leading edge. This location was selected because the engineers wanted to get the full effect of the change in downwash angle on the Tigercat's stabilizer for an automatic pull-out when they were deployed.

As a safety precaution on my first compressibility test dive in F7F-3 (BuNo 80330) on 9 October 1946, I started from a 40-degree dive angle at 35,000 feet altitude to penetrate the compressibility area at as high an altitude as possible. This would keep air loads as low as possible. When I rapidly exceeded .72 Mach number, the controls were instantly frozen solid, so I extended the dive recovery flaps. The aircraft immediately rotated up to 5Gs, yawed back and forth 10 degrees, started a roll oscillation, and began porpoising between 4 and 6Gs, buffeting violently. What I thought was going to be a smooth, run-of-the-mill test flight turned out to be hair-raising. When the Tigercat decelerated below .72 Mach number, the shock

*The number two prototype XF7F-1 (BuNo 03550) with the later and more powerful Pratt & Whitney R-2800-22C 2,100-hp engines. These engines verified the contract performance of 451 mph at 21,000 feet, establishing that the Navy now had a fighter as fast as the USAAC land-based fighters. It was the first aircraft to be tested in the new NACA (now NASA) full-scale wind tunnel at Ames, California. It was there from September 1944 to October 1946, but its all-too-late report provided no important information to Grumman because one month later the Navy ended its production. (Corwin H. Meyer Collection)*

wave effect disappeared and normal aircraft control returned. The maximum Mach number recorded was .78. After landing, the instrumentation showed that the aircraft structure had exceeded its limit load in several fuselage and tail areas when the dive recovery flaps were extended and all hell broke loose. Fortunately inspection found no indication of pulled rivets or skin-wrinkling damage. It was very clear, however, that the venturi effect between the fuselage and nacelles made this a grossly unacceptable location for the dive recovery flaps.

After talking to NACA they recalled that the position of the dive recovery flaps was outboard of the engine nacelles on the P-38. Grumman engineering relocated the Tigercat's there, too. At this location they performed much smoother. After some minor increases in angle adjustments were

made to the dive recovery brakes, I made a hands-off 4G recovery deep into compressibility, attaining a vertical, terminal-velocity speed of .805 Mach number. My maximum speed at the 20,000-foot recovery altitude was just over 600 mph. I was happy with our new knowledge of compressibility after the completion of these tests, as it would pertain to future aircraft.

## Conclusions

I never met a Marine or Navy pilot that didn't have the same loving regard for a Tigercat that Captain Trapnell expressed to me in such a candid manner. The Tigercat had claws, but any pilot felt he had tamed it completely after five minutes of his first checkout flight.

# Chapter 14

# Joint Army/Navy Fighter Conference

## 16 to 27 October 1944

In early September 1944 the U.S. Army Air Corps and the Navy decided to hold a Joint Army/Navy Fighter Conference at the Naval Air Station at Patuxent River, Maryland. They thought that cross-pollination between the manufacturers and the military would spur the attainment of President Roosevelt's goal of the 50,000-aircraft-per-year program that he had launched in 1941. Attendees included Bob Hall, Bud Gillies, Pat Gallo, Fred Rowley, and myself.

### The REAL Attendees

I could have cared less about the human attendees. I was only interested in the total number of new fighters that I would be able to evaluate. A Focke-Wulf 190 was supposed to have been present, but it was held up at Wright Field for maintenance. The list of fighter aircraft attendees, however, was very impressive to me. It included:

Grumman F6F-5 Hellcat
Grumman F6F-5N Night-Fighter Hellcat
Grumman F7F-1 Night-Fighter Tigercat
Grumman XF8F-1 Bearcat
Vought F4U-1C and D Corsairs
Vought X4FU-4 Corsair
Goodyear FG1 and 1A Corsair
Goodyear XF2G-1 Corsair
Ryan XFR-1 Fireball

*Lockheed P-38L Lightning
*Republic P-47M Thunderbolt
*North American P-51D Mustang
*Bell Airacomet XP-59A Jet Fighter
*Northrop P-61A Black Widow
*Bell P-63 Kingcobra
*Fairey Firefly-British Navy
*Supermarine Seafire-Navy
*De Havilland Mosquito-British RAF
*Mitsubishi A6M5 Japanese Zero
*Hellcat with a G-Suit
*Hellcat with Mark-23 Lead-Computing Gun Sight
*Howard DGA-1 with Hoover Horizon
(Note: an asterisk* denotes aircraft that I flew.)

There were more than 40 aircraft for the pilot-attendees to fly. Most manufacturers had more than one of each model so that there would be less of a waiting line. But for the most interesting ones the waiting line became hectic, as you will soon see, because only one hour was allowed for each flight, with no maintenance, turnaround, or checkout time in between.

The aircraft listed with an X, for experimental, were not allowed to be flown by competitor manufacturer's test pilots. I wanted to fly the vaunted composite-powered (piston engine in front and jet engine in the rear) XFR-1 Ryan Fireball, but it was verboten. The Navy had previously impressed Grumman with its high performance qualities when we were in their doghouse for one reason or another. I also wanted to fly the Goodyear XF2G-1 Corsair with the Pratt & Whitney R-4360 3,000-hp engine. This was another aircraft that the Navy hung over our heads when necessary. We were to learn of the real lack of teeth in both of them during "The Race."

Although I had flown a P-51A, a P-38E, a P-40N, and a P-47C during 1943 in another joint program between the Army Air Corps and the Navy, I was looking forward to flying the "new and improved" models of the P-38L, P-47D, and P-51D to see what higher-powered engines did to them.

The pilot checkout procedure in these aircraft was sparse, to say the least. Each aircraft had a Pilot's Handbook firmly attached to the cockpit and an Air Corps Tech Sergeant or a Navy "white hat" was available to answer questions, but not to give lectures. It must have been sufficient because of the excellent backgrounds of the pilots, and there were no accidents. It should be noted here that 1944 was a long time before military cockpit standardization. The specific military mock-up board of each of the five services approved each contractor's cockpit. It took serious mental gymnastics to jump from one fighter cockpit to another—at least in my case.

The newest A6M5 Japanese Zero was the only aircraft for which its test pilot, Commander Andrews, the Navy tactical test project pilot, gave a complete checkout. The Navy in Alaska had laboriously retrieved the first A6M2 Zero. Shortly after extensive repair and flight-test, a Curtiss Helldiver pilot unwittingly taxied into it. It was completely chewed into chopsticks from the tail to the cockpit and it was a total loss.

Besides the flying there were formal discussion sessions on a large variety of interesting subjects, such as the Navy's desire for 20-mm cannons and the Army's diffidence to the same in favor of .50-caliber machine guns, and the strong difference of opinion as to the value of the new Mark 23 lead-computing gun sight, which everybody else but the Navy thought was unnecessary. There were many other unemotional Irish discussions that went on, interminably disrupting Happy Hour every afternoon.

## Let the Games Begin – Flying "The Fork-Tailed Devil"

One year earlier I had flown the P-38E (BuNo 17632) for two flights. I found it to be a very pleasant and easy aircraft in which to check out. It had excellent stall characteristics with both engines running, in both the clean and landing configurations. In the single-engine condition it also had excellent handling characteristics. This was because the slipstreams of the live engine acted on one of the two fins and provided such good controllability that the aircraft could be completely stalled without any chance of spinning. Most twin-engine aircraft that have single tails have minimum single-engine speeds below which the aircraft cannot fly. This is because the vertical tail is not in the powerful slipstream of the working engine, and thus is unable to provide sufficient rudder power to keep the aircraft at zero sideslip. If a pilot in the single-fin aircraft type accidentally goes any slower than the minimum single-engine speed he will surely snap roll or spin. Not only did the P-38 have reliable engines, obviating much of the need to shut down an engine, but also it was controllable and safe right down to the stall; a great combination to generate immediate pilot comfort in any twin-engine fighter.

The P-38 did, however, have the most cluttered cockpit of any aircraft I flew except for the British Spitfire. The

*The P-51D-17NA Mustang was an aircraft that belied its abilities by combining very low fuel consumption with excellent performance. I was interested in its bubble canopy and how it was tamed directionally by the very large dorsal fin ahead of the main fin. We installed a similar dorsal fin on the Bearcat as soon as we returned to Grumman with the XF8F-1 prototype that was at the Fighter Conference. (Corwin H. Meyer Collection)*

speed with little thought for its slow speed and high-altitude accelerated stalls. The P-51 would almost have to be a new aircraft for carrier acceptance.

My schooling was over for the time being. North American did their homework and seven years later made some excellent carrier jet aircraft starting with the FJ-1. Finally, the Navy got their wish. North American's great line of Navy jet fighters kept Grumman on its competitive toes for the following 10 years.

## My First Jet: Flying the Lethargic Bell XP-59A Airacomet

The United States entered the Second World War three years after European countries were committed. Preoccupied with meeting the production quotas for its own, and the allied air forces, U.S. military air forces and manufacturers were, understandably, quite late in getting into jet aviation.

The Germans flew the Ohan-designed axial-flow jet engine in a Heinkel 178 in

April 1941; the English Whittle-powered centrifugal-flow jet engine Gloster E.28/39 flew a month later. General Hap Arnold, chief of the U.S. Army Air Corps, visited England in May 1943 to see the Gloster prototype fly. He was so impressed that he ordered General Electric, maker of many ground-use turbines, to license the Whittle jet and pioneer the U.S. into the Jet Age. He simultaneously instructed Bell Aircraft to design a twinjet fighter. It was coyly named the XP-59 by hiding its identity behind a P-number of a defunct aircraft contract. While it was being towed up from Los Angeles it had a fake propeller on its nose to keep its identity secret. The propeller fell off halfway to Muroc.

Bell Chief Test Pilot Bob Stanley flew it on 1 October 1942 at the then-deserted Muroc Dry Lake (now Edwards Air Force Base) in California. It had a disappointing top speed of only 409 mph and had snaking characteristics, which made it a poor gun-aiming platform, but it was an acceptable introductory jet trainer for the next Army Air Corps' jet fighter. The

553-mph Lockheed P-80A made its first flight in January 1944. Deliveries of the P-80A began in April 1945 just as the European war was coming to an end.

Rumors of the uniqueness of the jet engine ran rampant at the Fighter Conference. It was said that a jet engine had only one moving part, it could burn any kind of fuel from corn husks up, and a jet engine made no noise, etc., etc.

Even though the poor high-speed performance of the P-59A was well known, and it lacked beauty (even without a propeller), pilots were lined up to be the first to test this wonder aircraft.

## My P-59A Evaluation

The first thing that I noted after getting into the cockpit was the pungent smell of kerosene. The cockpit stank of it. After connecting my oxygen mask I found that the cockpit was tolerable. It was orderly and devoid of any engine controls except throttles. The propeller, mixture, supercharger, oil cooler, and cowl flaps controls were happily withdrawn.

As a matter of explanation, jet engines had two quite different indications from piston engines. Their RPMs were stated in percentages instead of actual RPMs because they rotate at fantastic and different amounts of RPMs, some as high as 12,000, which would make reading exact RPMs on a small gauge a dizzying task. The other oddity was that their power is not as directly related to RPMs as in piston engines. For instance, 50-percent power could be as high as 80-percent RPMs in some jet engines. This, combined with the lag in jet engine acceleration time, required a more anticipatory throttle movement for correct power management in formation and landing approaches.

Start procedures were very simple. Rotate the jet engine turbine speed to 10 percent RPM, open the high pressure

fuel cock, and a small "boom" could be heard as the engine ignited. The turbine came up very slowly to an idle speed of 61 percent RPM. Exhaust temperatures rose way over the maximum flight limit while the engine was accelerating to idle, but that was par for the course on early jet engines. This generated a much stronger kerosene smell until the canopy was closed, even with an oxygen mask on. In hindsight, I guess that we had gotten used to the lovely smell of avgas. It was true that there was very little engine noise compared to a piston engine. Relatively speaking, this aircraft was quiet and vibration-free, compared to propeller aircraft. It was a pleasant but eerie sensation that took some getting used to. During flight I frequently had to look at the instruments to see if the engine was still running.

Taxiing required forethought because once taxi speed was lost and the throttle was re-advanced it took quite a few seconds longer than a propeller-powered aircraft to apply thrust to regain taxi speed. This lag would be more serious in landing approach to regain speed if the aircraft slowed below its desired approach speed.

Even with full throttle during takeoff the aircraft seemed to ooze forward with agonizingly slow acceleration. After a long roll the aircraft was lifted off to increase its speed to best climb speed, which was 100 mph faster than any propeller fighter. I learned after the flight that jet engines increase thrust with increase in speed, propeller thrust decays with speed. It was a great introduction.

Because the P-59A was so heavy and had so little excess thrust, I had no enthusiasm to try aerobatics. After experiencing the gentle stall characteristics of the P-59A and discovering that I really had to anticipate advancing the throttle four to five seconds sooner because of the delay in spool-up time of jet engines, I felt there was not much more to learn from the P-59A. The snaking, which impaired good gunnery, was quite evident. It was a poor gun platform. (We had the same problem in Grumman's first jet, the XF9F-2, and found its simple solution accidentally from a cup of coffee, which will be explained in another chapter.)

Except for the long throttle-to-thrust delay, the landing was unremarkable. However, I was now a jet pilot. I had flown without visible means of propulsion support. We were told by other jet pilots not to pass the word around about how easy jets were to fly. We, therefore, all proclaimed what heroes we were to neophyte prop-jocks and all other earth-bound persons who would listen.

I was not to experience my next jet evaluation in the Lockheed P-80A until August 1947 just before I made the first flight of the XF9F-2 Panther. The General Electric I-40 engine in the P-80A had a much better response time. The Rolls-Royce Nene engine in the Panther required no throttle/thrust anticipation time by the pilot, thank goodness.

## The Northrop P-61B-1 Black Widow Night-Fighter

Although the Germans did little night bombing in the early months of 1940, the RAF had anticipated the possibility and had flown the Bristol Blenheim twin-engine, radar-equipped, night-fighter in July 1939. Its first scored victory was in November 1940. The U.S. Army Air Corps and the Navy also realized the need for such a specialized aircraft and ordered the Northrop Black Widow and Grumman Tigercat, respectively, in early 1941. The first P-61A Black Widow deliveries began in October 1943. This three-place aircraft was as big as a B-25 Mitchell bomber and was very complex with its early radar system and new, remote-powered four-gun turret. It also had four 20-mm cannons located in a pod-like bump in the bottom of the fuselage. Despite its size it was very maneuverable and obtained its first victory in the air over Saipan in October 1944. By the end of the war the P-61 had shot down 63 enemy aircraft—a very good record for this new and most difficult fighting arena.

I was a half hour late for my scheduled flight in this impressively large aircraft. Because of my tardiness and my past familiarization with the P-61's similar Pratt & Whitney R-2800 engines installed in our Tigercat, I went through the cockpit checkout much too quickly.

Unfortunately, there were no radar operators available to fly with me. This could have made the flight much more profitable. I was interested, however, in the long circular arc spoiler-ailerons in front of the full-span flaps. This combination was reported to give this monster a very slow (un-Air Corps-like) landing speed and great rolling performance. This was the first aircraft designed with such novel pitch-control capabilities.

Takeoff acceleration was slow for a fighter. Immediately after becoming airborne I noticed a strange motion in the aircraft. It felt as if the seat was going up and down an inch or so with a continuous, regular frequency. I finally realized that it was the natural motion of a much more flexible aircraft than I was used to, so I attempted to retract the landing gear. I tried to move the handle up—nothing. I tried to move it sidewise—nothing. I pushed it in—nothing. I tried rotating the handle—nothing. After getting frantic, I pulled that handle out an inch and the gear retracted. I had gone through my cockpit lecture much too quickly. For the rest of my checkouts I listened diligently for details.

By this time I was about 20 miles from Patuxent, still at takeoff power, so I zoom-climbed the aircraft to 10,000 feet and proceeded to evaluate the aileron/flap system. It had exceptionally low control forces to full deflection, and fast rate of roll up to 300-mph dives; the highest speeds I tested. It was a break-through in pitch-control systems. I found the P-61A to have the same excellent rolling qualities at approach speeds and near the stall with both engines running, or with one engine wind-milling at idle power and the other at full power. It had greater rolling power to correct wing dropping at the stall than aileron-equipped fighters. Its pitch-control handling qualities over the entire speed envelope were the best of any aircraft I had ever flown. I talked to the Grumman engineers about this fabulous pitch control. We did put a similar circular-arc spoiler/aileron system in the Grumman Tracker S2F-1 in the early 1950s. Grumman also installed full-span flaps with hydraulic-powered, full-span spoilers ahead of the flap for their carrier fighters up to and including the F-14.

Now that I knew how to actuate the landing gear, my landing was a slow, most un-Army Air Corps-like 90 mph. My calm was not to last long as my evaluation had been an hour and eaten up a half hour of the last scheduled flight of the day. Waiting for me was a very tired and irate Marine colonel. Before the engines had stopped, Col. John Harshberger, a famous night-fighter pilot, climbed up the ladder to the cockpit and chewed me out most articulately until I was long out of the area. I'm sure glad that he didn't know my connection with Grumman. The Marines were our very good customers. Years later when we became good friends I related the story, which he denied immediately, but with a smile.

## Another Lesson Learned in Aerodynamics AND Diplomacy – The Bell P-63A-9BE Kingcobra

In order to support the Russians against the German invasion until the Russian aircraft industry could be moved out of the fighting areas, over 73 percent of all of the 12,892 Bell P-39s and P-63s went to Russia as Lend-Lease weapons. Therefore, these two aircraft never received the popularity and acclaim in the U.S. Army Air Corps that the P-40, P-38, and other U.S. fighters received. The Russians may not have given them much acclaim, but the Russians used both continuously to the very end of the war.

I had not flown the P-39 Airacobra, predecessor of the Kingcobra, but I decided that an aircraft with its engine in the center of the fuselage was oddity enough for me to want to determine if such an arrangement had any handling quality assets or drawbacks. The engine was located in the center of the aircraft so that a cannon could be mounted in the very slim forward fuselage to fire through the propeller gearbox and still have enough room for ammunition. It was a very good idea. The Kingcobra also had a much bigger fin and rudder than the P-39.

I asked Bell Chief Test Pilot, Jack Wollams, why this fin and rudder change was made, and he stated most candidly that it was to improve the less-than-acceptable spin characteristics of the P-39. There had always been a strong and persistent rumor that the P-39 would tumble end over end in certain spins. It was never proven, but the rumor persisted and the P-39's reputation probably suffered because of it. I was not going to try to prove Jack right or wrong on his statement. Bell was not paying me as a test pilot, either.

## Evaluating the P-63A Kingcobra

With its 1,320-hp Allison engine and its light 8,800-lb gross weight, performance was quite sparkling up to 20,000 feet where I discontinued the climb to evaluate the flight characteristics of the bird. Generally it had good to excellent handling qualities throughout its entire speed range, including stalls. After hearing Jack's commentary about the bigger fin, I tried several aggravated spin entries and recoveries. They seemed satisfactory. I didn't do any complete spins. It seemed to have plenty of directional stability at slow speeds. It was clear that a hastily trained pilot could become rapidly proficient in the Kingcobra. It is interesting to note that the later P-63C model had an extended ventral fin under the aft fuselage to further increase directional stability. Perhaps there were certain flight conditions that could only be found in performing actual spins to evaluate Kingcobra spin or spin recovery problems that required a ventral fin.

The only unacceptable item I noted was that this latest P-63 had very poor visibility in the day and age of bubble canopies. Maybe the Russians had liked the unique door entrance to the cockpit, necessitating the bulky structure that cut down fighter-needed visibility, but I didn't.

Another old wive's tale I had heard was that Kingcobra pilots disliked the knowledge of having a shielded engine-to-propeller drive shaft rotating between their legs in flight. It didn't cause me any sexual trauma.

The P-63A was the last of a long line of distinguished Bell fighters that were available in large production numbers throughout the war when the Russians and we really needed them.

## The Supermarine Mk III Seafire – A Navalized Spitfire

The Fleet Air Arm did not decide to adopt a Navy version of the famous RAF Spitfire until 1941. After 400 fixed-wing

*The Russians used thousands of Bell P-63A-9BE Kingcobras extensively and they developed quite a name in both air-to-air fighting and in the fighter-bomber ground support roles. Although the U.S. Army Air Corps used its forefather, the P-39, in the early days of the war, they purchased very few P-63s. (Corwin H. Meyer Collection)*

Mk IIs were made, they finally decided in 1943 to put a double folding wing on the Mk III. The Royal Navy finally had a modern British fighter on their carrier decks along with hundreds of Lend-Lease Grumman Martlets, Hellcats, and Corsairs. The Seafire that I flew at the Fighter Conference was a Mk III.

There is no argument that the Spitfire/Seafire was the most beautiful fighter ever to emerge from a drawing board. Its elliptical wing and long, slim fuselage were most delightful to the eye. Its flight characteristics were equal to its beauty. The decision to produce the Seafire was probably not taken sooner due to the requirements of the RAF and the U.S. Army Air Corps, which had used up the entire production of Spitfires for the Battle of Britain and African campaigns.

The Spitfire and Seafire series had only two unacceptable features to aggravate a fighter pilot. One was caused by configuration and the other was the gross negligence of the design team. The long nose and its attendant-steep angle on the ground provided impossible forward taxi visibility. The slimness of the fuselage alleviated the problem somewhat, but continuous S-turns while taxiing were mandatory. The cockpit internal layout was a disaster. It was laid out as if the blindfolded engineers were pinning tails on a donkey. Important switches, instruments, and controls were unlabeled, small, and hidden. Unimportant items were labeled, large, and always in the way. I wonder how many of the 20,000 Spitfires and Seafires produced were made this way on purpose. However, pilots forgot these two drawbacks immediately after becoming airborne.

Two soon-to-be-famous Royal Navy lieutenants checked me out. One was Mike Lithgow, who became chief test pilot of Supermarine, and a good friend. The other was Peter Twiss, who became chief test pilot of Fairey and set the world speed record on 10 March 1956 in the Fairey Delta 2 by flying the first military aircraft to exceed 1,000 mph in level flight. They were not only friendly check pilots but also very helpful in getting me off the ground and back onto the flight line.

On the flight before mine, the pilot reported that the brakes had failed on landing. Inspection showed that the air compressor that provided air power for the wheel brakes had failed. Peter Twiss confidently suggested that they had filled the air accumulator. It would provide enough braking to get airborne, but it might run out of air during the landing runout. He further said that if I made a "docile" landing and taxied off the runway into the grass, they would retrieve the aircraft. With such encouragement, I decided to "give it a go."

With the thrust of its 1,340-hp Merlin engine, its big wing area, and a powerful rudder, I gave no further thought to the dead brakes. The terrific acceleration of this lightweight interceptor-fighter was thrilling once the tail was raised and I could see the rest of the airport. The Seafire left the ground after less than 500 feet of roll into a 20-mph wind and started climbing like a Japanese Zero. Anything offbeat in this aircraft was forgotten for the rest of the flight. Stalls were friendly with little wing dropping and at an unheard-of 66 mph. (The Hellcat had an 85-mph stall speed.)

Spins were like a training aircraft, with instant recovery as soon as the controls were released. Even if I could find the trim tab controls handily, which I couldn't, I didn't need them. The stability about all three axes of the aircraft was low enough to be a fighter pilot's dream and high enough to fly hands-off in mildly turbulent air. It was a great combination. Aerobatics were a pleasure. The aircraft responded right after the thought came to the pilot's mind, seemingly without effort.

It had such delightful upright flying qualities (and knowing that it had an inverted fuel and oil system) that I decided to try inverted figure eights. They were as easy as pie even when hanging by the complicated but comfortable English pilot restraint harness. I was surprised to hear myself laughing like I was crazy. I have never enjoyed a flight in a fighter as much before or after and felt so readily comfortable in it at any flight attitude. It was clear to see how so few exhausted, hastily trained, Battle of Britain pilots were able to fight off Hitler's hordes for so long and so successfully. I finally learned the depth of Winston Churchill's famous phrase honoring those RAF hero-pilots, which ended with the words, "Never in the history of armed conflict did so many owe so much to so few."

Alas, the gauge from my Seafire's one and only all-too-small fuel system beckoned to me to attempt a brakeless, "docile" landing without a ground loop. Like a martini high, and by landing in the same 20-mph wind, it seemed as easy as everything else had been for the last delightful hour. I nudged my new friend, the Seafire Mk III's rudder, and civilly went off the runway into the grass. I called the tower, notified them of my predicament, and awaited my kind, newly made English friend's arrival with a tug.

The Lend-Lease Royal Navy Wildcat, Hellcat, and Corsair fighters were only workhorses. The Supermarine Mk III Seafire was a dashing Arabian stallion!

## The British Firefly Naval Fighter

The Firefly was a follow-on growth version of the pre-war Fulmar two-seat shipboard reconnaissance fighter. It was designed to the traditional Fleet Air Arm criteria, which saw the twin-seat plane as indispensable on board aircraft carriers even though its performance was clearly limited relative to single seaters. In comparison to the Fulmar, the Firefly had only 650 horsepower for 9,000 lbs additional gross weight and a wingspan decrease of two feet. These factors produced a large increase in wing loading with little increase in power loading, greatly inhibiting the Firefly's maneuverability and eventual fighting potential against more modern German warplanes. The Firefly Mk I became operational in October 1943.

Because of its external load-carrying capability and its top speed of 316 mph, I was interested in comparing it to our Grumman TBF/TBM Avenger, which although 45 mph slower, had 500 miles greater range and a much greater load carrying capability.

The 5 x 7-inch 45-page (minuscule by American standards) Pilot's Handbook provided a typically British succinct and candid description of its satisfactory and less amiable flight characteristics. The following are handbook quotes and my commentary.

"It has marked changes in trim forces about the lateral, directional, and longitudinal axes," meaning all three axes of the aircraft had to be trimmed constantly with all speed and/or power changes. "In large yaw angles the rudder forces lighten," meaning the pilot should use the rudder without anger. I noted rudder forces reversed and began to overbalance over half rudder deflection under 150 mph. "In the power approach stall (carrier landing configuration) the nose or either wing drops and if the controls are mishandled, the aircraft may flick over on its back," meaning don't even roll your eyeballs if you get near the approach configuration stall. "Flick maneuvers not allowed," meaning no snap rolls unless, of course, you "mishandle" the controls in the approach condition. "If flown solo the aircraft needs 200 pounds of ballast in the rear seat," meaning that the aircraft can't get its tail down on landing without something big in the rear seat. These statements were much more articulated than my words could ever be. This beautiful aircraft with its splendid Spitfire-like aerodynamic lines did not inherit the delightful stability, control, and gentle stall characteristics of its likeness.

Even though the aircraft I flew was built in 1942, it had a lead-computing, manual-ranging gun sight installed long before it was available in American military aircraft. It also had four 20-mm cannons in the wings; two items of very superior armament design. Although there was no armament in the rear seat for aft protection, the Firefly had patented Youngman flaps that, when extended, gave it quite a wide speed range for evasive turning in combat, unfortunately little-used in World War II. With the Youngman flaps retracted the Firefly did not have satisfactory fighter turning agility.

As a fighter the Mk I Firefly could not be rated very highly among its competitors and adversaries. Later models, such as the NF, had the ASH radar for use as a night-fighter. The ASW model, used for anti-submarine warfare, finally brought its two cockpits into practical combat usage, but long after the war was over. I would presume that its two-place fighter role was a hangover from World War I aircraft similar to the famous two-place Bristol F-2B Brisfit biplane fighter that had such a glorious record. It was standard equipment in the RAF until it was finally phased out in 1932 just as the Firefly, Fulmar, and Blackburn Skua were coming into inventory.

## The Canadian-Built British Mosquito Mk 30 Night-Fighter

As a bomber of wooden construction the Mosquito was unique; in its multifari-

ous forms it was outstandingly capable in each mission, and it possessed that highly desirable but all-too-rare ability to make its pilot feel part and parcel of his aircraft on the first flight.

The Mosquito was originally designed in October 1938 to be a twin-engine bomber. It was subsequently used in the fighter, fighter-bomber, photographic, night-fighter, high-altitude recon, pathfinder, and mine-laying roles among many others. About the only capability it didn't have was to land on water more than once.

The aircraft I flew at the Fighter Conference and again a month later in New York was the fourth production Canadian-built aircraft and I was unable to form an opinion on this new British radar. Unfortunately, we experienced radar failures on both flights. Grumman was interested in this aircraft because the fighter version had four 20-mm cannons plus four .303 guns installed. As a night-fighter it performed a mission quite similar to the F7F series Tigercat with close to the same armament.

Although it won the worst cockpit award at the Fighter Conference, the human assets of the side-by-side, two-man crew and the general good visibility from the cockpit both on the ground and in the air made it an aircraft that the pilot felt comfortable with after his first flight.

The Mosquito lived up to its reputation in the air with sprightly performance and pleasant stability and control that perpetuated pilot-friendliness almost throughout the entire mission. Two inconveniences were noted at landing time: a large reverse trim was required for flap extension, and high power was required to offset very high landing flap drag. They were the only negatives noted from my first flight impressions, neither of which seemed nearly as much of an irritation on my second flight. Although the 121-mph stall speed was remarkably high for the time, which required a 135-mph approach speed, the unbelievably short landing rollout would have been satisfactory for operations from a 4,000-foot runway without excess braking. I did not have any problem with the British hand/foot brake system that other pilots commented on adversely. In my opinion braking operations at the top of the stick were found to be more gently applicable with one's hands than with one's feet on the rudder pedals, as all U.S. aircraft are so designed. Rudder pedal motions, in combination with hand pressures, were easily coordinated to turn the aircraft on the ground.

I only performed single engine simulations with a fully retarded throttle and an unfeathered propeller on one engine and with the other engine at cruise power. I presumed that with its small rudder and fin the Mosquito would have had a single engine minimum control speed approaching the 140-mph speed of our original, small-finned F7F-1 Tigercat—and would be equally unacceptable. It was. However, neither the single-fin Mosquito nor the Tigercat had the fabulous low speed control of the twin-finned Lockheed P-38 Lightning and Northrop P-61 Black Widow fighters, which could be flown single engine down to their stall speeds with acceptable control.

The Mosquito, with its few tolerable iniquities, was a very impressive, pilot-friendly aircraft. Its side-by-side seating always seemed to me much more amenable from the human standpoint for crew efficiency than the fore and aft isolated seating of the F7F-1 Tigercat. An English Mosquito pilot friend of mine said it much more candidly; "The ground-bound designer just doesn't understand how well another warm, friendly body in your cockpit close to you and within sight kept mission ghosts and goblins well outside of the canopy glass on a dark night."

## Epilogue

From the Grumman standpoint, and from my own education, it was a very successful meeting. Plans were in the offing for another Joint Army/Navy Fighter Conference when V-E and V-J Days fortuitously arrived.

Over the many years of my continued aviation education I also noted that when 20 pilots discuss any aeronautical subjects except wine, women, and song, you will get at least 40 firm, positive, well reasoned, and respected but vastly different opinions.

# Chapter 15

# The Japanese Zero – A Test Pilot's Report

## 21 October 1944

Anyone who grew up in the 1920s and '30s learned very quickly that "Made in Japan" meant cheap cost and poor quality. Almost everything bought in the Woolworths or Kresages Five and Dime stores had that tag. I remember that it was impossible to purchase anything imported from Japan that would not wear out or break after a very short useful life.

That fact and the secrecy of the Japanese in the years before World War II regarding their military build-up anesthetized all of us regarding their real might. The average American believed that in battle Japanese military forces would crumble as fast as their products had done.

We were obviously wrong. They overran country after country and their air forces were superior to anything that could be put up against them. Americans learned to respect the words "Jap Zero" as defining the epitome of aerial superiority. "Made in Japan" now had an entirely different meaning in just one day—7 December 1941.

When I arrived at Grumman on 11 November 1942 and started flying the Wildcat fighter I was immersed in the life and death struggle of Wildcat production. It was the only U.S. Navy fighter that could beat the Zero. All that we heard from the communiqués was that we couldn't

*The beauty of the Zero can be seen in this photograph. It flew as well as it looked until the speed went much over 250 mph when the stick then felt like it was frozen in cement. It had a very limited dive speed and, therefore, couldn't dive away from a fight. It didn't have any pilot armor plate protection or self-sealing fuel tanks. When hit directly by six .50-caliber machines guns of the Hellcat or Corsair it became an instant fireball. (Paul Koskela)*

build and deliver Wildcats fast enough. The story was still very fresh in everybody's mind about how Grummanites had volunteered to work around the clock for seven days after the Battle of Midway and delivered a much-needed 39 additional Wildcats to the fleet in only six days to replace aircraft lost during that pivotal battle. The reason that Grumman could not deliver more at that time was because we had run out of engines. So, I felt somewhat honored when I was selected to fly the vaunted Zero in October of 1944 at the Joint Army/Navy Fighter Conference.

Many historians have insisted that the Zero was either a copy of the Vought 143 (which the Japs had purchased) or the Hughes Racer. They did look alike, but the Zero used a much different design philosophy to get its weight lower than any other fighter of the time. Japanese designers reduced the loads on the structure by designing to very restrictive dive speeds and by dispensing with armor protection and self-sealing fuel tanks. They reduced weight further by moving the wing fold point nearly out to the wingtips.

## The Zero Creaks Out of the Hangar

My first impression of the Zero was that it looked every bit the fighter. It had very trim lines. Except for the canopy bulge, the engine was the biggest volume in the design and the slim fuselage behind it made it seem smaller than it was. It certainly had a magnetic drawing power to fighter pilots because of its reputation for unparalleled agility in dogfights.

During my walk-around I noticed that there were 1-inch bamboo rubbing devices attached to the wheel fairings, which the tires picked up as the gear retracted to close the wheel well door. The Japs were certainly using all the endemic materials at hand. Another item I noticed was that the

Nakajima Sakae 21 engine had an exact replica of the Pratt & Whitney logo complete with the eagle, with Nakajima in Japanese script, but the words "Dependability and Reliability" were in English. I did feel more at home with the Zero after seeing that mark of excellence.

Because of its rarity, the Zero was the only aircraft that had a pilot to assist in checkout. Commander Andrews, the Navy project pilot, would not even let a pilot start the engine until he was satisfied with his competence.

We started our cockpit checkout in the cool hangar. As we were talking, the aircraft was dragged out into the hot sun. I had previously noted that the fabric was drooped between the ribs of the ailerons, but had forgotten to ask Commander Andrews about it. Soon there were a lot of audible, metallic scraping noises. Commander Andrews then explained that the sun's heat on the fabric would cause it to become taut and the metallic expansion and retraction would stop after the aircraft had become acclimatized to the higher temperature outside the hangar. That is the only time I have ever "heard" an engineering weight savings in an aircraft.

This Model 52a Zero did not have self-sealing fuel tanks and pilot armor protection. That was to cost them 145 more pounds of empty weight in the Model 52c, which was just being delivered to Japanese squadrons when the Fighter Conference was going on. That weight penalty, plus others to come without an increase in horsepower, started an inevitable decline in the Zero's combat agility.

Its 8G maneuvering limit was the same as our fighters, but the maximum diving speed of our Zero Model 52a was only 410 mph. This allowed them to reduce airframe material sizes resulting from lower dive speed loads, which reduced the gross weight by several hundred pounds. That lower gross weight accounted for much of the Zero's outstanding dogfight maneuvering performance. In comparison, the Wildcat had a 460-mph dive speed limit. The F6F-3 Hellcat had a 485-mph speed that was subsequently raised to 525 mph in the F6F-5.

The Zero workmanship was superb, and comparable to American quality. This was amazing to us, in light of the quality of the prewar Japanese products with which we all had come in contact.

## An Interesting Cockpit for a Six-Foot-Three Pilot

During the cockpit checkout I noted that all the engine instruments and several of the flight instruments were calibrated in metrics such as kilograms/square centimeter (oil pressure) and meters (altimeter). I asked Commander Andrews to make pencil marks where the respective needles were supposed to be in flight so I would not have to remember so many unfamiliar readings.

To my surprise I found that the cockpit was large enough to make my six-foot-three body comfortable, from the seat bottom to the canopy. My feet, however, seemed tucked under me even with the rudder pedals full forward. It was uncomfortable but certainly not un-flyable. Even though visibility on the ground was only fair over the nose, the seat could be raised so that my eyes were several inches above the top of the open canopy for superb taxi visibility. Fighter-required visibility in the air was excellent, especially to the rear.

Another un-American feature that must have given the Japanese pilots mixed emotions was the protrusion of the two 7.7-mm Type 97 (.30-caliber) gun butts six inches into the cockpit on either side of the instrument panel. With all the cordite fumes I assume that Japanese pilots had good, 100-percent-flow oxygen masks. The nearness of the gun butts

must have been disconcerting and disfiguring in a crash. The rest of the cockpit interior was reasonably well laid out and easily adaptable.

Engine operation throughout the entire flight was very similar to American engines, as one might expect with the "P&W engine label" attached.

## A Great Dogfighter

Once the Zero started rolling on take-off, performance was impressive. It was considerably above its minimum takeoff speed when it left the ground after a 700-foot roll, and because its climb speed was 25 mph below the Hellcat, the angle of climb was stupendous. The only problem seemed to be that it took way too long to get to 10,000 feet, until I remembered that the altimeter indicated meters and not feet. At 3,500 meters indicated altitude I realized I was already well above 10,000 feet.

As a test pilot my training had always dictated that stall characteristics must be checked first to see just how much talent I was going to need to land safely and smoothly. In all configurations the stalls were gentle with little or no wing dropping. Accelerated stalls in either the clean or landing condition were as good or better than the Hellcat. The most interesting aspect of stalls was the airspeed. It was 25 mph less than the heavier wing-loaded American aircraft, which was a great tribute to the weight-saving program of the Zero's designers. It was apparent that inexperienced Japanese pilots would feel quite comfortable in the Zero. Our pilots flying P-40s, by contrast, had to cope with miserable stall characteristics that killed all too many young pilots in training and combat.

Prior to World War II, combat aircraft were rated on their turning performance—the ability to get on the other pilot's tail for the kill. Having no other aircraft to compete against made testing this quality

*This Zero is the same aircraft that I flew at the Joint Army/Navy Fighter Conference at NATC Patuxent, Maryland, in October 1944. It is the only Zero flying using its original Sakae 31 engine after 58 years of air show displays. Ed Maloney, owner of the Planes of Fame Museum, sent me a copy of the page in the Zero's logbook listing my flight and Charles Lindbergh's flight the next day. (Paul Koskela)*

difficult to quantify. I had learned to use the loop maneuver to check this ability when evaluating a fighter without an adversary aircraft. Actual combat is not as well simulated, but it comes very close. I began my first loop in the Zero at 170 mph from level flight. I completed it 1,800 feet higher than I started. It was my first loop and I was not pulling it in anywhere as tight as I could have, since I did not use its very low wing loading and stall speed properly, but still it was impressive.

My next loop was started at 140 mph and with tightening the loop to stall warning buffeting on the last half I pulled out 1,200 feet above my starting altitude. For comparison, a Wildcat needed a minimum start speed of 185 mph and it would end the loop several hundred feet below the starting altitude. It was easy to see why the Zero had gained such a fabulous reputation when it sucked the enemy aircraft into circling, dogfight combat. If the Zero was behind his enemy he could pull inside of him and get a good deflection shot. If the Zero was being tailed he could pull it in tighter than the enemy and stall him out before he could get a shot. If the Zero pilot was out of ammunition he could climb away in turning flight in complete safety. Our pilots learned the hard

way not to fight the Zero on its own terms. (The Grumman Bearcat was the only aircraft that could have bested the Zero at any speed, but it was two weeks too late for combat.)

## Dogfighter on a Short Leash – Very Inferior Limit Dive Capabilities

Because the Zero's high-speed level performance was well-known, I did not spend time and fuel checking that area. I next looked into the flight characteristics of the higher dive speed regimes. The weaknesses of the design stood out dramatically. At 230 mph the rolling stick forces were building up much faster than one would have realized for an aircraft with a limit speed of only 410 mph. The elevator maneuvering stick forces were also becoming quite heavy, thus rapidly diluting the Zero's turning superiority. The aircraft was showing itself to be a lead sled at a much lower speed than I had thought. At 275-mph airspeed the stick seemed to be "in cement" both for rolling and pulling Gs. It was most noticeable that the rudder forces were still very light and grossly out of balance with the other controls. I still cannot understand the rationale for the very low rudder forces when the ailerons, and especially the elevators, were practically useless. It was easy to see that the 410-mph dive speed limit was not much use for evasion when the pilot could not effectively use the ailerons or elevator. A lot of Zeros were shot down soon after American pilots learned that the Zero was not maneuverable over 300 mph in a dive.

## Wildcat, Hellcat, and Zero Comparisons

In comparison, both the Wildcat and the Hellcat had much more maneuverable stick forces up to their higher dive speed limits. The Model 52c Zero had heavier wing skins and structure to permit a dive speed of 460 mph. Unless the control forces had also been decreased by a large factor, it is difficult to see how this increase in dive speed would have assisted Zero pilots even during Kamikaze attacks.

Japanese test pilots and engineers had worked hard to make the Zero's flight-handling characteristics amenable to its dog-fighting regime. I immediately felt as though I had flown the Zero many times before. The balance of the controls, the cockpit visibility, the smoothness of the engine, the location of all the instruments, and the gentle stall characteristics made this one of the few fighter aircrafts I had evaluated that demonstrated almost all of the required qualities for rapidly putting a low-time pilot into combat with the confidence needed to survive.

## The Leash Shortens Again – Insufficient Wing Fold

Another less obvious but major Zero deficiency was that its wing fold span decreased its total span only six feet. This allowed only one Zero at a time to be on the elevator from the hangar deck to the flight deck for launch. Accordingly, the Zero's numbers on a carrier were limited by its 36-foot folded wingspan both on the hangar and on the launch decks. Having the wing fold at the tip saved a lot of weight over having it at the wing root. But it was to prove too great a sacrifice for weight savings/performance increase versus numbers of aircraft available per carrier during the very critical battles of the Coral Sea and Midway.

Both the Hellcat and the Wildcat had folding wings that decreased their spans 17 feet (from 43 and 38 feet, respectively), enough to allow five aircraft with wings folded to take the same area of two aircraft without wing-folding capabilities. This permitted a 150-percent increase in numbers of aircraft on the hangar or flight decks for the same size carrier and made deck elevators much more efficient by being able to handle two aircraft at a time. The folding wings also permitted U.S. carriers to get more aircraft airborne in less time than the Japanese due to higher numbers of aircraft able to be on the launch deck at one time. The value of greater numbers of available aircraft from the tight Grumman wing fold system paid off in spades in all of the air battles of World War II, despite each of their 210-lb weight penalties.

## The Leash Shortens Again – Sam Stumbles

The Zero stayed in production for the entire war even though it was outclassed well before the war ended. This is difficult to understand from an American viewpoint. We were continuously developing aircraft and were not distracted by the war going on around us. We also did not have the fixed conviction of our enemies that the war would be a short one, and we had a much larger manpower and material base for production, research, and development. Having been in the aircraft manufacturing business during World War II, Korea, and Vietnam it was stunning to me that the Japanese and Germans continued to develop new aircraft designs and had such incredible rates of production in the last years of World War II, despite the devastating 1,000-plane allied bomber raids.

Mitsubishi engineers proposed a great follow-on for the Zero in early 1942. It was an aircraft with the general planform of the Zero but sized up to fit the new 2,200-hp Homare 43 engine. It was fitted with all the armor plate, etc., that the war had finally convinced them was necessary. This aircraft was known as the Mitsubishi A7M2 Reppu and code named "Sam" by

P-38F Lightning.

the U.S. forces. Japanese Navy brass immediately dictated that it be redesigned to use a smaller engine. They then reversed their decision in late 1943 with the full-speed go-ahead it should have received when it was first presented. Because of this strange delay in the development program, only a few Sams appeared by the war's end. Had the Sam been pushed as it should have been, the Hellcat, Corsair, P-38, P-51, and P-47 would have met their match long before the end of the war. Because the Sam was hopelessly delayed, the only other option was to continue the over-worked Zero production line until the end of the war. There were a total of 10,499 Zeros of all models constructed; over 81 percent of all the fighters available to the Japanese air forces during the entire war.

The Zero was a fabulous fighter from 1938 to 1942 when dogfighting prevailed in combat. When allied fighter pilots finally understood its weaknesses, they should have been most grateful that the arrogant Japanese admirals and generals had convinced themselves that they did not need an improvement to the Zero even though the handwriting was on the wall. The Kamikaze mission was the Zero's last effort in regaining its usefulness as a weapon, fortunately only for a short time.

## Zero Versus American Fighters

In November of 1942, an earlier-model Zero 21 had crashed in Alaska and had been extensively repaired. A Hamilton Standard propeller exactly like the Zero's was fitted because the Zero prop was a copy of the Hamilton Standard. This Zero 21 had the 940-hp Sakae 12 engine installed. The model I flew had the 1,130-hp Sakae 21 engine.

The Alaska Zero was shipped to the United States, extensively repaired, and flight-comparison tests were flown against current American fighters. The aircraft in these evaluations all had at least 270-hp more than the Zero.

To cancel the temperature or turbulence differences that might happen if tests were done separately, flight-tests were flown in formation, at least up to the point where the aircraft could keep up with each other. All of the Army Air Corps' aircraft were the latest versions. The Navy did not compare the Zero to the Hellcat because there were only three Hellcats flying in November 1942.

## Summary Report Findings

The following is quoted from the Intelligence Summary Report. Statements in parenthesis are the author's comments.

## P-38F Lightning Versus the Zero 21

Both aircraft took off together. The Zero was at 300 feet when the P-38F became airborne. The Zero reached 5,000 feet approximately six seconds ahead of the P-38F. In level flight, acceleration started at 200 mph. The Lightning accelerated away from the Zero quite rapidly. Climbing from 5,000 feet to 10,000 feet, the Zero was about four seconds ahead of the Lightning. Comparable accelerations at 10,000 feet gave the same results as at 5,000 feet. Climbing from 15,000 feet to 20,000 feet, the P-38F started gaining on the Zero at 18,200 feet. At 20,000 feet and above, the P-38F was superior to the Zero in all maneuvers except slow-speed turns. One area where the P-38F was superior to the Zero was in the high-speed reversal of turns. This was because of the hydraulically boosted ailerons of the P-38 that gave it twice the rolling power of any other American World War II fighter.

## P-39D-1 Airacobra Versus the Zero 21

In a formation takeoff climbing to 5,000 feet, the Zero was at 4,000 feet when the Airacobra reached 5,000 feet. In level flight starting at 230 mph at 5,000 feet, the Airacobra had a marked acceleration away from the Zero. Climbing from 5,000 to 10,000-feet, the Airacobra reached 10,000 feet six seconds ahead of the Zero. Starting from 220 mph level at 10,000 feet, the Airacobra again accelerated markedly away from the Zero. Climbing from 10,000 to 15,000 feet, the Zero gained an advantage from 12,500 feet and began to pull away from the Airacobra. Climbing from 15,000 to 20,000 feet the Zero took immediate advantage and walked away from the Airacobra. The climb was discontinued as the Airacobra was running low on fuel. On a straight climb from takeoff to 25,000 feet, the Airacobra maintained the advantage until 14,800 feet and from then on the Zero pulled ahead, reaching 25,000 feet five minutes ahead of the Airacobra.

## P-51A Mustang Versus the Zero 21

During the takeoff, the Zero reached its climbing speed six seconds before the Mustang, and reached 5,000 feet six seconds ahead of the P-51A. At 5,000 feet in level flight at 250 mph, the Mustang accelerated sharply away from the Zero. Climbing from 5,000 to 10,000 feet and then to 15,000 feet, the Zero accelerated away from the Mustang in rate of climb. In level acceleration at 10,000 feet the Mustang accelerated sharply away from the Zero, but at 15,000 feet the Mustang's advantage became slightly slower than at 5,000 or 10,000 feet. At all altitudes tested, the P-51A could dive away from the Zero at any time. The tests were concluded at 15,000 feet because the Mustang's Allison engine failed to operate properly above that altitude.

## P-40F Warhawk Versus the Zero 21

The tests were not completed with the Warhawk because the P-40F's

*F4F-4 Wildcat.*

Packard Merlin engine could not obtain maximum performance. (Observation: the Zero kept performing for every flight while both the Allison and Packard engines couldn't keep up even with their optimum maintenance. Although it was in production by late 1941, no 2,000-hp P-47 participated in these evaluations.)

## F4F Wildcat Versus the Zero 21

The Zero was superior at all altitudes above 1,000 feet in speed, climb, service ceiling, and range. Sea-level speeds were the same for both aircraft. In a dive, both aircraft were the same except that the Zero's engine cut out during pushovers. There was no comparison between the turning circles of the two aircraft due to the relative wing loadings and the resultant low stalling speed of the Zero. In view of the foregoing, the F4F in combat with the Zero must be dependent on mutual support, internal protection, and pullouts or turns at high speeds where the minimum radius is limited by structural or physiological effects of acceleration. However, advantage was gained by the F4F's superiority in pushovers and rolls at high speeds, or any combination of the two. (Observation: This may sound overly critical, but the 1,200-hp Wildcat had a kill-to-loss ratio of 9-to-1 against the Zero in the Pacific. The 2,000-hp Corsair had only an 11-to-1 kill-to-loss ratio.)

## F4U Corsair Versus the Zero 21

The Zero was far inferior to the Corsair in level speeds and diving speeds at all altitudes. It fell short in climbs starting at sea level, and above 20,000 feet the Zero could not stay with the Corsair in high-speed climbs. The superiority of the F4U-1 was very evident and would persist even when carrying heavier loads. In combat with the Zero, the Corsair could take full advantage of its speed along with its ability to pushover and roll at high speeds if surprised. Due to its much higher wing loading, the F4U-1 had to avoid any attempt to turn with the Zero except at high speeds, and could expect the latter to out-climb the Corsair at moderate altitudes and low speeds. In this case, the Corsair should be climbed at high speeds and on a heading, which would open the distance and prevent the Zero from reaching a favorable position to attack. After reaching 19,000 to 20,000 feet, the Corsair had superior performance in climb and could choose its own position for attack.

## Summary

Do not fight with the Zero at low speeds. Keep the speed up on the attack. Push over, dive, and roll away because the Zero can't follow such maneuvers. The Zero 21 only had a 410-mph dive speed and all the other U.S. aircraft had dive speed limits of over 460 mph.

## Japan Learns a Fabulous Lesson in Building Quality Products

"Made In Japan" Zeros implied junk to Hellcat pilots after the Navy's unbelievably successful Marianas Turkey Shoot in 1944. But Japanese manufacturing magnates surely must have taken notice of "Made In America" quality when they

*F4U-1 Corsair.*

observed USAF and U.S. naval combat aircraft during World War II.

Immediately after the war, when Japanese industries were picking themselves out of the dust of war, they decided that they must vastly change their attitudes on the quality of their products to be competitive worldwide. It is interesting to note that they picked Dr. W. Edwards Deming from the United States, who was an outspoken quality-control advocate, but a prophet without honor in his own country, to come to Japan in 1946 and lead them in the competitive business race. They listened to him and followed his advice without question. It surprised the entire world of commerce to witness the rapid Japanese climb to world dominance in product quality in the world market places. The coveted annual Deming Award is prized by winning Japanese business leaders. His work is now praised worldwide as a Japanese innovation.

We all know the lessons U.S. manufacturers learned in the 1960s when Japanese automobiles, television sets, computers, and a myriad of other products started cutting deeply into worldwide competition. The Japanese nation may have lost a five-year war, but they won a 50-year eco-

nomic boom to bring back great "Made In Japan" products to American markets.

## One Aircraft the Japanese Didn't Copy

A story told to me by a Douglas executive many years ago proves the point that the Japanese didn't copy everything they bought. Just before the war they purchased the three-tailed, four-engine prototype DC-4E transport, which demonstrated 1940s state-of-the-art aviation. It was shipped to Japan and delivered to the military. The American flight and assembly crews thought that the Japanese would like to get checked out by them, but they were hustled off the air base immediately and told they weren't needed. A Japanese crew flew the aircraft the next day. The aircraft promptly crashed and burned on its first takeoff because the Japanese crew did not use the checklist and, therefore, did not remove the control lock prior to flying. After the fire there was not enough of the DC-4 left to copy. Had it not been abused it might have become a powerful bomber design for the Japanese Air Forces in World War II.

# Chapter 16

# Clipping the Bearcat's Wings

## 8 September 1944 to 20 February 1948

It is fascinating what the mind remembers and what it doesn't. I can't remember what I had for breakfast yesterday, but some test flights stick in my mind like they happened this afternoon. I vividly recall a program in which I intentionally broke large parts of the wings off a Grumman Bearcat in the air, and then landed minus more than 20 percent of the wing and half the ailerons. I remember every aspect of that program in infinite detail. A few folks have marveled that I have such a retentive memory. But when one was a 24-year-old bachelor who got paid for flying experimental fighters and hadn't found out yet that girls existed, such events are indelible in the mind's eye.

The concept of jettisoning large portions of an aircraft's wing in flight would appear to be insane until the nature of the times when the Bearcat was in its gestation period is examined. In early 1943 it had become clear that the Grumman Hellcat was a great improvement in fighting performance over the vaunted Zero fighter. But Japanese aircraft, which would have much increased horsepower and performance, were beginning to appear over Japan. All students of aerial warfare know that the fighting life of any aircraft in wartime, even the new Hellcat, would be limited.

In 1942 the Pratt & Whitney engine manufacturing company had gone into massive production of their 2,000-hp

*The front view of the Bearcat shows the thinner wing, stabilizer and fin, and more compact fuselage than the Hellcat, which made the Bearcat look a lot like the Focke-Wulf 190. With the same engine that was to have been installed in the 3,200-lb heavier and improved F6F-6 Hellcat, the Bearcat was 76 mph faster and had twice the rate of climb of that new model Hellcat which was never produced. (Northrop Grumman History Center)*

R-2800 engine. Newer engines of vastly increased horsepower were not on the near horizon for American aircraft designers. It was clear that to get further increases in performance over the Hellcat, Grumman designers would have to produce a much smaller and lighter fighter. Grumman would utilize the R-2800 engines that were currently available in production and count on this engine's performance improvements later in the upcoming R-2800 development cycle.

In early 1943 three Grumman officials were invited to England to see and fly captured fighters of the axis powers. The test team was LeRoy Grumman, Bud Gillies, and Bob Hall. Having been a Grumman engineering test pilot for only six months, I was too junior to be invited to that important educational trip.

Of all the aircraft they saw and test flew, they were most fascinated with the new German fighter, the Focke-Wulf 190A. It not only had sprightly performance, but it had excellent flight characteristics with a weight of only 8,750 pounds combined with 1,730 horsepower. The Hellcat was 3,200 lbs heavier with only 270 horsepower more than the Fw-190A. Both Gillies and Hall flight-tested the Focke-Wulf and immediately found it to be the aircraft that they would like to have designed instead of the Hellcat. It was exactly what the Hellcat follow-on aircraft should be. The only three U.S. Navy requirements that it lacked were sufficient vision angle over the nose for good gunnery lead computing, proper carrier approach visibility, and a structure that would withstand carrier operations. The Fw-190A impressed them so much they felt compelled to hurry home and put together a fighter of this performance class to utilize the soon-available Pratt & Whitney R-2800-C engine with 2,400 (War Emergency Power) water injection horsepower. This would give our naval

The Bearcat design team decided to use the latest Pratt & Whitney R-2800-C engine with WAR (War Emergency Power) and design the lightest carrier fighter possible from what they had learned from the Focke-Wulf evaluations. This would be timely in order to combat the latest 2,000-hp Japanese fighters – Jack, Sam, and George – which were expected to appear before the invasion of Japan scheduled to start in March 1946. It was a great challenge, and this Bearcat demonstrates the outcome of their Focke-Wulf education. (Northrop Grumman History Center)

aviators a big performance increase over the newer Japanese fighters soon to appear, and still inherit the proven performance and reliability of the engines presently installed in fleet Hellcat squadrons.

The F8F-1 Bearcat was begun immediately on the team's return to the United States. Mr. Grumman took a direct hand in its design. As the effort progressed it was easy to see that carrier aircraft catapulting and arresting loads, not required in the Focke-Wulf 190, were going to make attainment of the gross weight goal of 8,750 pounds difficult to obtain in the Bearcat.

Innovative measures were needed to meet the stringent goals that Mr. Grumman and his team were striving to attain. Many items that were considered standard Navy equipment were going to have to be sacrificed: these included the reduction of the number of guns and ammunition from six to four, reducing the

*This picture of the 2,000-hp Japanese Mitsubishi Jack showed the fine fighter that the allied pilots expected to have come into Japanese inventory in 1943. It was great for the United States that the high Japanese brass thought that the war would be a short one and kept producing more 1938-designed 1,100-hp Zeros, which delayed developing higher-powered fighters. Very few of these fighters made the scene before V-J Day. (Northrop Grumman History Center)*

internal fuel capacity from 250 to 162 gallons, and the elimination of the adjustable seat. The seat would be integral to the cockpit floor structure. Cushions or the parachute would have to be used in place of seat adjustment. The folding wing mechanism would have to be much simpler than the Hellcat and be moved further out from the fuselage to save weight. A single instead of a three-tank fuel system would simplify and reduce the weight, too. Even with all this ingenuity the goal of 8,750 pounds still seemed unattainable. Finally, Pete Ehrlensen, chief of structures, came up with a far-out but intriguing idea to save a further 230 pounds of wing structure, which was a large enough amount of weight to make the goal.

Pete remembered that during my Hellcat structural demonstrations I had four failures at the mid-span of the stabilizers when I pulled up into the unknown compressibility "buffet boundary." No previous Grumman fighter had experienced this disastrous phenomenon. We later found out that the Lockheed P-38, the Republic P-47, and the North American P-51 had all experienced this buffet boundary. A P-38 had twice lost complete tail sections, killing two pilots trying to meet their demonstration 8G

points. During operational combat flying Hellcat pilots had bent and even broken off stabilizers and elevators at mid-span, too, when entering the mysterious and unknown violent buffet boundary during high-G pullouts while fighting Zeros.

The stabilizers and elevators fortunately broke at their semi-spans just outboard of the mid-span hinge. After this excessive stress they reduced loads substantially. Fortunately, the structural failures left enough of the working elevator control to fly the aircraft back to the carrier and make a successful landing.

Pete calculated that if the wing was designed to have an ultimate breaking load of 7.5Gs at a controlled point about three feet inboard of the wingtip, the wing would relieve itself of the tip loads and the remainder of the wing structure would support a load of 13Gs, which was the standard ultimate (breaking) load of fighters. The amount of wing area remaining was calculated to be sufficient to make a safe, albeit somewhat faster, carrier landing.

Pete suggested that a carefully designed rivet joint be made at about half-span of the outer folding wing panels and a break joint be designed in the ailerons so that the two outer halves would also detach when the wing panels broke off. This would leave half the aileron connected by two of the three hinges to the remaining wing structure to provide adequate pitch control for combat and a carrier landing.

It didn't take much persuasion for the Navy to agree to such novel measures; wartime pressures dictated more and more climb performance requiring greater power-to-weight ratios. Grumman designers had an outstanding reputation with the Navy brass and pilots from experience in "Grumman Ironworks'" Wildcats and Hellcats. The Navy soon agreed to this unique suggestion for weight savings.

A very detailed ground test program was conducted to prove that the rivet joint would break consistently at 7.5Gs as promised. One must realize that wing loads were estimated and that even those measured in flight-tests were not too accurate. Before they approved of the idea at the inception of the program the Navy required that Grumman make an experimental installation on a Grumman F4F Wildcat. Grumman had to pull the outboard portion of the wing and aileron off in a 7.5G flight-test to demonstrate that the Wildcat had acceptable flight characteristics, that it could make a satisfactory carrier-type landing, and that Grumman engineers could predict these flight loads. A Grumman F4F Wildcat was then rigged up with the wingtip rivet joint and aileron severance capability. Test pilot Carl Alber demonstrated this unique theory in one flight in December 1943. Everything worked as predicted in the air, and the aircraft demonstrated more than sufficient maneuverability and control for a satisfactory carrier landing at a speed not much higher than the normal Wildcat approach speed. The Navy and Grumman were now satisfied that the F8F-1 could be operationally satisfactory with such an installation.

In the F8F-1 Bearcat wingtip demonstration the Navy also required that Grumman make take-offs and landings

with both, and then alternate removed right and left wingtip and aileron panels, one at a time, to demonstrate acceptable flight characteristics, and be able to land safely aboard a carrier. I had the duty to fly those tests on 5 April 1945 in the second XF8F-1 (BuNo 90461). Although it was obvious that there were minor unsymmetrical pitch and directional flight deficiencies, the aircraft was easily flyable and landable if only 15 degrees of flap were used and carrier approach speeds increased by only 10 mph. World War II carriers were well capable of handling those requirements. Both Grumman and the Navy agreed with the results.

In clear hindsight it would be easy to think that such meager ground and flight-testing was grossly insufficient for such an unconventional innovation. Remember, however, that late in the war, with the invasion of Japan imminent, high production rates were paramount. For instance, during a single month, March 1944, when the Bearcat was in its ground and flight-test phase, Grumman delivered 620 Hellcats (a U.S. record), and 85 other aircraft including the F7F Tigercats and amphibians. In the rush of the times it seemed to Grumman and the Navy that the testing program was indeed sufficient. As you will see, we both underestimated the quality and the quantity of our design and testing phase, by an order of magnitude, in order to get squadron quantities of Bearcats to the Pacific Theater ASAP!

By early 1945, the F8F-1 had entered Fleet Squadron VF-19 led by Commander Joe Smith. Pilots found that it was indeed a great shot in the arm to have such startling performance available because, as we had expected, the Japanese had introduced the new 2,200-hp Homare 43-powered Mitsubishi A7M2 Reppu fighter (code named "Sam"), with much improved performance over the Zeros, Hellcats, and Corsairs.

The timing of the Bearcat as an addition to the fleet was perfect. Not only was it an exciting aircraft to fly (one could see the Focke-Wulf 190A heritage), it was 55-mph faster than the Hellcat (without water injection) and took off in 200 feet of deck space compared to the Hellcat's 325 feet. It had an amazing rate of climb of 5,340 feet per minute, more than twice that of the Hellcat's. It had the fastest rate of climb of any propeller-driven fighter in the war. Its rate of climb endeared it to Navy pilots because getting on top of the enemy has been the criteria of aerial combat success ever since World War I. You can imagine that naval aviators also enjoyed the fact that the F8F-1 Bearcat could easily outperform all the latest P-51, P-47, and P-38 Army Air Corps fighters at the time.

After a few weeks of glowing operational reports on the Bearcat, word came back that an operational pilot had shed only one of his two wingtips during a practice dive-bombing pullout and had been fatally injured in the crash. Several others followed, and the Navy and Grumman became greatly concerned. The wingtips weren't coming off as predicted, so Grumman hurriedly sent a team of engineers to visit all F8F-1 squadrons to study the remains of crashed aircraft to find out what had gone wrong. It became apparent that the severe vibrations that the wing outer panels received from constant hard carrier landings and the very strong wing oscillations when the aircraft pulled into the buffet boundary at altitude put a strain on the special wingtip rivet-joints than had been predicted. Grumman or the Navy in the rush of getting the Bearcat into production and service hadn't even considered these strains. It was also determined that the rivet-joint was not getting the sufficient quality control attention in Grumman production that this new and unique idea merited.

Squadron VF-19 sailed from Hawaii to the Pacific Theater of Operations to be launched into the combat zone just as the war ended. Now operational accidents were looked at with a much more critical eye by the Navy. The flight envelope was now severely restricted from high-G buffet boundary combat maneuvers.

Because of the Navy's continuing need for the availability of the Bearcats with their superiority of performance over any other enemy fighters of the time, Grumman needed to find a better way to guarantee wingtip separation, one which did not depend solely on a rivet-joint that took such a beating in the Bearcat's two tough flight regimes. Ideas were suggested, but one that seemed to solve the problem

The remarkable NASA-designed dive recovery flaps that were installed on all production Bearcats after I had tested them on the Thunderbolt at the Joint Army/Navy Fighter Conference in October 1944. Although they were small, they were God-sent if a pilot dived into compressibility and had all of his controls frozen from the compressibility shock wave that formed. When he extended these small flaps just 20 degrees the aircraft came out of compressibility immediately with little effort on the pilot's part. (Northrop Grumman History Center)

was to install a 12-inch strip of prima cord, a rope-type explosive used to detonate dynamite, just outboard of both wing rivet-joints on the lower wing skins with a set of electrical micro switches at both break joints. These would activate the other tip's explosive device if only one wingtip came off. We called these "ice box" switches, which shows our status in technical nomenclature antiquity. The ground tests were spectacular, to say the least. After several successful tests we rigged a Bearcat with this Fourth-of-July system for flight-test.

For a practical test one of the wingtips was structured to come off at 5Gs. According to theory, the "ice box" micro switch in the other wing would electrically activate the prima cord to blow the other tip off at exactly the same instant.

The demonstration point was selected to be 450 mph at 7,500 feet altitude in a 30-degree dive angle. We had movie photographers on both sides of my Bearcat in the rear cockpits of F7F-3N chase aircraft to record the action. I pulled 6Gs to insure that the 5G rivet-joint would fail and activate the other wingtip explosive.

Lo and behold, the genies of fate urinated on the pillars of science again. With an impressive flash of fire, smoke, and debris, the weakened tip left the aircraft at 5Gs as predicted, but the other one remained as fixed to the wing as ever. I looked out and saw that not only had the standard short wing become even shorter, but also the other one was full of jagged holes. That got my immediate attention. One of my chase pilots came in close and inspected the trauma that had occurred to the wings. He observed a large hole in the bottom skin of the wing that had indeed proved that the prima cord had fired as predicted, but the wingtip remained firmly attached even though the 12-inch explosion hole was in the most critical stress area in the wing. Good old

*Four F8F-1s from the Naval Reserve Squadron based at NAS Glenview, Illinois, in 1950. The step-up formation in this picture was only used for photographic demonstrations. The usual formation for combat was step down so that pilots would not run into each other making rapid combat evasive turns. The Bearcat was used for reserve squadrons until 1953, long after jets were in inventory. (Northrop Grumman History Center)*

Grumman Ironworks! Fortunately, as might be expected, this did not cause any aerodynamic disturbance. I landed the F8F with one tip removed.

It was quite obvious during the debrief that there were a lot of very perplexed engineers. Finally, one non-program engineer timidly offered the suggestion that possibly the powerful slipstream's effects had not been considered sufficiently, so it was back to the old drawing board.

The project engineer then suggested that 26 inches of prima cord be used on the next flight. Ground tests were run. They checked that the new length of explosion should cause proper wingtip severance in the air. On the next flight when I pulled 8Gs, both tips departed as planned amid much smoke and debris flying from the aircraft. Even though the prima cord made a deafening explosion during ground tests, slipstream noises cancelled all explosion

*The Director of the Grumman Worldwide Service Department, Roger Wolfe Kahn, had a commercial G-38 (F8F-2) Bearcat that he used to visit Naval Air Stations across the United States from 1947 until 1960, when he died from cancer. This aircraft had the Pratt & Whitney R-2800-C 2,100-hp engine. It was a flashy and plush way to arrive at a Naval Air Station. I used it several times for business visits to NATC Patuxent River, Maryland. With its 150-gallon external tank it had a range that could cross the country with only one fuel stop. (Northrop Grumman History Center)*

noise in the air. Both chase pilots were much more excited than I was. They were able to see the visual effects that I couldn't see because I was monitoring the cockpit accelerometer. They said that it looked like the aircraft had blown up when both tips blew and the ailerons and wing sections departed from the bird. There were two very smoky explosions with two wingtips and two aileron halves coming off in rapid succession, along with much shattered metal from the explosion areas. Both wingtip ends were cleanly severed as planned. There weren't even small metal shards remaining on the wings or ailerons to suggest that an explosion had done the surgery. Both the Navy and Grumman considered the test a great success again. Incidentally, we stuffed both of the departing wing sections and ailerons with kapok so we could pick up those pieces as they floated in the Long Island Sound over which we were performing the flight-tests. Again we failed in our preparations. The wingtip pieces floated but the aileron halves sunk because their heavy balance weights overcame the buoyancy that the kapok provided.

We could now guarantee that both wingtips would come off simultaneously.

However, with the advent of peace the Navy now required Grumman to do a complete flight envelope demonstration versus the one-shot demos that we had previously performed. Consequently, a 10-flight program was developed that pulled the wingtips off from 250 to 525 mph, the limit speed of the Bearcat. The

*Number two production F8F-1 (BuNo 90438) with two 500-lb bombs on the wing racks. The streamlined bombs required for the much higher flight speeds finally superseded these stubby World War II bomb designs. The Bearcat was not just designed for the air-to-air combat role; it could carry 2,000 pounds of bombs and all Bearcats were delivered with four wing racks for 5-inch HVAR rockets. It was designed to be a great fighter-bomber, too. (Northrop Grumman History Center)*

Sixty-eight-year-old Marine Major Alford "Al" Williams flying his Gulfhawk 4 over Central Park, New York, in mid-October 1947, just after he had taken delivery of it at Grumman. I had the privilege of checking out this very famous prewar World War II and postwar aerobatic demonstration pilot who was backed by the Gulf Oil Company. He only flew this aircraft for 58 hours before he landed it on 18 January 1949 at New Bern, North Carolina, gear up to avoid a thunderstorm in his flight path. The aircraft was consumed in flames when his drop tank ignited while scraping the runway. He was uninjured. (Northrop Grumman History Center)

Navy also required that they be pulled off in a vertical dive for the final demonstration. For an extended period of time, when I left for work in the morning, I knew I'd be blowing wingtips off of a Bearcat all day long—just another day at the office.

During the previous wingtip severance at 5Gs I had noticed that the aircraft had pitched up one more G than I had planned. Having practiced complete and accurate structural demonstration pullouts for the Wildcats, Hellcats, Tigercats, and Bearcats I had made hundreds of pull-ups and had always come within one-tenth of a G of my target, so this excessive G bothered me somewhat. I talked to the engineers about it but they suggested that I was probably nervous; strongly implying pilot error as they usually did when they couldn't find an immediate answer for a mistake they might have made. I

promptly and wrongly put this slur out of my mind.

We then beefed up both wingtip riveted-joints to the full 7.5G Navy demo point, armed the prima cord devices, and proceeded with the full-blown program. On the first pullout I aimed at 8Gs to be sure that one or the other joint would fail. They both came off with the usual fireworks and after it was all over I noticed that the maximum G recorded was 9.5! I came back and emphatically stated that I couldn't have overshot that much and demanded an explanation from the aerodynamics department using some indelicate, seldom used, four-letter motivational engineering terms. After a little re-thinking, another non-program aerodynamicist observed that, of course, the aircraft would pitch up without pilot effort when the span, area, and aspect ratio of the wing with the tips off had increased the aircraft's

A carrier deck taxi accident crash on the USS Leyte on 8 July 1947 between Bearcats number 110 (BuNo 95203) and number 117 (BuNo 95192). My neighbor, Lt. John Fisk, was just taxiing over the retracted Davis Barrier when number 117 taxied too fast up the carrier deck after being released from his arresting wire. None of the men on "Vulture's Row" watching the accident seem to be as excited as John Fisk was when he heard the propeller of 117 chewing up the back end of his fuselage. Fortunately, the pilot of 117 stomped on his brakes sufficiently to keep the accident from becoming worse. As the old Navy adage so succinctly states, "There is no acceptable excuse for any pilot causing a taxi accident." (Northrop Grumman History Center)

pitching moments so drastically. He also calculated that 9.5Gs was exactly the amount of G increase the F8F should have pitched up to. So much for pilot error when engineering couldn't explain a phenomenon.

I was exonerated, but I learned that engineers who have a proprietary interest in a program might not always think as widely and objectively as professional test flying requires when the answer is not patently obvious. That hard-won experience stood by me during all of my years as an experimental test pilot when I couldn't get answers that would rationally satisfy me. I began seeking two or more professional opinions long before that was an accepted practice in difficult medical prognostications.

We finished the program without much ado, and the increased pitching problems were noted in the Pilot's Handbook now that we had a satisfactory engineering explanation. The Navy was happy with the Bearcat for full operational utilization and all aircraft were fitted out with the now-proven 26-inch explosive release system.

But our travails were not over, not by a long shot. As you might have guessed, the prima cord was actuated electrically but had been designed with no safeguards for possible ground maintenance mistakes. Shortly afterward we received word from a squadron that during a maintenance fix there was a short circuit when making some electrical ground tests and the wingtips of one aircraft blew off on the hangar deck. That incident fatally injured a Navy maintenance white hat.

The Navy now said that they had enough of this weight-saving fiasco and suggested that the wingtips be fastened firmly to the wing without the prima-cord device and that the aircraft flight envelope be limited to 4Gs. With the strains of carrier landings and pilots frequently exceeding 4Gs during target fixation in practice air-to-ground work and not reporting it, the Bearcat soon had its wings coming off in the air, breaking at the wing root! A steel strap fix was installed to give the Bearcat sufficient strength for carrier landings and 7.5G pullouts, but it was soon supplanted in operational squadrons by the much faster Grumman F9F-2 Panther and the McDonnell F2H-1 Banshee jet fighters with much higher speeds and no wartime weight-saving gimmicks.

F8F-1s and -2s were retained, however, by the Navy Blue Angels from 1946 until 1949 when they were supplanted by the Grumman Panther. The remaining Bearcats were put into the training command where they were flown with an excellent safety record. In 1956 all Bearcats were relegated to the Arizona storage fields, where all aircraft, good and bad, eventually retire to rest.

The structural weight savings of the detachable wingtips was a great idea theoretically, but its short-cut wartime flight-testing, design, and production implementation just didn't allow enough time for Navy shakedown to pass real-world tests. However, had the war continued, the Bearcat would have given Navy pilots a great speed and climb advantage over all Japanese types it met in combat.

In early 1945 a Navy Bearcat set a time-to-climb record from a standing start to 10,100 feet in 91 seconds. That record stood long after the advent of jets. Even in 1989 a souped-up Bearcat, flown by Darrel Greenameyer, set a world speed record for piston-powered aircraft of 501 mph. Not bad for an aircraft that was designed very hastily during wartime well over a half century ago.

## An Embarrassing Epilogue

As the project test pilot of the Bearcat, I flew it in many air shows. Immediately after the war Grumman hosted the *New York Daily News* model aircraft meet and I flew my usual routine air show with one addition—a never-performed-before, eight-point slow roll.

Previous Grumman fighters had too much lateral stability to make a slow roll with hesitation eight times during the roll. I thought I was good at them and performed two in that air show. My wife was in the audience and I asked her what she thought of my fantastic eight-point roll performance. She said, "I thought they were beautiful but one of the two little old ladies standing in front of me said, 'Why can't he make them smoothly like the other fliers did?'" That was the last eight-point slow roll I made in Bearcat air shows.

## Conclusions

Looking back on all of the fighter aircraft I have been privileged to fly, I still put the Bearcat at, or near, the top of my list of favorites. It was an absolutely wonderful handling aircraft with unbelievable performance. When a Navy pilot wrapped a Bearcat around him for flight he knew he was playing in the fast lane with a very classy pussycat from the Grumman Ironworks. But every pussycat will occasionally show its claws at the wrong time. And so it was with the Grumman Bearcat.

# Chapter 17

# The Best Fighters of World War II

## June and July 2003

When *Flight Journal* asked me to write a dissertation of all of the great World War II fighters to determine which one was the best, I thought... what an ego trip! This selection would be easily dug out of my dusty flight report files during World War II when I had evaluated eight types of World War II fighters, and from research books in my collection.

I was fortunate to have flight-tested several versions of these fighters during the Joint Army/Navy Fighter Conference at NAS Patuxent in October 1944, and with fighters that were passed around between Navy and Air Corps contractors for test pilot evaluations. They were: F4U-1, -D, -4 Corsair; P-51-B, -D, -H Mustang; P-38-D, -M Lightning; P-47-B, -D, -N Thunderbolt; P-40-N Warhawk; P-63 Kingcobra; F4F Wildcat; F6F Hellcat; Supermarine Seafire (carrier version of the famous Spitfire); Fairey Firefly; De Havilland Mosquito; and the Japanese A6M5 Zero.

These World War II flight evaluations were not just joyrides to add hours to my logbook. They were set up to investigate known good and bad flight characteristics and performance capabilities of these fighters during simulated gunnery runs against other fighters and during dive-bombing runs against targets. I then wrote a comprehensive report on each fighter to illustrate all of these findings so that Grumman engineers could incorporate, or steer clear of, these features in forthcoming fighter designs.

Picking the "best fighter" involved a very complex series of operational factors. On top of that, because there was a great geographical difference between the land-based war in Europe and the island-hopping Japanese war in which carrier-based aviation played such a vital part, these two basic theaters must be discussed separately.

## "Best Fighter" Selection Criteria

### Continuous Production Improvement in Combat Capability

General Nathan Bedford Forrest, the famous southern Civil War cavalry officer, coined the phrase, "Git Thar Firstest with the Mostest." That axiom of combat probably had been defined in many other languages for ages before General Forrest, but his statement was so succinct that it has become the prescription for victory, even in air combat. It's a simple matter of numbers—more aircraft available for a greater length of time. To limit the number of contestants in this beauty contest, I have selected only examples of fighter aircraft that were built in quantities of over 10,000. They will then meet General Forrest's criteria of "the Mostest."

### Four Missions Capability

The principle characteristic for a "best fighter" must be its continuous contribution to the destruction of the enemy ground and air forces in its four tactical roles; fighter-to-fighter, air-to-ground troop support, bomber protection, and photo-recon missions. To compare them only in the exciting, ace-making fighter-to-fighter role would be an omission of three-quarters of their other capabilities where they were tactically and strategically useful and necessary to win the war. Most of the combatant air force pilots in World War II were trained in all of these roles, and most fighters could perform all of these missions to varying degrees. During my operational training in 1944 at Naval Air Station Atlantic City, under the personal tutelage of Dauntless and Wildcat ace Commander Swede Vejtasa, I was introduced to these roles in a Grumman Hellcat. I was amazed and embarrassed to discover that so many of my fighter preconceptions were inaccurate.

### Pilot Compatibility

The fighter must also be comfortable for a 200-hour, wartime-trained pilot, have docile flight characteristics, high performance, good cockpit design, visibility, comfort, armor/self-sealing fuel tanks, and a resulting low accident rate.

### Service Record

United States records from the European and Pacific theaters of operations were easy to obtain and will clearly show what each fighter type contributed in its different roles.

### The Would-Have-Been "Best Fighter" If...

A good example of a supposedly perfect fighter, hailed by many historians as the greatest fighter of World War II, is the German twinjet-powered Messerschmitt Me-262. It was faster and had the most powerful fighter-to-fighter armament of the World War II fighters consisting of four centerline-aimed 30-mm cannons. But it had three serious combat problems: the engines were extremely sensitive to throttle movement, which could blow out their combustion chambers easily, they were exceedingly hard to air restart, and they had no propeller drag for speed control with power changes, which all World War II fighter pilots used for combat

*A well-marked twinjet Me-262 superbly restored by the Smithsonian Institution. This aircraft was modern in many ways. It had one of the first bubble canopies, a tricycle landing gear, and a very thin .87 critical Mach number. The Me-262's top speed was about 100 mph faster than that of allied fighters. One of its drawbacks was not being equipped with an aerodynamic brake for airspeed control necessary during gunnery and formation flying, which was mandatory for jet aircraft with such high-speed diving capability. (Smithsonian Institution)*

The P-40N-1-CU that I almost became a stall/spin accident statistic in on 30 July 1943 while trying some inept aerobatics at a very low altitude. The P-40 had a very high stall-spin accident rate, which I didn't pick up on during that flight even though I had seen several P-40 pilots spin in at the Boston Logan airport in 1941. (Northrop Grumman History Center via Corwin H. Meyer)

maneuvering. Thus, the Me-262 had very poor speed control capability required for two-plane fighter combat and formation flying. Even with those problems, however, it would have been a "best" if not for one other little problem. Not enough of them were built or put into combat to make any worthwhile contribution to the German war effort. Thanks to an incredibly shortsighted series of decisions on Hitler's part, only 160 hurriedly flight-tested Me-262 aircraft were available for combat operations just four months before the end of the war.

In 1944, after adamantly and ignorantly deciding that this fighter must be only a level bomber, Hitler finally gave top production priority for that fabulous aircraft as a fighter on 10 March 1945. Therefore, it cannot even be considered a contender. Was it a good fighter? Absolutely! Could it have been good in the ground attack role? Probably. Did it make a major contribution? Of course not.

Another would-be contender might be the 13,733 Curtiss P-40 Warhawks delivered from 1940 to 1945. Although it had some well-known limitations, it was

in the USAAC official list of "On Hand Overseas in All Theaters" from the beginning to the end of the war, but in much lesser numbers than its three other U.S. peer fighters. Many had been built and they were greatly used to stem the enemy tide until more powerful fighters could be deployed, but they did not have the continuous development required to meet the demanding combat requirements for the last half of the war. The following USAAF records are the aircraft that were deployed to the battle zones.

| | Aircraft Type | | | |
|---|---|---|---|---|
| | P-38 | P-40 | P-47 | P-51 |
| Dec. 1941 | 0 | 466 | 0 | 0 |
| 1942 | 506 | 1,601 | 10 | 0 |
| 1943 | 1,168 | 1,327 | 1,910 | 368 |
| 1944 | 1,866 | 351 | 3,702 | 2,918 |
| Aug. 1945 | 1,588 | 71 | 3,111 | 3,101 |
| Wartime Total | 5,128 | 3,816 | 8,827 | 6,381 |

Note that the P-47 had an earlier entry than the P-51, and higher numbers in the field than either the P-38 or the P-51 after 1942.

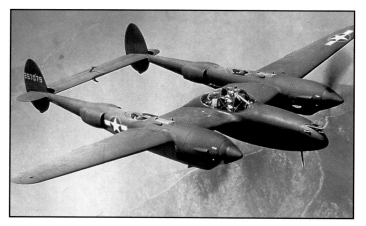

*The P-38 had many qualities that the pilots liked; most popular were its twin engines, which gave it a great high speed and rate-of-climb advantage over any Japanese fighter. And it would bring its pilot safely home if one engine had been damaged by a lucky shot from a Zero in combat. Its four .50-caliber, nose-mounted machine guns made easy kill shooting for its pilot. (Corwin H. Meyer Collection)*

## Best Fighter in the ETO

*Number Seven —*
*the Lockheed P-38 Lightning*

Lockheed's twin-engine Lightning had a great potential to be the number one fighter. Its first flight occurred on 27 January 1939, early enough to have been deployed before Pearl Harbor. It had much more horsepower than ever before had been installed in any previous fighter. Its tricycle landing gear greatly simplified pilot training. Its five centerline guns, unhampered by converging wing gun aiming problems, made gunnery much less difficult for its pilots. Its turbo-supercharged engines gave it a great altitude advantage over enemy aircraft. It had many combat assets and should have been a pushover program, but...

It was the very first twin-engine fighter ever put into service by the USAAC and took a much longer time for training, maintenance, and world-wide spares support. It was the first fighter ever designed for top-priority mass production by Lockheed when they were already encumbered both in design and manufacturing problems with a very large backlog of other military aircraft contracts. Its engines and turbo-superchargers had not completed their military acceptance programs. The massive P-38 program require-

ments dictated that Lockheed expand their manpower and manufacturing space in Los Angeles, a city already overloaded with many other top-priority military aircraft programs. It was the first fighter to enter the unknown and destructive compressibility regime in dives, which caused the loss of several of its prototypes and early military aircraft. Having two engines in a larger aircraft, its manufacturing time and deployed maintenance support hours were much higher than single engine fighters. For the above reasons the number of Lightnings deployed to all theaters of the war was only able to reach 80 percent of the P-51 and 58 percent of the P-47 numbers.

The P-38 endured a lot of growing pains when it was first deployed to Europe and did not have sufficient range for the required bomber-escort missions. The P-47 and P-51 soon replaced it. The Lightning did, however, show its magnificent combat abilities in the African and Pacific theaters in the air defense, fighter-bomber, and photo-recon missions.

Pilots who flew the Lightning in combat quickly became accustomed to their fighter's excessive thrust and appreciated its single-engine safety potential. Later in the war, when the P-38 received its hydraulic-boosted ailerons, it demonstrated a greater combat advantage over enemy

## Number Six — Messerschmitt Bf-109

Twenty-nine Messerschmitt Bf-109Bs had been in combat by two combat squadrons in JDG Group J-88 in the Spanish war against Russian fighters from July 1937 to 1939. Thus it had pre-World War II war experience. It was produced in the largest numbers of any World War II fighter without interruption; and it was manufactured until the very end of the war. It was a promising fighter, but... fully 11,000 of the 33,000 Bf-109s built were destroyed in takeoff and landing accidents alone, which accounted for one-third of its combat potential.

I was most amazed when my late friend, 176-kill ace General Johannes Steinhoff, related this fantastic landing accident rate to me in 1956. During its lifetime, such accidents reduced the Bf-109's combat numbers by 11,000 aircraft—more than all of the 9,936 Lockheed P-38 Lightnings manufactured. It seems incredible that the primary cause of this outrageous statistic, a splayed-out wheel landing gear of known disasterous geometry, was not rectified immediately. After the war, Josef Hubert (chief aerodynamicists for the Messerschmitt Me-163 rocket fighter, who came to Grumman in 1946), told me that Willie Messerschmitt adamantly refused to compromise the Bf-109's performance by adding the drag-producing bumps and fairings on the wing surfaces that would have been necessary to accommodate the wheels with a known proper geometry. This would have given it a normal military fighter accident rate and made it a world standard.

As a fighter-bomber, the Bf-109F-l/B was a borderline failure. It couldn't carry enough external stores to justify the risk. The best it could do was to carry a single 1,000-lb bomb on a centerline rack. There are good reasons why you seldom see a picture of a 109 carrying bombs—it was not a powerful fighter-bomber.

*The standard Bf-109 had quite unstable vertical wheel angles for takeoff and landing rollouts because designer and test pilot Willie Messerschmitt refused to install bumps on the upper and lower surface of the Bf-109's thin wings necessary for this angled wheel to have the lowest drag after retraction. General Johannes Steinhoff, a 176-shoot-down ace of the Luftwaffe, told me this caused the destruction of over 11,000 aircraft – one-third of its total production – during takeoff and landing accidents during the lifetime of this German fighter. German combat pilots described the landing rollout characteristics as "malicious." (Luftwaffe)*

fighters. And, when it finally had dive recovery flaps installed, pilots no longer had a fear of fatally over-diving the P-38 into compressibility.

Major Bong was a Lightning pilot who shot down 40 enemy aircraft, the highest number of any U.S. fighter pilot. He, along with many other P-38 pilots, considered the Lightning a very useful combat tool in all theaters. However, it had too many teething problems and limitations to rank nearer the top of the list.

Steinhoff also related the story of ferrying 200 Bf-109s from Germany to France just before D-Day in June 1944. Because of weather, lack of sufficient pilot training, and other operational problems, only 23 made it to their destinations—177 aircraft were lost.

Early in the war the Bf-109 made hundreds of high-scoring aces below top scorer Erich Hartmann (with 352 kills) and it was considered an outstanding defensive and offensive fighter. But with its mediocre fighter-bomber capability, and with an accident rate designed into it, it could never be rated as the "best."

### Number Five — Russian Yak-1 and -9

In 1938, 32-year-old Alexander Yakovlev won the contract for building a line of very simple, straightforward Yak series of fighters that would provide over 30,000 fighter aircraft to the USSR air forces during the war.

The Yak-1 fighter started out with a wooden wing, steel tube and fabric fuselage, and tail surfaces. After a move east from Moscow to Kamensk Uralski, Yakovlev's first aircraft rolled off the lines three weeks after the arrival of the jigs and tools. This was an amazing feat. The Yak-l was powered with an 1,100-hp M-105PA engine, which gave it a speed of 311 mph at sea level, and 363 mph at 16,000 feet. Range was penalized by a fuel capacity of only 107 gallons. The Russians, however, learned quickly and the Yak series of aircraft was continually redesigned and improved. As its designations moved forward (and backward – the USSR had a strange model numbering system) it got faster, more lethal, and carried heavier bomb loads. The primary role of the Yak-9M was to support the ground forces and keep the sky clear of Luftwaffe fighters and bombers. They also escorted Russian IL-2 Sturmovik fighters and Petylakov Pe-2 bombers on bombing runs over German airfields. It could easily out-climb the Messerschmitt 109 and later models had enough range to escort allied B-17 shuttle bombers from Britain through Russia to Italy.

There is no question that the Yak 1, 3, 7, and 9 series (which, for some reason, were not deployed in that order) of fighters contributed greatly to winning the Russian segment of World War II. It was entirely a run-of-the-mill design produced using the materials and labor available.

All Yakovlev fighter models had many attributes in common: mass-production availability, continuous development which stayed ahead of the enemy, and excellent stability and controllability at high angles of attack combined with extremely powerful combat capabilities. The 30,000 Yak fighters produced and combat-available for their three major fighter roles for the duration of World War II were able to operate and be easily maintained under conditions that would have grounded their refined allied contemporaries. Had any specific combat mission data been available, such as aircraft shot down, bomb load carried for ground support, and bomber support, this aircraft would probably have been a very strong contender for the "best fighter."

## The Fighter Beauty Queen Selection Becomes More Difficult

From now on, the facts for the determination of the following four fighters will rate them closer to each other because they were all first-class aircraft.

### Number Four — North American P-51 Mustang

Many military historians have lauded the 15,686 P-51s that served in all of the theaters as the greatest fighter of World War II. It was an excellent fighter and served our country and Great Britain well for the rapidity with which it was put into production and the length of time it was in service.

The development of the Mustang with the fortuitous British combination of the Rolls-Royce Merlin with the basic design of the early P-51s they had purchased, are well known events and I can add nothing to that great legend. I can, however, make personal observations on the aircraft.

All three Mustang models that I evaluated (the B, D, and H) had great cockpit layouts, good visibility, and were a delight to fly, but had two rather powerful vices. I found that the Mustang's poor rolling characteristics during stall recovery gave it strong tendencies to enter snap rolls and accidental spins when in a landing condition final turn and during combat gunnery runs in the clean condition. If you pulled hard at the wrong time, it was all too will-

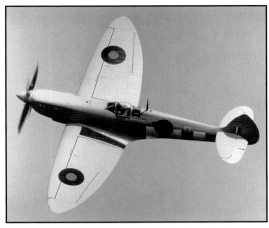

*The Spitfire's beautiful elliptical wing planform and light wing loading made it a great fighter against Bf-109s in turning combat. However, its highly visible engine oil and coolant systems under the wings were very vulnerable to aerial and ground attacks. (Royal Air Force)*

*Four Eighth Air Force P-51Ds of the 361st Fighter Group based at Botisham, England, with two 90-gallon under-wing tanks giving them a range of 2,000 miles. With this range they could easily protect the bomber fleets to Berlin and return and have fuel left for combat or ground attack. The P-51D had six .50-caliber guns and great visibility from its bubble canopy. It had the greatest P-51 model production run of 7,956 aircraft. Its major vulnerability to enemy ground and aerial gunfire was from its oil and engine coolant system radiators located in the aft fuselage. (USAF)*

ing to snap over the top of the turn into a spin.

Its other far worse vice was its vulnerability when shot at from the rear. The engine-cooling radiator was located in the belly of the aft fuselage and was an easy target, which could be quickly fatal to the engine's combat life. (Note: The air-cooled radial engine of the P-47s, Hellcats, and all of the other radial engine powered aircraft had no liquid coolant engine-stopping vulnerability and their oil coolers were usually buried safely behind the engine.) Many unfortunate P-51 and P-38 pilots had to bail out over enemy territory because of this drawback and spent the rest of the war in very inhospitable German stalags (prisons).

Mustangs played a continuous role in the war in all four of the fighter roles, missions, and worldwide theaters.

### Number Three — The Supermarine Spitfire/Seafire Team

The Supermarine Spitfire had a 20-year background of high-speed aircraft design from their Supermarine S-4, S-5, and S-6B seaplane racers that finally won the 1931 Schneider Cup outright for Britain with a world-record speed of 406.99 mph. So it is understandable that from the Spitfire's 1935 prototype to the final postwar versions all were high-spirited combat mounts. I also considered the Spitfire a wonderful aircraft to fly, but it wasn't without its operational problems.

Few World War II aircraft saw the amount of development that was lavished on the Spitfire's basic design. It grew from 1,030 to an incredible 2,375 horsepower in the Griffon-powered versions, and performance followed suit. The increase was awe-inspiring: speed increased from 362 to 439 mph, altitudes from 32,000 to 43,000 feet, and rate of climb from 2,530 to 4,600 feet per minute. It could really perform. However, the aircraft had extremely short legs. Its low internal fuel capacity and limited ability to carry drop tanks wouldn't let it fly very far or fight for very long. It carried less than half the internal fuel of the Hellcat, Thunderbolt, Lightning, and Mustang, which greatly limited its radius of action for bomber support.

Being short of fuel, the Spitfire's major drawback was in the fighter-bomber role due to its low weight of stores or external fuel-carrying capability. Provisions were

Because of the Fw-190's short range with internal fuel, many Fw-190 sorties carried a 71-gallon tank on the centerline rack. This fuel increased their range by 260 miles. The air-cooled engine of the Fw-190 with its oil cooler located just behind the engine was much less vulnerable to air and ground fire than the liquid-cooled Spitfire, Mustang, and Warhawk. (Luftwaffe)

added to late Mk V series' to carry one centerline 500-lb bomb or a 170-gallon drop tank. In the 5,665 Mk IXs built, the bomb load was finally increased to 1,000 pounds. Several later models carried six wing racks for 5-inch HVAR rockets. This limited external stores armament list remained the same until after the Mk XVI model ended wartime production.

All pilots who evaluated it described the Spitfire's flight handling characteristics: a highly bred, swift Arabian steed compared to the American workhorse fighters.

Spitfires filled the short-range defensive fighter and long-range photo-recon roles but they were too short "legged" in the fighter-bomber, ground attack, and bomber escort roles to be competitive with other World War II fighters to be "best fighter."

The British Royal Navy built 1,620 Seafires before the end of World War II, but it didn't do well in the carrier environment. According to Royal-Navy Captain Eric Brown, "The Seafires had very limited range for combat air patrols and the Seafire's deck landing accident rate resulted in more operational losses than combat successes." He listed the Hellcat, Zero, and Wildcat at the top of his list of the best shipborne fighters. The Seafire was not even on this short aircraft list.

### Number Two — The Focke-Wulf 190

Although the Focke-Wulf 190 was the first fighter designed by this company, it was a fortuitous design for future multi-role development. It had a stable, crosswind-compatible landing gear compared to the accident-prone, unstable gear of the Bf-109, and an outstanding bubble-type canopy long before this amount of fighter visibility was considered necessary in combat. It was far ahead of its German Messerschmitt Bf-109 competitor in these regards.

At the time of its presentation in 1940, the radial engine was not favored for Luftwaffe fighters, the in-line engine was. General Ernst Udet's change of decision for this radial-engine future asset for the Fw-190 came as a surprise to the Focke-Wulf management.

The Fw-190A had other positive attributes, including: flight handling characteristics were rapidly learned by a 200-hour pilot, an outstanding cockpit layout, and its canopy that set new standards for fighter visibility. On top of this impressive list, its structural design not only provided for exceptional performance but also, more importantly, it was ideally suited for mass production.

The Fw-190 was continuously updated with larger engines and from the very beginning had good range and load carrying capability that only got better as the war continued. It had a highly developed "tank buster" fighter-bomber variant with a variety of heavy-caliber cannons and bomb racks. The Fw-190's wider range of development programs exceeded the Bf-109's and provided the most versatile, mass-produced fighter and fighter-bomber aircraft for the Luftwaffe. The 20,001 Fw-190 fighters and fighter-bombers delivered gave the Luftwaffe many splendid offensive weapons. Unfortunately for the Germans, when the Fw-190's talents were really needed in the wide Russian fronts and after the D-Day invasion, massive logistics foul-ups prevented them from contributing much, if any, service to the final defense of Germany.

### Number One — The Republic P-47 Thunderbolt

The 15,683 P-47 aircraft delivered from three major factories was the largest aircraft production in American fighter-plane history. Republic's prewar production lines of the 463 similarly designed and constructed P-35 and P-43 fighters signifi-

This group of RP-47Bs is flying over Long Island, New York, in the winter of 1942. They are in training to be the first P-47 squadron to deploy to England. Squadron leader Col. Zempke is in number one and Lt. Bob Johnson, who was to become a very high scorer in his P-47s, is in number 26. One day at about this time five P-47s crashed into the Great South Bay of Long Island producing evenly spaced holes in the ice. They had been following their leader in aerobatics and had performed a half roll followed by a half loop to recover but they were all too low to have enough recovery altitude. (Warren Bodie)

cantly assisted the P-47's rapid production build-up rate and military introduction. Republic P-47s delivered: 1 in 1941, 532 in 1942, 4,428 in 1943, 7,065 in 1944, and 3,657 in 1945. Compared to the Fw-190 enemy, Thunderbolts were faster over 15,000 feet, and their massive firepower of eight .50-caliber guns soon began making a definite impression on the Luftwaffe. With the Thunderbolt's 445-mile range, high-altitude escort capability for the American B-17 and B-24 daylight bomber raids became available. At the end of 1943, there were 10 P-47 Groups and by June 1944 there were 17 P-47 Groups stationed in the ETO.

By the end of 1943, Thunderbolts were beginning to use any remaining fighter escort ammunition for low-altitude strafing runs. Their successes led to

the adaptation of the P-47 to its most successful role: that of the offensive fighter-bomber role.

There were 31 AAF P-47 Fighter Groups in all combat areas by the end of 1944. The only theater in which the P-47 did not operate was Alaska. In addition, 730 P-47Ds were sent to the RAF, and 446 P-47Ds flew in seven squadrons with the Free-French Air Force, Russia, Brazil, and Mexico for their air services in all theaters of World War II.

The original Thunderbolt was an impressive eight .50-caliber gun, high-altitude fighter with a belly rack for a 500-lb bomb or a 75-gallon fuel tank. The later series P-47D-20-RE with its "universal" wing and fuselage racks was fitted for various combinations of up to 2,500-lbs of bombs, two 150-gallon wing tanks, and one 75-gallon ventral tank. The P-47-D25-RE model introduced the bubble canopy, which greatly improved combat visibility. P-47D-27-RE fighters added 10 outer wing stations for 5-inch HVAR rockets and it was also equipped with the 2,400-hp R-2800-59 engine with water injection. That greatly reduced its heavyweight bomber escort takeoff distance. It was also equipped with electrically operated dive recovery brakes, which completely counteracted the compressibility effects that had resulted in the loss of many earlier Thunderbolts when dived too steeply.

The last model produced, the longer-wingspan 467-mph P-47N, with an increase of internal fuel to 556 gallons, combined with external tanks, gave it a combat range of slightly over 2,000 miles for B-29 bomber support. The only fighter role that it did not participate in was photo-recon because the usual camera location in the aft fuselage was filled with the massive turbo-supercharger and its plumbing.

The P-47 was well fitted to the 200-hour war-trained pilot. Its cockpit was roomy with all of the controls, switches,

gallon fuel tank or a 1,000-lb bomb. It also had a 1,000-lb bomb rack on the right wing stub. Bob Hall flew the prototype on 30 July 1942. Commander Fred Trapnell flew it for only two flights in September 1942 and gave it the Navy's approval for mass production. Grumman delivered 12 in 1942 and 2,566 in 1943. By January 1944 the production rate was up to 500 a month. In March 1945 the production rate hit 620 per month to set a United States fighter production delivery record for the entire war.

In addition to the fighter, fighter-bomber, and bomber support roles, 229 Hellcat F6F-3Ns and 1,432 F6F-5Ns, with the APS-4 and -6 radars mounted on the right wing, were used successfully as night-fighters. The Hellcat also performed the photo-recon role as the F6F-3P and -5P with cameras in the aft fuselage. When the F6F-5 production started in early 1944 it had a second 1,000-lb bomb rack on the left wing stub and six wing-mounted 5-inch HVAR rocket racks, which increased its armament. It could now carry 3,000 pounds of bombs. No SBD Dauntless or TBF Avenger bomber was ever lost to aerial attack after the Hellcat began bomber-support operations.

As the war progressed, Hellcat numbers were constantly increased on all carriers to take over the strike/attack duties of the SB2C Helldiver and the TBF/TBM Avenger. Navy records show that within the total of the 100 combat-aircraft capacity of the *Essex, Saratoga,* and *Enterprise*-class carriers, the numbers of Hellcats increased from 36 in mid 1943 to 54 in mid 1944 and to 73 in November 1944.

Navy pilots repeatedly suggested that their 12,275 Hellcats came from the Ironworks because of its ability to take so much combat punishment. It performed to the end of the war in all of the four fighter roles, including night-fighter, and was considered a "grandfather's aircraft" for its gentle handling characteristics.

## World War II Fighter Kill Records in the Pacific Theater

| | Enemy Kills | Aces | U.S. Kill to Loss Ratio |
|---|---|---|---|
| **U.S. Navy/Marines** | | | |
| F6F-3/5 Hellcat | 5,156 | 306 | 19 to 1 |
| F4U-1 Corsair | 2,140 | 93 | 11 to 1 |
| F4F-4 Wildcat | 1,006 | 62 | 9 to 1 |
| | | | |
| **U.S. Army Air Corps** | | | |
| P-38 Lightning | 1,700 | 90 | Not Available |
| P-39 Airacobra | 243 | 1 | Not Available |
| P-40 Warhawk | 706 | 27 | Not Available |
| P-47 Thunderbolt | 697 | 32 | Not Available |
| P-51 Mustang | 296 | 5 | Not Available |
| P-61 Black Widow | 63 | 1 | Not Available |

Note: The above U.S. government figures tell the story very well.

## Conclusions

The Grumman Hellcat accounted for 62 percent of all enemy aircraft shot down by the Navy and Marine Corps and 43 percent of the total shot down by all U.S. fighters in the Pacific. This more than gives it the top score for the air-to-air fighter role in the Pacific Theater. Its fighter-bomber ground support, photo-recon, night-fighter, and bomber support role capabilities qualify it as the "Best Fighter" in the Pacific Theater of Operations.

Chapter 18

# Lessons Not Taught at Test Pilot School

## 1942 to 1947

The average person's impression of a test pilot: Possessed of the highest education baccalaureates, speaking computerese with the fluency of a native IBM-er, thousands of hours of accident-free military flight time, military and wartime experience, a graduate diploma from one of the prestigious Test Pilot Schools, and, of course, young, handsome, and dashing.

This may be true today but was not so in November 1942. On-the-job training was the only way to understand test piloting. It came while a test pilot was listening to his managers, engineers, and mechanics, but that was not where all the classrooms were. The following lessons were learned without such erudite people as mentioned above. These tales come from all the many other less scholarly "classrooms" I attended. It amazes me where all of my many shards of wisdom came from.

To let you know that my "Test Pilot School by on-the-job training" was not all champagne and roses, time has now permitted my ego to release some true stories and brag a bit about them. I only have one remaining story that I still haven't aged sufficiently enough or had enough to drink before being able to confess.

*The Grumman Widgeon in which Corwin H. Meyer learned a prime lesson flying as a co-pilot. A co-pilot should always ask detailed questions of the pilot's flying experience before starting the engines, even if he is a quiet FAA (Federal Aeronautics Administration) test pilot who tries to act like he is Lindbergh. (Northrop Grumman History Center)*

168
CHAPTER EIGHTEEN

## My Almost Fatal Case of FAA "Inspectoritis"

All neophyte aviators believe that FAA inspectors are the "Wizards of Oz" when it comes to their absolute knowledge of flight and their ability to recite the thousands of FAA Penal Laws and Regulations. They would imply to the bystander that they were better test pilots than Wilbur, Orville, Glenn Curtiss, and Chuck Yeager all put together. Many times in the 1940s I had to face these inscrutable despots of the air to obtain the proliferation of certificates necessary for my six ratings. I began trembling with inspectoritis hours before I faced them and didn't stop until I had the signed certificate in one hand and a strong drink in the other. However, I had yet to meet the real ogre of the FAA.

In 1945 Grumman wanted to obtain a small increase in gross weight for the certificate of the G-44 Widgeon amphibian. I had performed all of the flight-tests and soon the inevitable day arrived when a very taciturn FAA Inspector came to check our calculations and flight characteristics for this relatively simple addition to our certificate. After the Grumman design paperwork preliminaries were completed I suggested that he fly from the left seat, presuming that he had all the proper ratings, abilities, and experience for the necessary flight-tests he might perform. Wrong!

After he was seated I positioned the single-wheel, throw-over control to his side of the cockpit and we took off. I didn't realize that action almost tossed my accidental-death insurance policy out of the window.

After takeoff he asked where he could check the water-landing characteristics. These maneuvers were not necessary for the certification, but out of politeness I suggested that the Great South Bay, which

was about 10 miles south of our airport, would be satisfactory. With no discussion as to his intentions he soon started a landing approach, holding a steep nose-down attitude at 90 mph while descending toward the water.

I should have asked him about his intentions because the normal approach speed should have been 70 mph in a slightly nose-up flight attitude, but believing in his omnipotence I reverently remained silent. As our descent passed through 20 feet above the water without his starting a flare-out, I realized in panic that he would submerge us if we continued. Having no control wheel on my side of the cockpit I grabbed the center positioned control column with my left hand and yanked it back just as the nose struck and dug deeply into the water. A colossal water loop occurred with the nose of the aircraft veering abruptly 30 degrees to the left, fully submerging the right wing pontoon. By that time the violent aft elevator control motion that I had applied in panic took effect and the aircraft flipped out of the water at a very nose-high, almost stalled, attitude. I shoved the control column ahead, jammed the throttles full forward to keep from stalling, and flipped the control wheel over to my side of the cockpit.

Barely able to control my emotions, voice, and blood pressure, I asked him just what the hell he was trying to demonstrate. He stated very calmly that he had been told that the Widgeon would water loop if it touched down on the water above 90 mph and he wanted to check it out. It didn't seem to faze him at all that he almost killed us and that I had to perform such a violent recovery from the lethal landing approach he had set up. Several service reports of the Widgeon in such water landings had resulted in the nose of the aircraft instantly breaking off at the cockpit and fatally injuring all persons aboard the aircraft.

Without any quibbling on his part I demonstrated all of the air maneuvers required to pass the test. After we landed I called his boss, who Grumman had worked with for many years, to ask about that flight inspector's seaplane qualifications. His boss told me that he not only didn't have a seaplane rating but that he had never made a water landing before that date. I told him the story of his stupid aerial actions and asked that he never return to Grumman again. I was happy to find out later that he was relieved of his position and left the FAA.

The years of on-the-job training revealed two fundamental truths. The FAA is not as omniscient as all aviators are forced to believe. But even more importantly, I would never again be politically reticent from inquiring in great detail about the certification, talents, and proficiency of anyone who flew an aircraft in which I was a "passenger," ANYONE!

## The Art of Trying to Get Fired

The first of my tales of woe will prove that I am the only Grumman test pilot in the company's history to receive two weeks off without pay for bringing new and unappreciated flight-test techniques into their midst.

One of my unintended vacations was self-inflicted when I was enjoying an air show too much. I was putting the first one on for Navy brass in the experimental XF7F-1 Tigercat with 23-year-old exuberation. I was nearly eliminated by the steeple of a very venerable building in my flight path while approaching the runway at 450 mph. In my abrupt pull-up and subsequent nose-down recovery to get over the steeple I firmly convinced all the spectators that I was about to complete the show by crashing into the center of the runway where the audience was positioned. I received a radio call demanding

my immediate presence to my boss Mr. Gillies' office after landing to receive his very colorful and loud "respects." My comeuppance of a week off without pay ended the discourse. Because I was the only pilot checked out in the experimental Tigercat I was called in to fly the following day. The "without pay" clause was fulfilled in spite of their urgent need.

## My Second Week Off Without Pay

This was another self-perpetrated act where I decided to demonstrate the combat aerobatic capabilities of a special Hellcat that had an inverted-flight oil system to an unsuspecting naval aviator flying an open-cockpit N3N biplane trainer below 3,000 feet and without any pre-arrangement. This show was as illegal as murder in the eyes of the CAA. I made gunnery runs on this little N3N, flew upside-down formation with him, and other maneuvers that must have scared the hell out of him. He saw me land at Grumman so he followed me in. I taxied to Plant 5 and forgot the subject. He landed and taxied to Flight Operations in Plant 4. He went in and asked just who that test pilot was who scared him out of his wits. All the production pilots laughed at him so he decided to fly back to Navy Roosevelt Field and complain to his Navy boss. His boss called Grumman and demanded retribution; my hide, my license revocation, and my immediate transplant into the walking wartime army – all of which were possibilities if it was taken to the CAA. One of Grumman's executives, a well-known and famous former naval aviator, Commander David Rittenhouse, who knew the naval officer's boss, inveigled my pardon. It was accompanied by a second "stripe" to be added to my previous lashes in lieu of the Navy boss's much more strongly-motivated multiple destinies for only a second week

*This pilot probably doesn't understand the additional expertise that he can learn from taxiing on new sod that has been rained on. Sixty years ago it provided me with some talents that I have fortunately never had to use again. (Northrop Grumman History Center)*

off without pay. I was one very penitent pilot, however, to be so simply "pardoned." Commander Rittenhouse was my best friend for life.

## The First Meyer Park

About two weeks into my Grumman career I was flying a production test flight in an Avenger on a very soggy, rainy day. I had completed the test, landed, and was rolling to a stop when the tower called me and said, "Clear the runway immediately." Two of the runway exits were now behind me and the third one was about 200 yards ahead of me so I immediately exited the runway on the sod. Where I was trained, "clear the runway," meant right now. The wheels sunk down and I needed a lot of power to get to the next cement area 100 feet ahead in front of the tower. After taxiing to a parking place I went into Flight Operations to present my data. I was beset upon immediately by Bud Gillies and told in no uncertain terms that I was never to do that again. I was always to taxi to the next exit to leave the runway.

I didn't know at the time that it was very fresh sod and was Bud's pride and joy

at his just-completed Flight Operations plant. He then told me, in front of other production test pilots, that I should put some big winter flight boots on and stamp down the 100-foot length of my three deep ruts to level the sod again.

I spent the next three hours in the drizzling rain doing just that until they were as even as my 220-lb weight could perform in simulating a steamroller. My episode was visible all too long, and I was reminded of his words every time I flew with the production test pilot group who aptly named it "Meyer Park."

## An All-Too-Short Friendship With a Fabulous Mentor

When I came to Grumman I was a pretty raw young man of 22 with only 423 hours of flight time. For their first 30 days, each new Grumman test pilot had to wear a red baseball cap so the other pilots would know he was a neophyte and steer well clear of him for their own safety. None of the 41 production pilots would let me within a country mile of them to learn formation flying. But Bobby McReynolds took it upon himself to spend the time to teach me that touchy and necessary skill. We became so adept at it that we put on many official and unofficial air shows together. Bobby was such a great production test pilot that he had been selected to do experimental testing now and then, so I looked up to him as a very important teacher. He was 11 years older than I and I had great respect for him. He was very easy to get along with and his constant happy-go-lucky manner made flying with him a pleasure. He liked to fly steep S-turn landing approaches after his air show performance to delight his fellow Grummanites on the ground. I followed him on several occasions when he flew so close to the stall speed that I had to break away and go around to make another approach. Formation flying during these steep turning patterns was more than I was able to handle.

On a sad October day in 1943 I was flying about 200 yards behind him during his landing approach after we had put on a war-bond air show over Westbury, New York. Bobby was S-turning the first experimental night-fighter Hellcat with a large radome on its right wing during its first flight. Less than 100 yards prior to his touchdown, his Hellcat stalled and spun to the ground from an altitude of less than 100 feet. He skillfully directed it between two houses that were less than 50 feet apart, thus preventing any other deaths or injuries but his own. We found out later that the radome on his wing gave this Hellcat quite different stall characteristics from the standard Hellcat. I never again made another S-turn landing approach in any aircraft. After flying with him for 11 months I found that I had lost a friend who had taught me a lasting set of rules for

*In a heavily loaded Panther I relearned that runways should always be used even though an apparently hard-packed 30-foot short cut between runways looked good to me. After this event I could have easily performed making love standing up in a canoe in a thunderstorm. (Northrop Grumman History Center)*

proper test flying procedures. I can still see his broad grin when he would say to me, "Son, let's go up and noodle around." That meant, "Let's go up and do some aerobatics in formation." Bobby was a wonderful mentor to a young fellow who really needed to be taken in hand by a great aviator. I am still alive 62 years later thanks in great part to his wonderful mentoring.

## A Second Park Named Meyer

There is also another Meyer Park at the Grumman Bethpage airport. Just before the Korean War began I rushed to get airborne with a very heavy load of external stores in a high-priority Grumman Panther jet demonstration test flight. Because of my haste I opted not to taxi to the paved runway exit on my left and U-turn to taxi to the end of the runway but to taxi directly across 20 feet of sod to the runway to save time. I attained 18 feet in the crossing without making a dent in the hard ground when the main wheels sunk in up to their axles. At my ignorant insistence, and over the plane captain's violent objections to towing the aircraft out of that miserable condition, the nose wheel down-lock broke when the towbar's built-in break joint failed to live up to its supposed test results. It was supposed to break first when towed under such conditions. As I was now stuck with my aircraft half on the main runway, this fiasco required that the 15 Grumman aircraft production test flights now had to land at Republic Airport, four miles distant from the Grumman runway.

The new emergency crane arrived on the scene but we found it had never been ballasted or tested properly and it almost fell over on my aircraft in its first attempt to lift the nose of the Panther off the runway. It required 20 or so of the management on-lookers to stand on the back of the crane to replace the missing ballast.

This display was performed right in front of Plant 5 with all the rest of "Management Row" looking down upon my self-promoted disaster and me. Somehow, I always performed stage front with standing room only.

Two hours later the aircraft that had landed at Republic were called back to Grumman. I also learned that the Panther towbar had never been tested for this task. Thus my bio should show that I am the only Grumman test pilot who tested nose towbars beyond their calculated structural limits. That area was also given the name of "Meyer Park" by all too many test pilots, mechanics, and management.

## I Get a Military Pilot Education

In the summer of 1943 Bud Gillies put out a memo asking if any of our 41 Grumman test pilots wanted to get Navy Operational Training. I was the only one who said yes. I guess it was the greater age and marital status of the other pilots that caused them to view this challenge with more reluctance than I did. Bud flew me to NAS Atlantic City and introduced me to Commander "Swede" Vejtasa, a very famous World War II ace (amazingly enough in a Douglas Dauntless divebomber). Swede agreed with the idea. It was a done deal. Since I was in the middle of the Hellcat structural demonstration, Swede agreed that I could come down any day it was convenient with my schedule and he would fit me into his squadron with no problem. On that basis I went through complete operational training including FCLP (Field Carrier Landing Practice). It was the best government furnished on-the-job training in the world.

During the first dive-bombing phase of the training I was most pleased that all of my 10 scores were in the bull's eye. I was patting myself on the back until Swede told me that the Navy would fur-

*I thought that the Grumman test pilots had taught me well in polite, parade formation flying. Commander "Swede" Vejtasa taught me how to fight for your life in head-swiveling, high-G-turning combat formations. (Northrop Grumman History Center)*

nish 10 burials at sea for me, one for each of my 10 dives. He then explained to me for the second time (I was in seventh heaven the first time he warned me so I guess I didn't listen) that pullouts must be made above 3,500 feet or enemy ground gunfire would most surely shoot me down. On my next flight I scored well below my previous backslapping score when pulling out above 3,500 feet.

I did notice on my lower altitude recoveries that the Hellcat had recorded over 8Gs on my accelerometer during some pullouts. I was getting target fixation and after dropping my bombs I finally realized my closeness to the ground and pulled out without looking at the accelerometer. I was intent on looking at the ground, which was all too close at the bottom of my pullout.

This was very surprising to me because in my Navy demonstration flights at Grumman I had encountered strong buffeting in 6G pullouts that I was making at the Navy-specified demonstration altitude of 10,000 feet. I had experienced several bent stabilizers during those pullouts, too. In my dives at Atlantic City there was no buffeting or bending of stabilizers. Needless to say, I was very interested in talking to the engineers at Grumman about this revelation. As a comparison, in the Wildcat I had pulled 8Gs at 10,000 feet with no buffeting or damage to the stabilizers. I had heard some vague engineering conversations about the possibility that the much heavier wing loading of the Hellcat might be getting us into the unknown "compressibility." This word was used for a new phenomenon that was really Mach number or transonic effects, or terms yet to be coined. We made pullups at 20,000 feet in the Hellcat and found the maximum Gs that could be attained when buffeting began were much less than at 10,000 feet so we named the effect, "the buffet boundary," an appellation that is still used today. Soon afterwards we found that all the other aircraft being manufactured with as heavy a wing loading as the Hellcat, with its higher dive speeds, were encountering this same problem. It is difficult to believe now, but each manufacturer had so many problems to solve and so few people to do just that, that little or no information was being exchanged between aircraft companies during the war years.

My 19th on-the-job training flight with Swede Vejtasa's training squadron was edifying to my specific test pilot education in the many roles of navy combat training and also in understanding the buffet boundary.

Swede was kind enough to write me a three-page letter of commendation using all the flatering words: "exceedingly rapid progress... excellent, experienced pilot... genuine desire to learn Navy methods, etc." He was also kind enough not to include notification for my 10 government-furnished funerals in his letter. His kindness started me on a long mission to complete Navy Operational Training by actual carrier qualification.

## I Attended Navy Test Pilot School With a Zero

Several years later my illegitimacy as a "real" Navy test pilot was recognized and certified by Captain "Tex" Birdwell as Director, U.S. Naval Test Pilot School, when he sent me a framed parchment complete with the Test Pilot School Crest of Arms. It has hung on my wall with great pride for many years. It reads as follows:

KNOW YE ALL TEST PILOTS AND OTHER FORMS OF LOWER LIFE, THAT: MR. CORWIN H. MEYER, HAVING SUFFERED THROUGH THE EARLY DAYS OF TESTING NAVY AIRPLANES IN 1943, 1944, AND 1945, AT AND AROUND THE FLIGHT TEST DIVISION, NAVAL AIR TEST CENTER, PATUXENT RIVER, MARYLAND, AND HAVING RECEIVED INSTRUCTION FROM AN ESTEEMED GROUP OF PRE-TEST PILOT SCHOOL FLIGHT TEST EXPERTS FOR LACK OF ANY OTHER SOURCE OF FORMAL EDUCATION IN THIS AREA, IS HEREBY DECLARED A MEMBER U.S. NAVAL TEST PILOT SCHOOL, CLASS "ZERO."

CAPTAIN "TEX" BIRDWELL JR., CAPTAIN, U.S. NAVY, DIRECTOR U.S. NAVAL TEST PILOT SCHOOL.

## Conclusions

In November 1942 on-the-job training was a great way for me to learn, especially when the Deans of my school were Bud Gillies, Bob Hall, Captain Trapnell, Carl Alber, the entire team from Mr. Grumman to the fellow who made my "Box Seat" in the experimental hangar, Bobby McReynolds, Commander "Swede" Vejtasa, and the esteemed group of Class Zero of the Navy Test Pilots School.

# Chapter 19

# Blowing a Panther's Nose

## 10 January 1951

Aviation historians have long speculated why Grumman was the last major U.S. fighter manufacturer to get into jet fighter production. The long-term Grumman policy of cautious prudence in approaching all new challenges was the only answer. Having been the project test pilot for the F6F Hellcat, F7F Tigercat, and F8F Bearcat, I was privy to the decisions that affected the design of every new fighter. While Grumman's conservative approach caused it to be the last of three competitors in the jet fighter field of development, the fact remains that when

they finally started production with the F9F-2 Panther jet fighter they supplied 87 percent of all the jet fighters and fighter-bombers that the Navy deployed in the Korean War.

As you have heard before, Grumman's policy in selecting power plants for every new model was to use the very latest squadron-reliable engine currently in production, never to install a new engine in a new aircraft.

This sound policy produced a remarkable result. In testing over 100 experimental types and 30,000 production

*The first takeoff of the experimental Panther on 21 November 1947 from Grumman's runway. The aircraft was off much sooner than I expected in less than 2,000 feet from the start of the roll. The Navy ordered the Panther to land on the 8,000-foot runway at Idlewild (Now John F. Kennedy airport). They thought the Grumman 5,000-foot runway was much too short. On my first landing I rolled less than 3,000 feet. It flew like a trainer. (Northrop Grumman History Center via Corwin H. Meyer)*

aircraft, from startup in 1930 until 1980, Grumman lost only four prototypes. No other military aircraft company came close to this record.

## Gestation Gymnastics for the Final Panther Design

Following the Joint Army/Navy Fighter Conference at Patuxent in October 1944, Grumman engineers began to search for the ideal jet engine to power the company's new fighter. They wanted only the best engine in the free world for the plane that would be named Panther.

Several of us Grumman test pilots had flown and evaluated America's first jet-powered fighter, the Bell YP-59A. Along with our unenthusiastic reports, John Karanik, head of the Grumman propulsion department, had studied several jet engines still under development. These included the Westinghouse J-19 and the upcoming J-34 engine, General Electric's I-40 centrifugal flow and J35-GE-7 axial flow engines, and Allison's J-33. They all came up wanting by Grumman's standards for the degree of reliability necessary for a single-engine carrier-based fighter.

Karanik then went to England to investigate the Rolls-Royce Halford, Derwent, and Nene engines. The Nene was the most powerful. He also was convinced that Rolls-Royce had the best record of trouble-free ground and flight-testing for the Nene engine of all the companies that he had reviewed.

Congress had previously dictated that no foreign engines could be imported into the United States for production aircraft. Therefore the Navy induced Pratt & Whitney to obtain a license to build production Nenes in the United States. Our experimental Panthers were equipped with these excellent British-made Nenes, which gave only very minor problems

during hundreds of flight-test hours. Turbine blade shedding was the bane of all jet engines of that era. None of the English-built Nenes, Pratt-built Nenes, or later-built Tays ever had a single blade failure in testing or in hundreds of thousands of hours of operational flight in over 3,300 Panther and Cougar aircraft.

Although Grumman's philosophy often kept it from being in the forefront of experimental naval jet aviation, it did provide the Navy with the vast majority of squadrons of needed front-line jet fighters for almost 20 years.

## The XF9F-2 Panther Evolves

Grumman had a team begin working on a single-engine aircraft powered by the Rolls-Royce Nene. They convinced the Navy to revise the existing large, four-engine XF9F-1 night-fighter contract to accommodate the new XF9F-2 aircraft instead of cancelling the XF9F-1 contract outright. The XF9F-1 contract was amended into the XF9F-2 contract on 9 October 1946 for three single-engine prototypes; two with English-built Nene engines, a structural ground test article, and design data for a swept-wing version. The engines to be used in these experimental aircraft were to be the British-built Nene engines with the American Allison J-33s as production backups in case Pratt & Whitney delayed the American J-42 production Nene.

## A Panther Finally Flies

The Navy inspected the two prototype mock-ups in January 1946. Only minor changes were required. The first flight of the Nene-powered aircraft was conducted by the author and occurred on 21 November 1947. It was made under the foulest weather conditions of any first flight in my flying experience.

*The nose cone being closed on the experimental Panther prior to its first flight. This is the stuffy compartment that housed the four 20-mm cannons. It could be opened about two feet further for easy maintenance of the guns and electronics equipment housed there. My explosion showed that they didn't get along very well with each other. (Northrop Grumman History Center via Corwin H. Meyer)*

Because Grumman had declined the Navy's request to ship the Panther prototypes to the long runways of the Naval Air Test Center at Patuxent River, Maryland, for the first flight, the Navy then insisted that we make the first landing at the yet unfinished Idlewild (now JFK) Airport's 8,000-foot runways 40 miles away. This was an order I did not relish because I would have to fly half that distance over the densely populated Long Island suburbs of New York City in our first brand-new jet fighter. I was pleased, however, that the reliable Rolls-Royce Nene powered the Panther.

As always happens in prototype flight-test schedules, it was much later in the day than we had planned when I took off from Grumman's Bethpage 5,000-foot runway. Increasing clouds all day had finally lowered the ceiling to 9,000 feet. Immediately after I had gained altitude I performed stalls to see if I could get the Panther back down safely. It performed like a J-3 Cub. It had very gentle stalls with no wing dropping. These stalls demonstrated that I could easily land on the Grumman Bethpage 5,000-foot runway. I radioed the Grumman tower to request permission to land back at Grumman. I was told in no uncertain terms that Flight One (Mr. Grumman) had

replied that I was to proceed to Idlewild. With my new management-assisted good judgment, combined with dark clouds in the direction of Idlewild, I directed the aircraft there immediately and landed uneventfully under a ceiling of 3,000 feet. My Bearcat chase aircraft decided to orbit Idlewild to better observe the deteriorating weather conditions.

I found out after landing that Grumman's only external-power jet starter truck was limited to 35 mph by an engine governor and would arrive one hour later at Idlewild. By the time the truck arrived a light rain had started but the chase Bearcat now reported a 1,500-foot ceiling over Idlewild and a 5,000-foot ceiling at the Grumman Bethpage airport.

## A Rather Wild Second Flight

I took off with a heading that I thought would take me directly back to Grumman. At my first observation outside the cockpit after takeoff I saw that I was in heavy rain now and rapidly speeding along at 1,000 feet over the Atlantic Ocean. I immediately began a 5G, 90-degree left turn in a steep bank with the rain coming down more heavily now. The next thing I saw was Mitchell Field about 10 miles west of Grumman, so I rapidly

*The flight-test team patiently waiting at Idlewild for the starter truck. It is interesting to note the bucolic farm scene in 1947. It was not to be that way for long. Although our landing was the first landing of any airplane on that airport, I don't think there is any plaque so honoring that auspicious event. The rains, however, were just about ready to ruin my parade anyway. (Northrop Grumman History Center via Corwin H. Meyer)*

turned again about 50 degrees to the right and immediately popped out of the rain to a fairly good ceiling and decent visibility. I could see the Grumman airport about five miles ahead. I felt much better now about my stupid decision to return to Bethpage in such miserable weather conditions. But I was soon to receive a second jolt.

For the first time since takeoff I looked at my airspeed indicator. It was indicating a shocking 450 mph—200 mph over the maximum speed limit I had been given for the Panther's first flight! I immediately chopped the power to idle and deployed the speed brakes for the first time. When I finally reached the Grumman airport I was shaking considerably but flying at a stately 200 mph. In a false but cool test-pilot voice I asked for landing clearance. The landing was anticlimactic. When I brought the aircraft to a stop I sat in the cockpit for about 10 minutes writing anything on my note pad I could think of until all the tremors had left my body.

I had just unintentionally demonstrated over 50 percent of the complete structural envelope of the XF9F-2 in a seven-minute second flight under partial instrument conditions. The Grumman Ironworks designers had again come to my rescue.

## First Flight Epilogue

A few weeks after my first flight in the Panther, my friend Woody Van Hoven, a World War II naval aviator and president of the United States Aviation Insurance Group (USAIG), the world's largest aviation underwriter, told me that his company had provided the insurance for my first flight. My head swelled a bit in appreciation of his deep concern for me during that episode. That was until he informed me that USAIG only insured the entire Idlewild Airport from any accident that might have been caused by my landing there.

## The Structural Demonstration

The next 100-plus flight-test hours went by uneventfully. I performed the full structural demonstration to 650 mph and 7.5Gs. The power plant and aerodynamic demonstrations afforded very little need for changes or fixes. The only major problems we had were directional snaking oscillations at high speeds, especially at reduced fuel weights. This would have given the Panther unacceptable gunnery aiming and tracking capabilities. We made several fairing changes around the tailpipe and under the fin with little effect. Because it didn't occur with full fuel tanks, someone decided that maybe fuel sloshing in our two large, cup-like tanks was causing the problem. We installed two levels of 6-inch, horizontal, shelf-like baffles around the insides of the tanks. This cured the problem, but only temporarily. Upon opening the tanks for an inspection a few days later it was discovered that all the baffles and their fasteners were lying on the bottoms of the tanks. The fuel sloshing was more powerful than the designers had planned for. A stronger baffle system finally cured the problem.

## The Ejection Seat That Wasn't All There

In 1947 development of ejection seats was sporadic. Each jet aircraft manufacturer designed and tested its own seat from scratch. The Bell P-59 jet aircraft I flew in 1944 was not even designed for an ejection seat. I have few memories of my checkout during the two evaluation flights I received at Wright Field on 24 July 1947 in the Lockheed P-80A jet fighter. I vaguely recalled that the plane captain pulled several pins, with long red streamers attached, from the seat before I taxied out to fly and told me, "The seat is now hot."

After the first two flights in the Panther I casually asked my plane captain Rudy Wincher why HE didn't have any be-ribboned pins to pull to make the ejection seat hot. He calmly answered that the seat had no propellant system installed and was, therefore, inoperably "cold." I then consulted the ejection seat engineers. They told me that they hadn't made sufficient test firings of the seat to be sure that it would function properly. Thus they reasoned that if I used the seat it might injure my back if the propellants were installed and actuated. When I suggested that I would rather have a bad back than no head they agreed and promptly installed the propellants. They also speeded up the seat test completion.

Although the Grumman-designed ejection seat tests were then given top priority, the three experimental Panther aircraft never had seats that were approved to be used under 5,000 feet. They lacked many of the now-developed automatic features. Without them it required way too much time to get the pilot separated from the seat for complete

The Panther with the speed brake extended. Without this device formation flight, rapid descents, and deceleration for landing would have been very tedious and difficult. This speed brake did the same speed control job as a propeller did for previous fighters. (Northrop Grumman History Center via Corwin H. Meyer)

main parachute deployment. It wasn't until many years later when the famous English-designed Martin-Baker zero altitude, zero airspeed seat was perfected that ejection seats came into their own and greatly reduced pilot losses in combat and test operations. A lot of well-known civilian and military test pilots were lost before Martin-Baker seats were installed in many U.S. aircraft.

## The Panther Waited Until After the Air Show

On the eighth flight I was authorized to perform an air show for a large number of news media personnel. The custom of Grumman, contrary to that of most aircraft manufacturers, was not to demonstrate a new plane until top management was satisfied that the aircraft was performing well enough to trust it to a public demonstration. Most companies had their big public relations splash during a non-flying aircraft completion rollout, weeks before a first flight. Grumman management almost did not wait long enough this time.

The Panther air show was normal and completely uneventful until after I landed and got out of the cockpit. With all the media standing about I saw fuel gushing from the belly of the aircraft.

The Panther was immediately dragged out of sight of the media and inspected. The results were frightening. The large-diameter main fuel line had come off the nipple of the engine inlet because its clamp had not been secured more than finger tight. The good Lord had been looking over my first flights very carefully by not letting that hose uncouple until my ninth landing rollout! A re-inspection of the entire aircraft was put into instant motion. Several other discrepancies were found that were also missed before the first flight.

## Captain Trapnell, the Navy's Premier Test Pilot, Arrives

I delight in telling you of an earth-shaking event I had with the Navy's premier test pilot, Captain Fred M. Trapnell, in a Tigercat discussion.

Captain Trapnell was the only test pilot in the Navy whose word was law, both in Navy and industry flight-test circles. As an example, he came up for a three-hour evaluation of the first XF6F-3 Hellcat right after its first flight and gave the official Navy go-ahead for mass production that day. It finally passed its contractual demonstrations two-and-a-half years later, after more than 8,000 Grumman aircraft had been delivered to fighting squadrons. Trapnell understood what an easily flyable fighter could do for its pilot. The Hellcat went on to set a record 19-to-1 kill-to-loss ratio.

My first meeting with Captain Trapnell was when he came to Grumman in a Tigercat to perform the preliminary evaluation of the Grumman Panther in early 1948. I was the only Grumman test pilot who had flown the Panther before he did. At every opportunity during his three-day evaluation I tried as hard as I could to find out his conclusions. He said nothing except to give a few grunts every time I tried to pry opinions from him.

Finally, at the end of his evaluation, we were walking out to his F7F-4N Tigercat for his return trip to the Naval Test Center. I proudly told him that I was the project pilot of the Tigercat from 1943 to 1947. He immediately burst into a diatribe of the many deficiencies of the Tigercat naming over-cooling of the engines, under-cooling of the oil system, lack of roll stability, excessive high dihedral rolling effect with rudder input, the high minimum single engine control speed, etc., etc. He ended his oration with my exile sentence; "If I had been the chief of the test center at that time I would have had you fired!" Every one of his comments was absolutely true. I was devastated and fervently wished I hadn't gotten out of bed that day.

Just as we reached his Tigercat I finally blurted out, "If you dislike the Tigercat so much why do you always fly it everywhere you go?" He continued: "The power in the two engines is great for any aerobatics, the forward visibility in the carrier approach is the best in any fighter ever built, the tricycle landing gear will make much faster pilot checkouts, the roll with the power-boost rudder is faster than the ailerons, it has the greatest range of any fighter in inventory, etc., etc." He was absolutely right again. As he climbed up the ladder to the cockpit he turned around, grinned from ear to ear, and stated, "It's the best damn fighter I've ever flown," closed the canopy, and disappeared over the horizon. I realized he had thrown the entire test pilot school book at me with his few words and that he and I were pretty close regarding characteristics that make up a really good fighter. I went home happy that night. His full report on the Panther had only one minor hydraulic system deficiency that I had failed to note.

The ailerons were assisted by a highly boosted (33-to-1) hydraulic power system. When this failed, the manual pitch forces required to fly carrier landings were high but I had thought they were acceptable. He did not. We then designed a mechanism in the system so that when the boost failed, the stick was then provided a double mechanical advantage. He approved it with a grinning comment, "I'm a little older than you are, Corky."

## Tip Tanks Are Added

The Navy also decided from Trapnell's evaluation that the range of the Panther was insufficient. We were asked to install 120-gallon fixed (not jettisonable), fuel-dumpable tip tanks. These tanks gave the Panther a mission time of just over two-and-one-half hours and permitted a radius action that the Navy needed so that flight deck crews had time to re-spot the deck between squadron launchings.

During our flight-tests we found that these tanks did not cause any measurable reduction of cruise, high speed, stall speeds, or flight characteristics. The engineering explanation was that the tanks acted as aerodynamic end plates to the wing, thus giving it a theoretically higher wingspan than it actually had. The

The third production F9F-2 dumping fuel from the tip tanks. These tanks had to be rapidly purged before combat because they could not be jettisoned. During one of my air shows, Butch Voris, the leader of the Blue Angels Navy air show team, saw this startling effect and used it with three aircraft dumping red, white, and blue water during their round of air shows. (Northrop Grumman History Center via Corwin H. Meyer)

Grumman designers had not predicted that blessing. The only tank installation drawback was that they reduced the aileron power of the aircraft when full of fuel, but not to an unacceptable degree. Tanks were usually empty after the initial climb to the Panther's 40,000-foot cruising altitude. This quickly removed the onus of the reduced rolling power.

## The Panther Behaves Better at Its Second Air Show

The grandest and largest airport of the three New York terminals, Idlewild opened to great fanfare on Sunday 1 August 1948. All the available dignitaries, including President Harry S. Truman, joined the millions of New York area residents in saluting the aerial might of some 900 aircraft of the United States Navy, Air Force, Army, and Marines. It was to continue for five days. I was asked by Navy coordinator Captain Roy Sempler to perform in the Navy's newest Panther fighter.

The 500,000 people on hand opening day were given the most massive air show ever to be seen, before or since. Within the three-hour afternoon offering, these air forces displayed hundreds of different World War II bombers, the massive new B-36 atomic-bomber, and hundreds of World War II propeller and jet fighters as well as transport aircraft. All of these war machines were tightly orbiting Idlewild in massive formations of 50 to 100 aircraft, all waiting to be called in for their low passes over the field. It was pandemonium flying in that unbelievable gaggle and a miracle that there were no mid-air collisions. Coordinating the various players of that massive air show was so time-consuming it seemed like slow motion.

The Navy was given only a half-hour for its review. It consisted of a smoke-bombing raid on the field by five squadrons of Hellcats and Corsairs, launching and retrieving Bearcats on a simulated carrier deck equipped with field operated catapult and arresting gear, a very short Jet Assisted Take Off (JATO) with its steep climb out staged by a Lockheed P2V Neptune, and a helicopter rescue by a Piasecki twin-rotor helicopter. I was the last act, making a low-altitude, single 625-mph pass in front of the President's reviewing stand. The new Panther jet was to be the crème de la crème of the Navy show.

With the help of high humidity from the nearby Atlantic Ocean surrounding Idlewild, a massive white visible shock wave occurred on the back half of the Panther during my very low pass over President Truman's grandstand and continued until I disappeared in a steep climb out.

I still have the next day's issue of the *New York Times*. The headlines on the front page blared out, "Truman Dedicates Idlewild Airport; Hails it as the 'Front Door' For the UN." Right under that was, "Navy Steals Show. Navy experimental jet in spectacular run. Eyes can scarcely follow it," and much more. I ate it up, humbly, of course.

The next day Grumman received a message from Washington stating that they would like to have Captain Trapnell, a naval officer, fly the remaining air shows (instead of a "civilian"). I was un-delighted. A few hours later Washington relented. Trapnell asserted that he didn't have the experience that I did in the Panther and that I should continue the remainder of the shows, which I did with great pleasure. What an ego trip for me.

## My First Unexpected Flameout

During the Panther's altitude performance program, Pratt & Whitney had asked us to check out engine operation while making manual switch-overs from the normal to the emergency engine fuel control. I started the tests at 5,000 feet and the switchovers were normal until I got to 25,000 feet. At this altitude, when I went from normal to emergency, the engine growled a bit and the tailpipe temperature rose somewhat, but not over the limit. At 30,000 feet the switchover showed the engine to have more aches and pains. The growl was very loud and the tailpipe temperatures almost went to the limit. I should have stopped but the Pratt and the Rolls-Royce engineers assured me that I would have no trouble with air-starting the engine. I later found out that they gave that edict with absolutely no experience in Nene air starts!

During the switchover at 33,000 feet the growl shook the aircraft, the tailpipe temperature went over the limit, and the engine flamed out. I was now riding in a silent but very heavy glider, descending with cabin pressurization disappearing rapidly. I went through the air-start procedure at the correct windmilling RPM and nothing happened. The Rolls-Royce representative had told me that air starts would probably be more attainable below 25,000 feet, so I waited. The engine didn't start at 25,000, 20,000, or 15,000 feet, so I now kept trying at each 1,000-foot interval, getting more apprehensive at each failure. I tried minor different engine windmilling speeds to no avail. I was over a previously measured 10,000-foot potato field about a mile north of the Grumman airport. I had decided before the flight that if an engine-off landing were required I would use that 10,000-foot open field instead of Grumman's 5,000-foot runway, which had houses located on both ends.

At 3,300 feet I gave up all starting efforts on this miserable engine and concentrated on a 360-degree flame-out landing pattern for a wheels-up landing in my selected field. Without any help from me, all of a sudden a great blast of energy shot out of the engine, the tailpipe temperature soared way over the limit, and the engine RPM started increasing rapidly to about 30 percent thrust. It stopped, fortunately, where I had unknowingly left the throttle position. After things, including myself, had settled down, the engine seemed to be running smoothly at sufficient power for my landing. Now with wheels and flaps down I made a much less eventful landing at the Grumman airport than I had planned a few seconds earlier while unhappily heading towards my favorite potato patch.

After I shut the engine down, mechanics looked up the tailpipe and found that the air-start igniters were burned to a crisp and twisted and warped so much that they could not be removed to be tested. They also told me that they had seen the flames shoot out of my tailpipe about 100 yards when the engine had overcome my vain efforts and kindly started of its own accord.

The Pratt representatives, however, gave me the usual look of "pilot error" during our debriefing after the flight. They could find no rational reason for my catastrophe. Their inspection report also stated that there was no possibility the igniters could have started the engine because they had been burned beyond any usefulness. Because of the excessive over-temperature during the air start the engine was removed and returned to Pratt & Whitney for complete tear down inspection.

## Pratt Eats Crow

Pratt then received one of our two XF9F-2 prototypes and began an air-start program near Hartford. I was told later that they considered Grumman test pilots incapable of running such a program properly. They soon pleased me for their rude assessment of my ignorance. On their

*Three types of aircraft used in the Korean conflict are seen on this carrier deck. A few propeller-driven Douglas AD-1 Skyraiders are in the foreground. In the middle are two squadrons of Panthers, and in the background are McDonnell Banshees with wings folded but without the range that tip tanks provided. (Northrop Grumman History Center via Corwin H. Meyer)*

first fuel control switchover test flight the engine flamed out at 33,000 feet, the same as mine had. Their much more professional chief test pilot worked frantically all the way down to the ground without re-light success and was forced to make a dead-stick landing on Brainerd Field's 4,500-foot runway. He blew both tires skidding off the end of that runway. The problem was then pontifically deemed by Pratt no longer to be pilot error but British material failure. A new air-start ignition design called "shower of sparks" was installed and it did a great job of air starting over 25,000 feet altitude by Pratt & Whitney's test pilot. It soon gained a great reputation for immediate starts for the rest of the Panther's operational life. Thankfully, I was never blessed with another attempt to air start a Panther, even with the "shower of sparks" ignition. In service the Navy found that this ignition system worked up to altitudes of 35,000 feet.

### The Panther's First (of Very Few) Test Accidents

Because the Navy had the carrier suitability demonstration requirements, our prototype XF9F-2 soon went to Patuxent for these trials. On his first arrested land-

ing the Navy project test pilot, Commander Butch Davenport, received the cut and snatched the wire easily with his arresting hook. The rear half of the fuselage immediately parted company with the aircraft at the engine removal disassembly juncture. It remained connected to the arresting wire by the hook. Thinking his hook had missed the single wire of the arresting gear, Commander Davenport immediately applied full throttle to go around the pattern and make another attempt. Fortunately, a fast-thinking ground crewman successfully radioed the problem to Butch, and Butch, trying to become airborne without the back half of his Panther, did not further compound the accident. The entire tail assembly joint was redesigned and the Panther program never had another such failure.

### The Panther Gets Added Capabilities For the Korean War

In January 1950 Grumman received very high-priority instructions from the Navy to install bomb and rocket racks on the Panther's wings. The inboard rack was stressed for 1,000-lb bombs or 150-gallon drop tanks. The other three outboard racks were stressed to carry 250-lb bombs

185

or 5-inch HVAR rockets. As project pilot I was assigned to this program with full motivation for its top priority rating. I was to re-demonstrate the Panther's aerodynamic and structural integrity flight envelope carrying these many external stores.

During a 400-mph buildup dive with two 1,000-lb bombs, I got a large, sudden change in yaw and a pitch-up. My chase pilot closed in and told me that the fins of both of the bombs were bent, rotated, and twisted completely out of shape. Their use was then restricted to 300 mph, which meant that the Panther would be in range of ground fire much longer than necessary. The bombs we used for demonstrations were similar to the blunt, stubby, ancient World War I bombs, which were designed to fly and launch at one-fifth the speeds that jets were now flying. These bombs were discovered to be from World War I surplus storage.

The Navy then sent us their newest high-speed bombs, which were aerodynamically slimmer, with very strong fins. These bombs could withstand the pressures of all the flight conditions the Panther could attain. We later learned of large numbers of World War II bombs in storage which would have to be used in

combat before the more streamlined bombs would be available in mass production. We always seem to be fighting the last generation's war in each subsequent conflict that we enter.

I have often speculated that these bombs, which were surely plummeting much faster than 400 mph after being launched from high altitudes in World War II, must have had the same or worse fin distortion as they picked up speed on their way down. This might have accounted for the Army Air Corps' change from precision bombing to carpet bombing after they had been in the European Theater of Operation for only a very short time. This is an interesting possibility because there was no way of testing bomb fins from such high altitudes in World War II.

## Blowing the Panther's Nose

Grumman did not have responsibility for gun-firing tests for the Panther program. The Navy performed these flights shortly after my structural, spin, and aerodynamic demonstrations at Patuxent.

During the first part of the action in Korea the Navy noted that some Panthers were showing a tendency to shed their sliding noses during high-altitude gun firing.

*A picture of a Panther that landed on the carrier without a nose cone. It was not a very streamlined shape. After blowing the last nose off of a Panther in the air I was glad that neither any Navy pilot nor I ever had to fly it in that miserable configuration again. (Northrop Grumman History Center via Corwin H. Meyer)*

This was caused by the gases emanating from the four 20-mm guns located in the nose compartment exploding for some unknown reason. Grumman top engineers (having no experience in Panther gun firing) stoutly denied any responsibility for these problems and any need to redesign this area for gun gas removal.

After a few more such in-service aerial nose departures the Navy mandated that Grumman would have to perform a gun-firing program. It would take place at 35,000 feet altitude, with a spark igniter system in the nose gun bay to prove that it was or was not a gun gas explosion problem.

Grumman flight-test requisitioned two production Panthers, installed government-furnished igniters, and conducted a 200-flight program with absolutely no gun gas explosions. In their unbiased minds they were now fully exonerated and had produced a 2-inch-thick final report proving that this was absolutely NOT Grumman's responsibility.

## Meyer Emerges to Further "Assist" the Grumman Engineers

They were about to forward the report to Washington when I asked if I could add a flight to the program because I had never fired four 20-mm guns. Permission was granted. Another Grumman test pilot and I proceeded 40 miles south of Long Island over the Atlantic to the gunnery range. I must note that it was a very cold day in January with a 100-plus-mph wind blowing from the north (out to sea) at our firing altitude.

The other pilot fired first. His deceleration from 300 mph to 230 mph was quite impressive when he fired his full 20-second load. I then fired my full load, and after the clattering had stopped I moved the igniter switch to the "on" position. A loud explosion instantly followed and the entire sliding nose section of the aircraft blew forward on its sliding tracks and disappeared over the top of cockpit. My aircraft had already decelerated to 230 mph from the firing, but now with a very blunt nose, then continued to slow down at such a high rate that I had to go to full throttle to keep the aircraft from stalling. I didn't relish the thought of ejecting into that cold, turbulent Atlantic Ocean with a 100-mph wind assisting me to Bermuda during my descent. Deceleration finally stopped at 135 mph (only 15 mph above the aircraft's stalling speed) but it required a continued high rate of descent while I was making a rapid 90-degree turn back toward the safety of the now very distant Long Island.

It seemed that my ground speed had come to a standstill. As I continued my forced descent I finally reached lower altitudes and found that my headwind was decreasing. Still needing to be at full power, however, my fuel gauges seemed to be going down faster than I was making headway toward the shoreline. It seemed to take an interminable length of time to make landfall. During that time everybody on the radio became quiet, well understanding of my situation. Just before landfall Carl Alber, who was flying the amphibian chase plane, said, "Corky, I'll take your boots." That broke the tension beautifully and conversation began for all of us. In this same manner he was a blessing many times with his commentary as a chase pilot. As my fuel was now down to the "frantic" level, I decided to make an emergency landing at Republic's airfield. It was about five miles nearer to my position than the Grumman airport. My engine flamed out during my landing rollout. I slowly cooled off to 98.6 degrees in the cockpit while I was being towed off the runway.

The Grumman test team brought a complete, new sliding nose section to

*A picture of an F9F-8 Cougar to illustrate the two of the four exit ducts installed in the nose compartment to correct the gun gas problem. They are just under the forward portion of the fuselage insignia. The other two are on the other side of the nose. A mean-looking set of armament. (Northrop Grumman History Center via Corwin H. Meyer)*

Republic, installed it, and I flew the Panther back to Grumman on Republic's gift of full fuel tanks. Immediately after I landed the gun installation engineers frantically asked for my comments. When I told them that I had turned the igniter switch "on" after my firing was completed they told me emphatically that that was the wrong way to do it. They insisted that I should have turned the switch "on" *before* firing. I postulated that my method demonstrated that their procedure only burned the gasses, and that my method exploded the gasses.

The Navy then demanded that Grumman install two gun gas vents on both sides of the nose skins, which Grumman engineering had previously refused to admit were necessary. Grumman also had to run another 200-flight-test program with the igniters turned "on" after firing to insure that the vent design was effective enough to remove all gun gasses. It did.

## The Gun Gas Problems Were Not Over By a Long Shot

When I asked the question to the inspector as to why the lock ring on the fuselage for the removable nose cone was not damaged when the nose was blown off, he answered that it was impossible to inspect the locking mechanism design. At my insistence several new, large inspection holes were placed near the lock mechanism. Inspection then determined that on all of the new production aircraft inspected, the nose lock ring could not be cinched up enough for it to enter the fuselage locking ring groove. A locking fix was immediately installed in Panther production. The Navy grounded its Panthers until all of the several hundred operational machines incorporated this change. My switch-timing mistake caused several Grumman management egos to be redesigned somewhat, too.

## The "Point-the-Guns-Anywhere" Emerson Turret

The third production Panther, F9F-3 (BuNo 122562), had the Emerson turret installed in its nose. This turret allowed the pilot to aim the four guns of the Panther in any forward direction he needed for firing. The guns could be rotated 360 degrees in combination with transverse movements back to 20 degrees behind the vertical. I believe this was an offshoot of a remote-controlled bomber turret.

Several of our pilots and I evaluated it. Although it was fun to fly in formation with another aircraft and fun to shoot it down, we couldn't determine just how any pilot could aim it with much accuracy. It also increased the Panther's empty weight by several hundred pounds. It was further evaluated at NATC Patuxent with the same conclusions and was never heard about again.

## The XF9F-5 Panther's First "Grumman Ironworks" Air Show

As the project pilot of the more powerful XF9F-5 Tay-engine Panther, I was asked to give a flight demonstration to a visiting group of admirals. On my first low pass down the Bethpage runway I was unintentionally 50 knots over the maximum airspeed that I had previously attained at altitude during the flight envelope expansion but was still under the preliminary engineering approved airspeed limits at sea level. I then pulled 5Gs for a vertical climb-out. The stick forces were normal at the beginning of my pull-out. Then they immediately reversed at about 3Gs, requiring a two-handed push force to keep from exceeding 8.5Gs. This was 1G over the structural design limit load of its new, much thinner, wing than the F9F-2 Panther's wing. Fortunately, I soon slowed down below 300 knots in my

vertical climb and the maneuvering stick force returned to normal. I was a very wide-eyed test pilot because the speed of my pull-up was 100 mph below what I had used in many air shows in the F9F-2 and -3 series Panthers. I cancelled the rest of the performance and landed immediately for a complete aircraft inspection.

When I asked the aerodynamic and structural engineers what had caused this frightening phenomenon, they speculated that it was due to the lower wing torsional strength of the thinner wing section as compared to the F9F-2. They also stated that fueled wingtip tanks under G forces aggravated the situation, but they were only guessing. They had just begun the F9F-5 wing structural tests and went back to the drawing board and did some masterful torsion redesign of the wing before completing the structural tests that provided the thinner wing F9F-5 Panther the same maneuvering structural flight envelope as the F9F-2 Panther.

Two years later, in 1952, the Air Force experienced a rash of complete wing failures on the Northrop F-89C Scorpion night-fighter equipped with tip tanks during low level, high-speed maneuvering flight because of severe torsional aeroelastic problems. After several crashes, one of which was into a gas storage tank in a Los Angeles residential area during an air show, all F-89Cs were grounded and returned to the factory for wing structural redesign. Grumman was fortunate to discover this problem before F9F-5 production deliveries began.

## Pratt & Whitney J-48 Engine Headaches

The more powerful Pratt & Whitney J-48 engines (English-built offshoots of the Nene) installed in the F9F-5 Panther experienced two very interesting growing pains after delivery to Grumman.

After I had flown our XF9F-5 aircraft for over 100 hours the Grumman instrumentation department routinely recalibrated the cockpit tailpipe temperature indicator. It showed that an incorrect bias had been installed in the test instrument prior to its first flight. This error had allowed the tailpipe temperature to reach a true 760 degrees Celsius while the cockpit instrument only indicated 700 degrees.

After reviewing the complete Grumman flight-test program on the J-48, the 150-hour ground test limit of 700 true degrees was promptly increased to 760 degrees by Pratt & Whitney without any further ground or flight-tests.

The second engine problem was a little more shocking to the Navy, to Grumman, and to me. I had just landed after attempting a full-power speed run to determine the max speed of the J-48-powered XF9F-5 Panther at sea level. I stopped the run and returned to Grumman long before accelerating to top speed because the air was extremely rough and shook the aircraft so much that it blurred the instrument panel and upset my stomach. During lunch my plane captain Rudy Winscher came in to inform me that my aircraft now had a hole in the bottom of the fuselage large enough to see a very damaged engine inside. When the engine was removed for further inspection it was found that the brazing joint had failed in the 90-degree fuel nozzle fitting within the bottom burner of the engine. The nozzle had then rotated 180 degrees downward in flight, blow-torching its way through the bottom of the burner and then the aircraft structure, thoroughly charring the main fuel line as it progressed. This engine was ahead of its time in demonstrating "vectored thrust."

The Pratt representatives declared this was an "isolated case" and another engine was installed in the XF9F-5 to continue the flight-test program. During the next several weeks F9F-5 squadrons reported five more similar events, which killed five Navy pilots in fiery crashes. The Navy then convinced Pratt & Whitney top management that these six "isolated events" were their immediate responsibility. All F9F-5s were grounded for engine inspections and replacement of its nine nozzles.

I have never spent much time wondering just what might have happened if the air had been smooth for my full power speed run at sea level. But, in looking back, I was very pleased to be able to have had lunch that day.

## A Simple Solution to a Major F9F-5 Carrier Suitability Problem

When the F9F-5 finally passed its carrier qualification tests with flying colors at Patuxent, we at Grumman thought that the Navy's glowing report would be the end of the Panther development program. It wasn't.

Shortly after the F9F-5 squadrons started carrier qualifications, Grumman received a very curt but clear naval message that stated, "The F9F-5 stall speed must be decreased by 12 mph or it will be removed from carrier operations." The future production potential was clear. The fact that the North American FJ-2 (navalized version of the USAF F-86E swept-wing Sabre jet) was now making its debut into Navy squadrons changed Grumman swept-wing design to top priority. The aerodynamics department was at a loss on how to decrease the F9F-5's stalling speed. Boss Bob Hall then directed me to have my Skunk Works personnel try a possible solution after I told him of one of my previous, but unused, aerial investigations.

During several of my flights in the F9F-5 Panther I had been concerned about a large area of possible turbulent airflow behind the discontinuous intersection of the leading-edge "droop snoot" and the engine air ducts when the flaps and the droop snoot were extended for landing. To satisfy my curiosity on one flight I had taped many 6-inch strings of yarn around the affected areas of the wing to visually demonstrate the airflow. I was amazed to see such a large area of turbulent flow extending to the trailing edge of the wing and also the instant reversion to smooth flow when the flaps and droop snoots were retracted. The Panther aerodynamicist had pooh-poohed my supposition that lift might be lost because of the turbulence. I had almost forgotten about that single, but informative, flight-test.

I then slid a piece of cardboard into the droop snoot slot at its inboard end, drew a fence outline for a template, and had the resulting stiff aluminum fence installed. I flight-tested it in our instrumented F9F-5 test aircraft. This was all accomplished within two hours after Bob Hall's authorization.

With the fence in place there was no airflow turbulence when the droop snoot was down and a 9-mph decrease in stall speed was achieved. We then sealed up several other places in the flap and wing-fold hinges where it appeared that airflow leakage might not be appropriate. We also made the large flap cutout door, for a very long special missile clearance, non-operative except when the missile was to be carried. These changes showed a further reduction of 4 mph in the stall speed. We now met the Navy requirement.

At NATC Patuxent Commander, (now Admiral) "Whitey" Feightner, flying a standard, non-fenced F9F-5 and I flew over 70 formation stalls from 15,000 feet to 5,000 feet. He soon agreed that we had indeed decreased the F9F-5's stall speed by the required 12 mph. (At the 1999 annual meeting of the Golden Eagles I had the pleasure of reminiscing with Whitey regarding this experience of 50 years past.)

All production and operational F9F-5s were provided with this simple fence package. It was considered such a good idea that all of the F9F-2s and -3s were also retrofitted with it. This small change alleviated many possible carrier accidents and gave the Panther a sizeable increase in external store-carrying capability.

During my flights in the F/A-18B Hornet in 1997 I noted a similar droop snoot configuration without a fence, which resulted in a lot of buffeting when the snoots and flaps were extended. I sent a very detailed letter, along with Panther fence pictures, to the Commander-Naval Aircraft Atlantic regarding our Panther fence success and received absolutely no response, not even a politically correct, "We will consider it" reply.

## Conclusions

In competing with the three other Navy jet fighter contractors, Grumman's prudence made them last to field a carrier-based jet fighter. Their patience, however, provided the Navy with a jet fighter that equalled 78 percent of all the carrier- and land-based jet fighter and fighter-bomber aircraft deployed by the Navy in the Korean War. Not bad for a late bloomer.

# Chapter 20

# Surviving a Spinning Cougar

## November 1951 to July 1955

## The Panther's Metamorphosis

Immediately after the end of World War II, Grumman and the Navy met to discuss the Navy Technical Team's information learned from their recent visit to captured German Aeronautical Research Laboratories. This information put firm emphasis on the much higher critical Mach number speeds possible with swept-wing over straight-wing fighters. They had also learned that many top German fighter designers had "migrated" to our new enemy, Russia. With this information now in the hands of the United States and Russia, the F9F-2 Panther straight-wing jet fighter contract had provisions in it for developing a swept-wing version. Grumman designers gave priority to the straight-wing version now under firm contract. Grumman was also under competitive pressure from McDonnell, whose twin-engine, straight-wing F2H-1 Banshee had been carrier-qualified since July 1946. The more powerful F2H-2 Banshee was almost ready to fly.

The unknown aspects of higher stall speeds inherent in swept-wing jet aircraft caused the Navy to have concerns about catapult and arresting gear capabilities of their many World War II Essex-class carriers still in operation. The Navy Bureau of Aeronautics decided that the proof of the pudding would be to fly a swept-wing experimental research aircraft equipped with leading-edge slats to see if handling characteristics and stall speeds could be made compatible with existing fleet carriers. The Navy put out a bid request to both Grumman and Bell Aircraft to obtain two flying prototypes in the shortest possible time. Bell judiciously proposed sweeping the wings of two P-63 Kingcobras—one with leading-edge slats and the other without. Grumman proposed a swept-wing version of the Wildcat requiring an all-new airframe design. Both of Grumman's proposals were far more expensive, thus Bell received the contract.

On 19 June 1946 I flew a Tigercat to the Bell plant in Niagara Falls, New York, to evaluate both prototypes. My flight in the L-39 with no slats was brief. This bird cavorted like a cat on catnip during the stalls, which required excessive altitude for recovery. The L-39 prototype with leading-edge slats was docile during stalls and accelerated stalls. Both maneuvers could be performed with little wing dropping and minimum altitude loss. These two prototypes made it clear that slatted swept-wings would provide carrier-suitable flight characteristics for swept-wing fighters. I soon found out that my L-39 flights were only Swept-Wing Course 101.

Efforts on Grumman's swept-wing Panther languished because of the higher Navy priority to produce straight-wing Panthers in large numbers for Korea. Therefore, the swept-wing Panther slowly evolved into a completely new aircraft with a variable-sweep wing for combat, the untested Westinghouse J-40 engine (without its afterburner as yet), and with very unorthodox roll and pitch controls. At that time Grumman engineering believed this design to be the only solution that would guarantee swept-wing carrier suitability. It later evolved into the XF10F-1 Jaguar.

The Navy Bureau of Aeronautics soon learned that Rolls-Royce had sold the Russians the Nene engine rights that Pratt & Whitney had purchased for the Panther. In 1950, when Naval Intelligence learned that the Nene was now flying in swept-wing MiG-15 fighters, the Grumman Panther and McDonnell F2H-1 Banshee straight-wing fighters just coming into Navy inventory became instantly obsolete. Needless to say, the revised swept-wing Panther design was now given top priority and the whole new XF10F-1 prototype was temporarily shelved. A priority study contract was awarded to

Grumman in December 1950, which re-energized the corporation to expedite the design of a swept-wing fighter utilizing as much of the Panther design as possible.

To make the Cougar (the name of the swept-wing Panther) a more straightforward and producible design, the Panther's fuselage, engine installation, wing center section, fin, rudder, and landing gear were retained. The wings had 35 degrees sweep and hydraulic-powered leading-edge slats installed, similar to the Bell L-39. The Cougar's wing area was increased 50 square feet to retain the same carrier approach speed as the Panther. The stabilizer was swept 35 degrees and made electrically trimable for supersonic flight. The prototype flew with hydraulic-powered spoiler flaperons inboard of the normal unboosted aerodynamic ailerons in case of hydraulic power failure. Panther tip tanks could not be installed on the Cougar because of the far aft location on the swept wingtips. The resulting reduction in fuel capacity was made up by increasing the length of the forward fuselage fuel tank by two feet and installing bladder tanks in the wing leading edges behind the slat mechanisms. The fuel capacity of the Cougar was 919 gallons, 84 gallons less than the

*After transitioning from their F9F-5 Panthers in 1953 the Blue Angels flew the F9F-6 Cougars until the summer of 1957 when they transitioned into the Grumman F11F-1 Tigers. The diamond formation shown here was one of many of their standard formation patterns for their fabulous air shows. (Northrop Grumman History Center via Corwin H. Meyer)*

Panther's. This provided the Cougar with a cruising range of 907 nautical miles at 500 mph.

A contract was finally signed 2 March 1951. Six-and-a-half months later, on 20 September, test pilot Fred Rowley flew the XF9F-6 Cougar on its maiden flight. The first Cougars were delivered to VF-32 in November 1951 just one year after the MiG-15 debuted in Korea. Cold War combat necessity was the speedy mother of Cougar invention.

## Cougar Growing Pains

As the Senior Engineering Test Pilot, I was asked to relinquish my Panther external stores program to another pilot and assist Fred Rowley shortly after the Cougar's first flight.

Checkout in the Cougar was very simple. The only change in the Panther cockpit was the flaperon/aileron pitch control system. This provided for an automatic changeover to the normal ailerons when the hydraulic power to the flaperons failed.

A temporary placard listing airspeed limitations was placed on the instrument panel indicating that the maximum allowable airspeed was 575 mph. This was just slightly lower than the Panther's limit dive speed at sea level. It was also going to be the Cougar's best climb speed. I ignorantly assumed that the Cougar had already been flown to its cockpit placard limits. Wrong!

As I was accelerating through 525 mph on my first flight I felt a hand-numbing buzz in the stick grip, which was quite visible even with my hand tight on the grip. I immediately closed the throttle, extended the speed brakes, and climbed for altitude. While decelerating rapidly through 500 mph the buzz instantly stopped. I landed immediately for a complete aircraft inspection. It showed no damage. I was then told

that no previous flight had exceeded 475 mph. On my next flight at 525 mph my chase pilot noted that the spring tab on the elevator, designed to reduce stick forces, was a 1-inch blur when the vibration was in progress. Upon landing, engineering soon realized that non-static balanced tabs, which had been used on all previous Grumman fighters, should have been 100 percent static balanced tabs when used on a 35-degree sweep control surface. The balanced tabs cured the problem by increasing the tab's flutter speed well above the Cougar's designed maximum limit speed of 650 mph. We were now enrolled in the "35-Degree Sweep University"

The next problem that we found was that the small wingtip ailerons floated at different angles during transonic dives without pilot input so much so that the aircraft was useless for gunnery tracking. We first tried installing small vortex generator vanes on the upper surface of the wing to smooth out the supersonic flow ahead of the ailerons, but they proved useless. It was then decided that the ailerons must be eliminated and the powered flaperons extended another six feet to the wingtips.

## A Seemingly Easy Test Flight

I was taxiing down the main runway again for an easy flight-test with the extended 12-foot spoiler flaperons. The shop had bonded a 12-foot sheet of half-inch aluminum to each of the original 6-foot flaperons, hopefully to double the rolling capability of the Cougar. I had attempted to fly this configuration the day before when I had a very eerie experience.

I had been sitting in the cockpit after finishing my pre-takeoff checklist and had a feeling that something was drastically wrong, but without a clue as to the problem. I was looking down into the left cockpit console to go over my checklist again when I noticed something offbeat outside the canopy in my far left peripheral vision. Swiveling my head 60 degrees to the left I could focus clearly on the left wing spoiler flaperon. I was shocked to note that it was 45 degrees up, which was full deflection with my stick still centered! I moved the stick right to bring it down flush with the top of the wing surface, but it remained full up. I then checked the right flaperon and it was also full up and not obeying stick motions either. Taxiing back to the line, I was pleased that I had found this discrepancy. Had I started the takeoff roll, the drag of the extended spoiler flaperons would have never permitted the aircraft to leave the ground. I was relieved not to have discovered the cause at 150 mph while tearing through the village of Bethpage at the end of the runway.

Inspection revealed that some basic ground tests had been omitted by engineering in the rush to get this change into the air. I was told that my full deflection stick motions to check freedom of the controls had pushed the flaperon linkage over dead-center and jammed them in the "up" position. With the flaperon system linkage problem now corrected, inspected, and tested by me to my satisfaction, I again taxied into the takeoff position and fervently thanked the Lord for coming to my assistance the previous day just in time.

With my checklist now completed, I took off uneventfully to make a full evaluation of this new flaperon extension. About 30 seconds after takeoff, my radio began a very high-pitched squealing and the cabin pressurization system cycled from minus 2,000 to plus 4,000 feet cabin altitude. With both of these irritations I thought my eardrums were going to come out of my head. At the same time the aircraft started vibrating so strongly that the instrument panel was a blur. My mind was completely overloaded by this screaming, pulsating, and vibrating monster in aircraft clothes. The shaking was similar to a complete Allison J-33A-16 engine failure I had experienced two weeks earlier when a large number of turbine blades departed the tailpipe, seriously unbalancing the engine.

Instinctively I slammed the throttle aft and pulled up to a vertical climb in case I needed to eject. I immediately turned the radio and the cabin pressure system off to rid myself of their part of the cockpit cacophony. A few very long seconds later the vibrations stopped and I found myself at 150 mph and 8,000 feet, so I leveled off to inspect the engine instruments to see if I was in another engineless glider once again. When I gingerly and hopefully pushed the throttle forward, the engine spooled up and the tailpipe temperature started climbing. After performing this simple motion once again I was convinced that my beautiful engine was still operable so I looked outside. I found that the entire left 12-foot flaperon aluminum plank addition had come unbound and departed the aircraft. Someone in Woodbury, New York, soon found a very large slab of aluminum in his or her front yard.

After waiting for my blood pressure to return to normal, I turned the now-quiet radio on for a few seconds to announce that I was returning for an emergency landing that was happily uneventful. This was the only time in my entire career that I had three unruly cockpit crises happen simultaneously. The radio and pressurization problems had simple equipment replacement solutions. The flaperon extension had fluttered and ripped off because the hinge at the outboard end of the aluminum flaperon had been made out of aluminum instead of steel. That event left the 12-foot aluminum slab totally at the mercy of a 300-mph tornado.

The third flight-test attempt with the flaperon extensions proved to be boringly uneventful. The extensions demonstrated a welcome increase in rate of roll over the former aileron set-up throughout the entire flight envelope. Elimination of the ailerons also eliminated transonic rolling tendencies that had previously made gunnery tracking unacceptable.

## Landing Configuration Stall Problems

The Cougar seemed to have satisfactory landing condition stall characteristics for the first few flights while other more pressing problems were being investigated and corrected. I decided it was time to look into landing configuration stalls and accelerated stalls, which could occur when lining up for a carrier landing and proceeding into the turbulent wake of the carrier island structure. These tests are always completed early in the company's flight-test program to be timely for the Navy's important carrier-suitable tests.

I was at 9,000 feet in the landing approach configuration at 20 mph above the carrier approach stall speed for my first check of this condition. I very carefully pulled the stick aft to force an accelerated stall that I estimated should occur at 1.5Gs. As the aircraft pitched up, all of my pull stick forces disappeared and reversed. Even after applying instant full forward stick the nose continued rising as stall progressed. With rudder still in neutral the aircraft yawed rapidly to the left and entered a spin. I immediately applied full right rudder and full forward stick (anti-spin positions). I was no longer the pilot. I was a rider in this beast and aghast at what had happened with only such a small aft-stick deflection. As it entered the second turn I could see the little village of Oyster Bay, New York, rotating rapidly directly below me. During the third turn the rotation showed signs of slowing down and after the fourth turn the nose slowly dropped to the vertical and the rotation stopped. I was greatly relieved but I immediately had another problem. I had to apply full power to pick up airspeed and recover to level flight. I was staring straight down into the main street of Oyster Bay only 1,000 feet below and much too low for me to eject. I then made as delicate a pullout as possible in order not to precipitate another accelerated stall. I was now between a rock and a hard place; not wanting to precipitate another accelerated stall nor collide with the homes of the good townsfolk directly below. My pullout bottomed at 300 feet over the city. I was totally washed out. During my recovery climb back to 2,000 feet I noted with great amazement that my landing gear was now retracted. I must have subconsciously retracted the landing gear, remembering that with extended tricycle-gear on the Panther and Tigercat, I had previously demonstrated much less directional stability in a spin. I do not remember taking that action. The beast was now totally unfit for any kind of accelerated flight. Something had to change radically for me to want to perform accelerated stalls again. I returned to Grumman and landed in a state of disbelief and shock from the Cougar's God-given recovery during its first landing condition accelerated stall.

In the following tests I now noted that the short yarn tufts taped to the wings to visualize airflow showed that there was considerable span-wise stalled airflow from the fuselage out to the wingtips, which promoted stalling of the entire wing. Because we were all neophytes in swept-wing stall aerodynamics I had suggested the fix for this problem should be the same as that used by the Russians. The MiG-15 had used large mid-span fences on the upper surface of the wing. The Cougar also had very sharp leading-edge contours just inboard of the slats that were supposedly designed to give proper stall airflow char-

An abortive attempt to cure stall pitch-up on the prototype Cougar. These fences, installed just outboard of the engine air duct entrances and vortex generators, at the 30 percent chord position at the wing outboard section, demonstrated no corrective airflow by the yarn tufts installed on the right wing outboard surface. Back to the old drawing board! (Northrop Grumman History Center via Corwin H. Meyer)

acteristics, a known solution for this condition in straight-wing aircraft. But I was over-ruled. At my now more-motivated insistence, fences were installed and the sharp contour was refaired into a normal rounded wing airfoil leading edge shape.

These two changes cured the landing condition accelerated stall/spin control reversal problem. The tufts now showed that at stall speeds the fences and the leading edge change in contour were stopping almost all of the low G span-wise airflow and restoring chord-wise airflow beyond the fences to the wingtips. It was a satisfactory fix for stalls but we really had yet to graduate from the kindergarten of swept-wing aerodynamics.

## The Buffet Boundary

All fighter aircraft of that era could only maneuver up to their designed 7.5G structural limit load at altitudes below 15,000 feet. This was because of transonic flow over the wings, which caused a strong, Mach-number-induced, intense buffeting during pullouts at higher altitudes. This strong buffeting occurred at lower and lower Gs during pullouts as the altitude increased and was called "the buffet boundary."

Pull-ups into the buffet boundary also showed an unacceptable reversal of stick forces and uncontrollable aircraft pitch-up. Wing tuft motions during these maneuvers clearly indicated that the inboard airflow was again jumping the fences and causing the problem. In the first buffet boundary pull-up attempt, the aircraft departed into another unexpected accidental spin similar to the previous one over Oyster Bay. This time the controls reacted better and recovery was fairly quick, with only a few thousand feet lost. This was still too much altitude for satisfactory recovery. Trust me, accidental spins starting at 40,000 feet are much easier on the nerves than those occurring at 9,000 feet.

Further increasing the height and length of the wing fences only partially improved the buffet boundary pitch-up problem. We also had to re-contour a 10-foot-long flat area of the upper wing surface adjacent to the fuselage into a 6-inch higher airfoil shape to finally cure the cause of the premature stalling. It now had acceptable high-altitude buffet boundary pullout characteristics without stick force reversals. With these changes wing tufts now demonstrated that almost all of the span-wise airflow jumping the fence was eliminated and became normal chord-wise airflow. Outer wing panel stall, which caused the pitch-up, was a thing of the past. The pilot could now release the stick at peak Gs and the aircraft would reduce its angle of attack immediately and return to 1G level flight. We had now graduated from high school transonic class, but college finals loomed ahead.

## The Cougar Finally Gets a Flying Tail

In engineering's usual conservatism, the Cougar had an electric trim adjustable horizontal stabilizer, and an unpowered elevator for simplicity and reliability. This was a similar configuration to the original North American F-86A Sabre. USAF test pilots soon determined that the F-86A must be equipped with the newer, dual hydraulic-powered system, the stick-controlled stabilizer dubbed "flying tail," for acceptable transonic and supersonic maneuvering combat flight. The trimable stabilizer was too slow to counteract the fast trim changes required for transonic gunnery and evasive maneuvers.

To follow up on the Navy evaluation request for better Cougar transonic control, I went to Edwards Air Force Base, California, to evaluate a North American F-86E Sabre (U 91849) on 23 April 1952. This was the first fighter to have the highly touted dual hydraulic-powered flying tail system. This user-friendly roll-control system instantly demonstrated that subsonic, transonic, and supersonic flight could become much more smoothly integrated. It also demonstrated much greater combat maneuvering capability in transonic and supersonic flight. Upon my return I heartily recommended it for the Cougar.

Grumman's conservatism again took over and engineering designed a single hydraulic system with the stick-controlled flying tail, which, when hydraulic failure

The F9F-6 Cougar with all of the final fixes that cured the trials and tribulations of uncontrolled spins and pitch-ups. The sharp leading edge from the duct to the fence is refaired. The wing fence is the final enlarged and lengthened configuration and the upper six feet of wing center section surface behind the upper duct lip refaired all fixes to prevent early stalling causing span-wise airflow that had stalled wingtips prematurely. (Northrop Grumman History Center via Corwin H. Meyer)

occurred, reverted to its original trimable stabilizer and elevator control. It had some complexities that took a short time to resolve but it was considered satisfactory by the Navy for the Cougar's long operational life ahead.

Previously, the F9F-6 Cougar could be dived vertically to 1.2 Mach number, but it was work counteracting a lot of transonic pitching during the attempt. When equipped with the flying tail it was most pleasant to reduce altitude by supersonic dives. But a pilot had to be very careful that a supersonic bang wasn't unleashed on unsuspecting villages below when the Mach meter hand easily jumped past Mach 1.

## A Major Problem With a Meyer Solution

With its swept-wing drag reduction, the Cougar was a much slicker aircraft to decelerate in the air with its single Panther speed brake. Its lower drag was immediately obvious to me when requiring speed

*F9F-6 (BuNo 130884) from Squadron VF-174 on the USS Midway in 1955 has had its hook freed from the arresting cable and it is taxiing over the flattened barrier. The barrier is erected for each carrier landing to stop the aircraft from going to the front of the carrier deck and crashing into parked aircraft in case of hook or arresting wire failure. This happened too many times on straight deck carriers and was not precluded until the angle deck became standard several years later. (Bob Lawson)*

*F9F-8 (BuNo 141058) of Squadron VF-112 on the USS Essex in 1957 has come to a stop after being arrested. Because the raised hook still retains the wire the deck man has just given the pilot the signal to release his brakes so the aircraft can roll back a short distance to free the wire from the hook. (Bob Lawson)*

*The final configuration of the F9F-B Cougar with the author's smiling face beaming from the cockpit. The last fix that added significantly to the overall flight performance was the splitter plate boundary layer bleed installed on the fuselage with a painted "V" at the engine air-duct entrance. The 1,988 Cougars delivered were the Navy's first swept-wing carrier aircraft to serve as front-line fighters, fighter-bombers, operational trainers, and in reserve squadrons for 20 years. (Northrop Grumman History Center via Corwin H. Meyer)*

reduction during rapid descents from high altitude and decelerating during joining a formation and coming into the landing traffic pattern. To me the drag effect of the Cougar's single speed brake appeared to have only half the effect that the same speed brake did on the Panther. I tried to persuade the Cougar Program Manager of my findings, but he adamantly insisted that they already met the Navy minimum requirement deceleration specification. Therefore, there was no need for further discussion.

I knew that the chief Cougar aerodynamicist had previously come to the same conclusion I had from his drag calculations. He had also completed a design for an additional set of speed brakes as a part of the inboard landing flaps. This addition would now provide twice the drag and give it the same smart deceleration capabilities as the F-86E Sabre had demonstrated during my evaluation.

Knowing that Grumman had a solution, I decided to take the problem to a higher level to muster more powerful

forces for a decision. Unofficially I called my old friend USMC Colonel Marion Carl, the legendary ace of Guadalcanal, who just happened to be the director of fighter flight-test at the Naval Air Test Center, Patuxent, Maryland. After relating my speed-brake conclusions, I suggested that he visit Grumman to evaluate the Cougar speed brakes. He flew up the next day. After a short evaluation flight he commented to the Program Manager that the present single speed brake deceleration capability was not acceptable. A new set of dual speed brakes was installed on the inboard wing-flaps of all Cougars with no further resistance from the Program Manager. He and I didn't get along quite as well afterward.

The F9F-6 Cougar was now over its major teething troubles and ready for squadron operations. It was too late for the Korean War, but it did provide the Navy with the first carrier-based transonic fighter that could compete with the MiG-15 and -17 during the long, hot era of the Cold War.

The last production F9F-8 Cougar (BuNo 144376) awaiting Navy pickup on the Grumman delivery line in March 1957. Single-place Cougar fighters remained in front-line squadron service for 13 years of active service until 1965. The two-place F9F-8T trainers remained in active service for 17 years and were not phased out until 1974 when the Douglas TA4-E two-place Skyhawk replaced them. (Northrop Grumman History Center via Corwin H. Meyer)

## The Cougar's Range Demonstration

On 1 April 1954 the speed and range potential of the F9F-6 Cougar was demonstrated dramatically by making a three-aircraft "routine" U.S. transcontinental record flight in 3 hours, 45 minutes, and 30 seconds. Equipped with in-flight refueling probes, the Cougars took off from NAS San Diego on the 2,438-mile flight to NAS Floyd Bennett in New York. They refueled only once over NAS Hutchinson, Kansas. Commander Francis X. Brady logged the record time of flight. Lt. John C. Barrow took an "appropriate" one minute and 30 seconds longer, as did Lt. Wallace "Bud" Rich.

## The Flex-Deck – A Hard Way to Make a Soft Landing

Before the advent of jet engine after-burners, which finally allowed carrier fighters to perform as well as land-based

Lt. Cmdr. Francis X. "Gus" Brady kneeling on the wing of his aircraft congratulating Lt. Wallace "Bud" Rich after setting a transcontinental record for crossing the United States on 1 April 1954. (Northrop Grumman History Center via Corwin H. Meyer)

Crane lifting the Cougar off the Flex-Deck to place it on the dolly. The Flex-Deck system should have been conceptually trashed without spending another cent after learning of the previous British Royal Navy and the USAF problems, fiascos, and decisions. (Northrop Grumman History Center via Corwin H. Meyer)

fighters, some genius in the British Navy came up with a great idea to increase carrier-fighter aircraft performance. They postulated that if the tricycle landing gear and all of its commensurate structure and equipment were eliminated, a fighter's empty weight could be reduced about 30 percent. This 3,000-lb weight removal would translate into a simple and stunning increase in naval fighter performance.

Their landing area design called for a 300-foot-long bed of air bags 5 feet thick to cover the aft end of the carrier deck on which the aircraft would land gently and stop with the usual arresting gear and tail hook. After the aircraft came to a stop and the hook released, it would be pulled forward off the bag area and crane-lifted onto a waiting dolly for the pilot to taxi this combination to the forward-deck parking area. For pilot taxi control the aircraft brake lines would be readily re-connectable to the wheel brakes of the dolly by a deck hand. It surely sounded simple on paper. It was named Flex-Deck.

The Royal Navy rigged a Flex-Deck installation at their Boscome Downs test facility and configured a navalized De Havilland Vampire jet aircraft for the Flex-Deck landing tests.

Shortly thereafter the British proved to themselves that these tests might be great in theory but were impossibly ridiculous in practice because of the extremely difficult after-landing handling problems. The Flex-

Deck was summarily consigned to the British R&D trash basket.

Not so in America. With solid indifference to recent British aeronautical history, the USAF and U.S. Navy decided to have a go at the Flex-Deck.

The Martin Company configured a straight-wing Republic F-84 Thunderjet with an arresting hook. The USAF set up a Flex-Deck installation at Edwards Air Force Base and started flight-testing this combination with an aircraft that had a 155-mph landing approach speed; 55 mph faster than the Vampire's.

I was flying the Grumman XF10F-1 Jaguar at Edwards at the time and witnessed several of the actual landings, and an even more striking, slow-motion movie taken during a landing by Martin's test pilot George Rodney. It was awesomely clear that when the Thunderjet touched down, George completely disappeared below the canopy side rails on every landing. During the program both he and another Martin test pilot broke their backs. The USAF R&D incinerator trashed their Flex-Deck intentions shortly thereafter.

After the failed USAF attempts at Flex-Decking, the Navy couldn't be left standing out in the cold of aeronautical history. Grumman was selected to perform a Flex-Deck evaluation for future carrier aircraft in order to obtain these fabulous increased performance possibili-

Grumman test pilot John Norris garbed in his back-stiffening and helmet-holding rig that he devised after flying the De Havilland Vampire on the Flex-Deck at Farnborough in 1955 in England. He and Navy test pilot John Moore used this rig religiously during Navy tests at the Naval Aircraft Test Center, Patuxent River, Maryland, and were not injured. Four other pilots seriously damaged their backs in British and USAF tests of the Flex-Deck system. (Northrop Grumman History Center via Corwin H. Meyer)

ties. Norm Coutant, one of our more gray-haired test pilots, was chosen as project pilot for the program. After making two landings on the English Flex-Deck rig in their Vampire, his maturity got the best of him. He declined further honor for both Grumman and the U.S. Navy. John Norris, a younger Grumman test pilot, flew several Vampire Flex-Deck landings in England and "being less equipped with sanity" (his quote), agreed to complete the Grumman program in a specially modified Grumman swept-wing Cougar.

During his first Flex-Deck landings it became evident to him that the fundamentals of physics on the pilot's body were the same in all the air forces in the free world. A very special full-body harness was then designed to keep John's head and upper torso locked up to prevent it from disappearing below the cockpit rails as George Rodney's had done. Besides this minor problem, it was abundantly clear to the Grumman test team that little thought had been given to how these landing-gearless aircraft and their hundreds of necessary wheel dollies would be handled and supported during the remaining 90 percent of the aircraft's long life cycle when they were land-based.

John completed his contract-required 10 landings and was most relieved to collect his extra-hazard bonus standing erect and without assistance. To be sure that the Navy had not been hood-winked by Grumman they requested Lt. John Moore, "a feeble-minded Navy test pilot" (his quote), who smartly requested John Norris's full-body and head lock-up harness, to perform 14 more of these hazardous landings before the program was abandoned. This was a stroke of luck for all future test pilots and naval aviators.

In July of 1999 the author spoke to both Norris and Moore to ask their opinions as to why the Navy persisted in such an expensive, harrowing, two-time looser and back-breaking program. Without hesitation they both retorted that the U.S. Navy must have had a humongous excess of research and development money that the brass forced them to "launder" before the end of that fiscal year.

## The F9F-6 Transforms into the F9F-8

In order to increase range, reduce carrier catapult and approach speeds, and carry more external stores than the F9F-6, Grumman began work on the F9F-8

The first prototype two-place F9F-8T trainer (BuNo 141667), Grumman Design 105, with an air-to-air mission load of four AIM-9B Sidewinders and two Aero-1C 150-gallon tanks ready for carrier Combat Air Patrol training. Four hundred Cougar F9F-8T trainers were delivered to the Navy Training Command between July 1956 and August 1960. They had a 17-year career and equipped five squadrons until they were finally phased out in 1974 in favor of the two-place Douglas TA4-F Skyhawk. The F9F-8T was the first U.S. military aircraft to have the zero-speed, sea-level, English-designed Martin-Baker ejection seats installed. (Northrop Grumman History Center via Corwin H. Meyer)

Cougar design in April 1953. I had the pleasure of making the first flight in the F9F-8 on 18 December of that year. The wing was redesigned to incorporate a fixed cambered leading edge to provide the same lift characteristics as the complex F9F-6 slats. This now–available wing space, coupled with an 8-inch extension of the fuselage, provided room to increase the internal fuel capacity by 144 U.S. gallons, thereby increasing its range from 907 to 1,203 nautical miles. The F9F-8 Cougar now offered a range capability that was only restricted by the endurance of the pilot's bladder.

The redesign also increased the wing area from 300 to 365 square feet, which reduced the stall speed by 13 mph. This welcome reduction in stall speed allowed the F9F-8 to carry a greater load of the newer and heavier ground-attack external stores.

The increased wing area was developed by extending the width of the wing, thus thinning it and giving it less drag, which increased the transonic and super-

sonic critical combat dive speeds by a welcome 50 mph, developed the increased wing area.

The F9F-8 Cougar had an in-flight refueling probe and a UHF homing antenna installed in its nose. Provisions for carrying two of the new Sidewinder AIM-8B missiles on each wing were also added. The 601 F9F-8 aircraft produced not only had a large increase in capability but also, without the slat mechanism, now required fewer hours to maintain.

The F9F-8B Cougar was the first and only Navy carrier-based swept-wing fighter able to carry tactical nuclear stores launched by the Aero 18C Low Altitude Bombing System (LABS).

The 110 F9F-8P aircraft had much larger nose sections, which carried a total of four bulky, state-of-the-art Fairchild cameras for the all-important photo-recon role.

## The F9F-8T Trainer

Grumman began development of a two-seat Cougar trainer version in

November 1953 to meet increased Cold War carrier swept-wing training requirements. Grumman was in competition with the popular Lockheed TV-1 and TV-2 straight-wing trainer versions of the USAF F-80 that had been in the Navy Training Command for years. After much salesmanship by Grumman, the Navy authorized them to redesign an F9F-8 airframe as a two-seat trainer prototype. It flew on 29 February 1956. The failure of the Lockheed TV-2 to meet its requirements later boosted the production numbers of the F9F-8T to 400 aircraft.

To provide space for the second cockpit the fuselage was extended 34 inches. The additional second cockpit space also required that the size of the forward fuselage tank be reduced, giving the F9F-8T 296 gallons less than the standard F9F-8 fighter, which was satisfactory in training aircraft. The rear cockpit was given a strong windshield to deflect the air blast when the canopy was blown off during crew ejection. To keep the empty weight close to that of the F9F-8, two of the four 20-mm cannons and their ammunition were removed. Provisions for a nose in-flight refueling boom and four under-wing Sidewinder missile stations were standard equipment.

The five F9F-8T Cougar squadrons had splendid 17-year careers with the Naval Training Command. They were finally phased out in February 1974, having proved vital to the supersonic training of thousands of pilots who flew combat from carriers in Southeast Asia while fighting in Vietnam.

As the Cougars came out of Navy operational squadrons they were placed in 23 naval and Marine reserve squadrons at 11 naval air stations around the country. They remained in this duty until 1967. Not bad for a 1951 fighter.

## Conclusions

After much lethargy followed by frantic on-the-job training for its transonic education, Grumman expeditiously produced 1,988 of the first, and for 16 years the only, carrier-suitable swept-wing fighters needed during the long Cold War years.

In 1958 the supersonic Grumman Tiger began flying with operational squadrons.

## Epilogue

As you have read in previous chapters, I began Navy operational training as a civilian in Hellcats at Atlantic City in 1944 and 1945 to better understand Navy use of Grumman products. I received a letter of commendation from the skipper of the squadron I flew with that stated I only needed actual carrier qualification to complete my education. In the Panther chapter, I told of receiving carrier-arrested landings and catapult takeoff shots at NATC Patuxent in 1951. I was turned down for further actual carrier landings several times after that before I asked now promoted and retired Admiral Trapnell if he would intercede and get me the permission. He did and Commander "Shakey" Thomas of Cougar Squadron VF-61 allowed me to carrier qualify in June and July 1954. After 26.1 practice hours with VF-61, I received the required eight take-offs and landings with no "Wave-Offs" (balked landings demanding a go-around) on the straight-deck USS *Lake Champlain* on 14 July 1954, which finally completed my Navy training. I was told that I was the first and only civilian to be so qualified in jets. I found out later that those two months had the highest accident rate on carriers since World War II, which was quite possibly the reason why I had so much difficulty getting approved.

# Chapter 21

# Grumman's Only Alley Cat – the Jaguar

## March 1952 to April 1953

Abraham Lincoln told a group of friends that although he was flattered by the prestige and the high position of leading a certain parade he would decline the honor of being ridden out of town tarred and feathered on a rail. I probably should have taken the opportunity of declining the honor of leading this aeronautical procession for one year immediately after the first four flights of the Jaguar.

The XF10F-1 Jaguar was designed with a variable-sweep wing (13.5 to 42.5 degrees) for one reason alone: to render a heavy, swept-wing, combat aircraft to be compatible with aircraft carriers of World

*The takeoff of the XF10F-1 Jaguar at Edwards Air Force Base at 7:52 AM on 19 May 1952. It had so many problems that presented themselves immediately after takeoff on the first flight that it was landed only 17 minutes later. This was to be the standard flight-testing program for this aircraft's 14-month flight-test program. Project Engineer Bob Mullaney stated, "You really flew 268 first flights until we junked it." We did learn a lot about variable-wing-sweep fighters, but everything else on the aircraft demonstrated that we had designed an aircraft with far too many seemingly good ideas that were all under-researched prior to installing them in a mass-production aircraft. (Northrop Grumman History Center via Corwin H. Meyer)*

*The rollout for the first engine run-up of the Jaguar. I was to be the only person who ran the engines because we only had one engine available. This engine was in two other Navy fighters at the time; the Douglas F4D Skyray and the McDonnell F3H-1 Demon, and they were also duds. Why the Navy put all of their apples in the unproven, young Westinghouse jet engine company in the early 1950s has yet to be explained. (Northrop Grumman History Center via Corwin H. Meyer)*

War II vintage. The very high takeoff and landing speeds predicted for swept-wing fighters were understandably arousing intense concern in U.S. Navy circles in the late 1940s and early1950s. Thus having a straight wing available on a swept-wing fighter for catapult and arresting seemed like a splendid idea to them.

As far as the achievement of this primary aim was concerned, the XF10F-1 program was a resounding success. The straight wing stalling speed of the Jaguar was 90 mph. This represented a fantastically low arrested landing approach speed for an aircraft capable of Mach 1 in level flight.

Many areas of the Jaguar swept-wing flight envelope were tested without difficulties. The XF10F-1 never encountered a critical Mach number or compressibility effects during any of the swept-wing dives made to its limit speed. The variable-sweep wing lived up to its design predictions. Little did Grumman know at the time, however, that we were to meet up with variable-sweep wings again in two future Grumman cats. Being the only

fellow to fly it, I swept and unswept its wing more than 150 times during its one-year flight-test program.

That is the only good news about this Grumman feline. The rest of the Jaguar testing was one continuous nightmare.

## The New Horizontal Tail Objects Immediately

On the only taxi run I made at the Grumman Bethpage, New York, airport, I accelerated the aircraft up to 70 mph and pulled back on the stick. The nose wheel lifted off, and the tail bumper hit the ground—and stayed there. I pushed the stick forward, but the innovative double-delta canard tail didn't move. There was not enough front delta elevator power to lower the nose. The only way to accomplish this was to hit the brakes. Doing so brought the nose wheel back to the ground with a thump. This sadly confirmed the high inertia and low control power of the horizontal tail, which was previously demonstrated in a wind tunnel

*Right after the end of World War II it was learned that the German Messerschmitt company had designed a variable-sweep-wing fighter but had not completed it for flight. The Bell Aircraft Corporation got the contract to make it a flying aircraft for NASA research and called it the X-5. It had made quite a few flights with very little useable research. Major Robson of the USAF was killed in it just before the flight in which I was supposed to evaluate it. In talking with other pilots who had flown it they were unanimous in their opinions of its very poor handling characteristics. (Northrop Grumman History Center via Corwin H. Meyer)*

and by control-line, powered model flight-tests. But the project engineer did not believe this. I was soon to receive more convincing news that I had a longitudinal control surface over which I had anything but control.

As project pilot of the Grumman XF10F-1 fighter, I was most pleased that Grumman elected to use Edwards Air Force Base for the Jaguar's initial test flights. The 8,000-foot runway extended into a seven-mile lakebed, which was as smooth as a billiard table when dry. The reasons for my elation were manifold. The engine of this very big and heavy fighter really needed its yet-to-be-developed afterburner. A working afterburner was not scheduled for delivery until 12 months after the Jaguar's first flight.

The Jaguar was also going squarely against the general industry state of the art by being designed for transonic flight without having any of the industry-standard hydraulic-boosted flight controls. The Jaguar also had very unique and unconventional designs for the elevator

and aileron controls, a variable wing sweep mechanism, a new and unproven electronically balanced six-tank fuel system, and it was a new engine/new aircraft combination because the Navy required this engine to be installed in the Jaguar. As you have heard previously, installing a new engine in a new aircraft went against Grumman's strongly held policy. The Jaguar really needed the Edwards eight-mile-long lakebed runway.

## Its Dubious Reception at Edwards

The Jaguar was flown to Edwards in a C-124 Douglas Globemaster. As we assembled it, many unsavory comments were offered about its size and strange configuration. USAF personnel immediately joked about its size as the "The Navy's Blue B-52 Bomber," and taunted us with the question: "We know it's a transport, but where are the windows?"

The lakebed runway was closed due to standing rainwater when I made my first Edwards 8,000-foot paved runway lift-off attempts. It soon became obvious to the Edwards audience that Grumman had come up with an aircraft that was going to fly strangely, if at all. Because of its 600-lb bulk, the elevator controls displayed so much inertia response delay that the Jaguar's stick felt like it was made of rubber when I tried to control it at planned takeoff speeds of 120 mph. The aircraft and I lurched up and down the 8,000-foot runway as if one, the other, or both of us were drunk. These attempts to fly went on for a week or so, to everybody else's hilarity. But it was a real concern to me because I could get only five to eight seconds of airtime to get the feel of its elevator control or have the guts to want to fly it higher than 10 feet from terra firma.

As the numbers of these 120 mph lift-offs built up, I became increasingly frustrated and reluctant to commit myself to fly the aircraft. On one occasion I lifted off for about 15 seconds and when I put the XF10F-1 back on the runway Bob Mullaney, our project engineer, heard a loud, "Oh S#*t," knowing well that I had flown way too far down the runway. Fearing the worst, he leaped onto the crash truck and found the Jaguar sitting a hundred yards off the runway in the boonies with two blown tires. That episode made up my mind for me. I could not commit myself to fly the aircraft until we could use the still rain-soaked seven-mile "dry lake" runway and fly it near the ground for at least a minute to really feel out this strange canard elevator control.

## The Jaguar Makes Its First Useless Flight

Eventually the lakebed was pronounced usable on 19 May 1952. I managed to get the XF10F-1 airborne at 160 mph for a minute and determined that the canard tail had sufficient control for its first official flight but only above 160-mph. It was, however, a disaster as far as accomplishing any quantitative flight-testing was concerned. Once I was in the air I found I was unable to fully retract the wing slats, so I could not fly above the limit speed of 190 mph. I then climbed to 8,000 feet to do some stalls, but when I tried to retract the flaps, I discovered that any small up or down change in flap position used up all of my fore or aft stick motion. I then throttled back from 100 percent RPM to make my first stall with the wing flaps fixed in the "half down" position. The aircraft oscillated violently and yawed 20 degrees to the right until 20 seconds later when I was able to accelerate the engine back to 100 percent RPM power. Most jet engines would accelerate from idle to full power in five seconds or less. Wait until you hear the story of the rest of this miserable engine's tribulations.

With stalls impossible to complete, there was very little else that I could do except to make a circuit of the field and land very carefully. Only 16 frustrating minutes had elapsed since takeoff.

We fixed the yaw problem by installing a large horizontal airflow fence on the bottom of the fin to keep the engine exhaust from impinging on the fin when power was changed. We eliminated the flap problem by mechanically gearing the stabilizer to the flaps, which moved the stabilizer automatically to eliminate the massive change in trim I had experienced during the first flight.

## The Untried J-40 Engine Gets Uglier

The second flight was attempted two days later. Now the flaps could be retracted without any change in stick forces and engine changes in power did not cause the previous wild skidding of the aircraft to the left. On a very calm morning at 12,000 feet above the lakebed, I was just about to

*The Westinghouse J-40 engine was 26 feet long with the afterburner, which was never developed in time for the Jaguar's flight program. If you look at the extreme right-hand side of the photo you will see a white box attached to the engine. That is the first electronic engine control box that Grumman had to determine by opening it just why the engine twice exploded in the air early in the flight-test program. I'm glad we did. (Northrop Grumman History Center via Corwin H. Meyer)*

stall the aircraft for the first time when it was rocked by a violent explosion from the engine, which pitched the aircraft nose up 10 degrees. My chase pilot told me that several very large balls of fire erupted from my tailpipe, followed by an abundance of black smoke. He told me later that he had heard the explosion, too. It surely scared the hell out of me. I hurriedly shut down the engine, got the aircraft back under level flight control, and began an emergency gliding descent back to the lakebed runway.

The accompanying T-33 chase plane pulled out ahead of me as I came in for my dead-stick landing. I suddenly saw that its pilot had forgotten to lower his wheels for landing. I radioed him instantly and his landing gear had just completed its extension cycle as he touched down.

I made an unbelievable landing due to the fact that I had placed my attention on my chase plane. The ground camera showed that the XF10F-1 leaped and bounced all over the place, practically out of control. The best that could be said of my landing was that it was short.

Once on the ground, we gingerly ran up the engine and checked everything, but could find nothing that could account for the explosion. We decided, therefore, to risk a further flight the next day. Thirty minutes into that flight another violent explosion took place in the engine bay. This time, I was completely spooked. No warning had preceded either explosion. I was not changing altitude, moving the throttle or controls; I was just flying sedately along, straight and level. The explosions were so loud and violent that Bob Mullaney and the ground crew heard them again. I shut the engine down and this time made a smooth landing on the lakebed. The Westinghouse technical representative could offer no explanation for the explosions. Bob Mullaney intuitively decided that the totally new state-of-the-art electronic fuel control for the engine was the culprit and that we should open it up to look for the problem. The Westinghouse tech rep told us we were not permitted to open up the control unit, which must be returned to the factory complete with the Navy seal unbroken. Unfettered by his problems, Bob and I decided that we would open it anyway, and open it we did.

## Pandora's Westinghouse Box

The unit was 24 inches in length and 10 inches wide. We removed all the screws around the edges of the lid and attempted to pry off the top. It refused to budge. Something was holding it firmly in place at its middle. All that was left were two screws on the manufacturer's identification plate in the middle. We removed one of them, and it proved to be short, merely holding the plate in position. The second screw kept coming out until its one-and-a-half inches in length were clearly in view. Inspection showed that it had penetrated deep into the guts of the fuel control. Some careless mechanic, running out of the required short screws, had selected this over-sized screw and driven it straight into a bundle of wires, crystals, diodes, etc. We installed another fuel control and that problem never repeated itself. Had the

unit gone back to Westinghouse first, the real cause of the problem would have been lost forever in the paperwork.

## Jaguar Almost Hits Mach 1

On the 20th flight on 11 October 1952, both the Jaguar and I struggled up to its non-afterburner service ceiling of 31,500 feet for the first high Mach number investigation. At 200 mph, the highest speed I could get at that altitude, I pushed the nose down sharply to a 55-degree dive angle and slowly attained Mach .975, which was 710 mph. I pulled out less than 5,000 feet above the lakebed! The accompanying F-86 Sabre chase plane was going flat out in its dive to keep up with me but was soon left trailing far behind. The 42.5-degree wing sweep angle on that dive demonstrated that the Jaguar was going to attain the designed supersonic performance that the Navy needed as soon as we received the afterburner, which would add 50 percent more power.

## An Almost Unplanned Ejection

Only nine days later, on the 23rd flight, I was determining high-speed level performance at 21,000 feet at a mere 602 mph when my entire Plexiglas canopy shattered completely, leaving only the frame attached to the aircraft. Buffeting around violently in the cockpit, I instinctively chopped the

*This picture shows two items that we had to install at Edwards for flight improvements. The triangular fins were installed to improve both the weak directional and horizontal stabilities. It did, but the hydraulic powered horizontal stabilizer did a much better job. To the far right you can see the vents we had to put into the speed brakes for formation control and combat gunnery. Without the vents, the speed brakes had intolerable buffeting when they were deployed. (Northrop Grumman History Center via Corwin H. Meyer)*

throttle. The next thing I remember was that the buffeting had greatly eased and I was down to 200 mph. I gingerly advanced the power to land at Edwards as soon as possible. The chase pilot, my old friend Captain Zeke Hopkins, thought that I was a dead duck since he could see me rolling around in the cockpit for about 20 seconds while he was trying to rouse me on the radio. I let him know all was well after the buffeting eased up.

I knew from my previous lift-off experience that the horizontal tail went wild from the disturbed canopy-open airflow when approaching below 160-mph takeoff and landing speeds. Consequently I knew that I had to put the aircraft on the lakebed very fast, flying at least 200 mph. Just before landing, Zeke called me to say that the ejection seat face curtain was fully extended and flapping on the back of the fiberglass section of the canopy frame, a fact I confirmed by a glance in my rearview mirror. I reached back, grabbed the rubber handle on the curtain, and put it between my teeth, thinking to myself, what a B movie this has become! As the face curtain was fully extended, I suspected the seat was "hot" (ready for ejection) but I also thought that there might be a check device on the canopy that should prevent ejection until the canopy frame itself had been jettisoned. I was not all that sure, however, that it would be effective with the canopy glass gone. After touching down and slowing to 100 mph, I hurriedly unbuckled, scrambled out of the cockpit, and straddled the front fuselage, hanging on to the windshield, facing aft. I had managed to get back on the ground, and I had no taste for ejecting with a seat, which needed 5,000 feet altitude for a safe ejection. Several miles later the XF10F-1 Jaguar came to a standstill on the dry lakebed after completing a wide circle.

We found out later that the safety pin in the seat, which would have been pulled free by a wire attached to the canopy frame, had been 90 percent pulled out of its retaining hole and was being held in place by only a quarter inch of its 3-inch length! Debris from the canopy had impinged on the unguarded wire, causing the pin to snap completely out of its retaining detent. I immediately had a guard installed on that wire. We found that the canopy had been designed by an "improved" process without any ground pressure tests. We went back to the old Panther/Cougar process for our next canopy.

## The J-40 Engine – Reliable But Poopless

The Westinghouse J-40 was heavy but operated at appreciably lower temperatures than those of its contemporaries. It had big bearings and casings, making it look more like a turbine for an electric locomotive or a hydroelectric station than a fighter. The XF10F-1, however, was never to fly with a working afterburner. I make that statement with pleasure. For the rest of my life I did not want to do any more Westinghouse engine test piloting.

After starting the J-40, I knew when the engine had warmed up because the aircraft stopped vibrating like a helicopter and smoothed out after a couple minutes of running. No other jet engine that I had flown shuddered during warm up. Every once in a while my chase pilot would announce that a very big puff of black smoke (without an explosion) had emitted from the engine's tailpipe. On the first several occasions I anxiously inquired if he could see any fire. After getting a negative response I realized that this was going to be an unwanted and disturbing regular event. Another feature that was even more troublesome was the extremely delayed engine acceleration time. It required 20 seconds to wind up from idle to 100 percent thrust. Other jet engines took less than five to six seconds. Those 20 seconds always seemed like an eternity. You will see why I had that opinion shortly.

## An Air Show for Dan Kimball, Secretary of the Navy

This air show on the ninth flight of the XF10F-1 almost had two catastrophic accidents, which again demonstrated the Grumman Ironworks' structural soundness in all Grumman designs.

My takeoff was very long because this air show was scheduled for the hottest time of the day with a calm wind. I was told afterwards that it didn't seem to make any difference to the Secretary that it took me over two miles to lift off. The massive cloud of dust raised from the engine tur-

bulence completely hid the aircraft until I was 100 feet in the air. My first pass was at 160 mph to demonstrate the aircraft in the carrier landing condition. A 350-mph pass followed it with the wing fully swept back. Just as I passed the group, this new spoiler/aileron system started an explosive aerodynamic flutter, wrenching the stick from my hands. The stick thrashed back and forth against my legs at a very high frequency, making it difficult to grab it with both hands to regain control. I immediately unswept the wing, which slowed the aircraft down rapidly, and the flutter ceased. (I discovered later that my leg and stomach muscles were bruised black and blue.) Such violent flutter at 300 feet above the ground usually leaves the pilot little or no time before the aircraft disintegrates.

*This picture was taken just moments before I hit the ground with a 22-foot-per-second force equal to that required for a maximum stress carrier landing because I could no longer push the stick any further forward. For normal landings this aircraft would have been at about half this nose-high angle. I learned from this wild air show that I should now practice the air show before the event. (Northrop Grumman History Center via Corwin H. Meyer)*

## The Longest Eternity

At 100 feet during the landing approach I retarded the throttle to idle too soon in order to demonstrate a short landing right in front of the Secretary's group. The Jaguar then slowed to 15 mph below any airspeed I had ever landed the aircraft before. I found myself in the unknown and, therefore, unexpected T-tail pitch-up stall range. (When it was later discovered in other T-tail aircraft it was called "Deep Stall.") I pushed full forward stick, but it was useless and provided the aircraft with no nose-down reaction. I was horrified. I was landing an aircraft with absolutely no control. I immediately advanced the throttle to full power in hopes of accelerating out of the pitch-up condition. Those next 20 seconds seemed like 20 years. The aircraft was now descending at over 33 feet per second and continuing to slow down without any effective control on my part to increase my speed except by power. The engine finally spooled up to full power 50 feet from the ground, slowing my descent rate somewhat. The XF10F-1 hit the lakebed at 22 feet per second as measured by the ground camera. This was one-foot-per-second more than the complete Navy carrier structural demonstration required! It should have crashed. However, I rolled barely 900 feet to a stop without braking. The Grumman Ironworks had twice saved the day for me.

The Secretary of the Navy was convinced that the XF10F-1 was the most phenomenal aircraft he had ever seen. The next day Bob Hall called me up and said: "I don't know what kind of air show you put on, but the Secretary thought it was great. He's added 81 more aircraft to the contract!" The Secretary sent me a personal letter of congratulations. Little did he know of the two near catastrophes that happened on that flight.

As far as I was concerned, this incident showed me that the paddle spoilers had to be blocked out. We then flew the rest of the test flights with only the small ailerons as a pitch control. This little aileron had such a low rolling capability that it would never have been acceptable to the Navy, however.

It was clear that the pitch control system would have to be redesigned to a standard hydraulic-powered aileron-only system. It was another great theoretical idea from NACA but without any flight-test background. That was the end for this "perfect, forceless" NACA-designed spoiler system to be installed on Grumman aircraft.

I also came to the conclusion that the double-delta elevator system had to be enlarged and hydraulic powered to give it proper control at carrier approach speeds.

## The Double-Delta Double-Cross

As you have already guessed, the greatest single source of trouble with the XF10F-1 was the aerodynamically balanced, double-delta canard horizontal tail. Previous aircraft had shown that a conventional stabilizer with trailing-edge elevator would shock out and be useless at transonic Mach numbers. Theoretically it seemed that positioning the elevator in front of the tail plane might avoid the problem.

Up to speeds of 130 mph the double-delta canard was way too sluggish to fly the aircraft. When the stick was moved, a long finite time later the tail decided to move. The stick activated the little canard servo-plane on the front of the horizontal tail boom, which eventually moved the stabilizer behind it. After applying progressively more control input, the tail would finally respond madly and had to be instantly corrected in the opposite direction. Above 160-mph it began to react more like a normal aircraft.

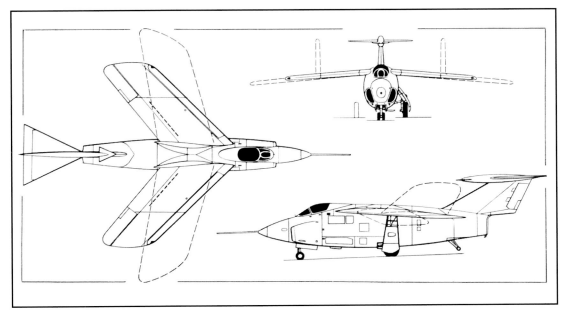

This three-view drawing should give the reader a better perspective of the hopes and failures in the Jaguar design. With a Pratt & Whitney or General Electric jet afterburner engine, a simple fuel system, hydraulic powered ailerons, rudder, and stabilizer this could have been a timely carrier fighter for the Cold War. Fortunately, the swept-wing Grumman Cougar was the Navy's first swept-wing jet available for deployment. (Northrop Grumman History Center via Corwin H. Meyer)

Various fixes were tried. We fitted counter-balanced springs, we changed the sizes, areas, and ratios of the stabilator and servo planes, and we put spring tabs on the servo plane. I even tried running a set of springs from the stick to the seat and instrument panel so that my hand would have something to work against, giving me a better idea where the stick was in relation to tail movement. Nothing really did the trick, and we never achieved positive control at slow speeds with this horizontal control. The tail always seemed to be doing its own thing and leaving me wondering how I could catch up with it. At high speeds the forces to maneuver the aircraft were also too high for combat. We never found the proper horizontal tail control design for the complete speed envelope of the Jaguar.

For the 24th flight on 9 January 1953, we fitted a 35-percent larger double-delta horizontal tail thinking that it might be more powerful. It had the same problems but magnified several times. On the last flight I made with the larger tail fitted, I found myself completely out of phase with the tail at 130 mph; the aircraft was bucking and skidding uncontrollably. I should have bailed out but couldn't get out of the cockpit. I shall never know how I regained control of the Jaguar. The instrumentation was too confusing to be read for an answer. Even project engineering couldn't decipher the 10 pertinent photo-panel time-history graphs during that out-of-control maneuver. I have not the slightest idea what the aircraft or I did to recover. One of the fellows looked up the word CANARD in Webster's and found the first definition listed as... HOAX. I could have told them that.

In the end, we admitted defeat and tested a standard hydraulic-powered tail similar to the design we had on the Grumman Cougar. It worked great.

Had we opted from the outset for a powered tail, as the original mock-up should have required, we would have saved ourselves a great deal of woe. With a powered horizontal tail any pilot could fly the aircraft easily from the 90-mph stall to the Mach 1 limit dive speed. That and an afterburner was all that was lacking now.

## The Fuel Tank Management System Had a Mind of Its Own, Too

In addition to sporting the first engine electronic fuel control system, the XF10F also had the first electronic, six-tank, automatic fuel balancing system. Nevertheless, the tanks never drained in any consistent manner. First one tank emptied and then the next, but never in the same sequence. We were never able to master that "new-and improved" system either. I, therefore, made every test flight well within gliding distance of Edwards Air Force Base because I never knew if the engine might flame out when any of the tanks emptied. In all my flights in the XF10F-1, I never lost the feeling that the fuel system knew much more than I did regarding where the fuel was going to flow next.

## Conclusions – Safely On the Ground

From the point of view of the only test pilot that ever flew the Jaguar, the entire flight-test program conducted with the variable-sweep wing was unbelievably interesting. We were continuously improvising—always changing things. As Bob Mullaney once put it: "Every one of your 150 flights was a first flight!" I had never attended a test pilot's school, but for me, the XF10F-1 flight-test program provided the complete curriculum. If it taught us anything, we learned the hard way that we should never again put so many basic, untested, and innovative items (including the engine) in one aircraft. For a year we tried to break all the rules of aerodynamics and common sense. The protracted development difficulties that were experienced, countered by the mass-production availability to the Navy of the more conventional fixed swept-wing Grumman F9F-6 Cougar, finally led Grumman and the Navy to admit defeat and abandon this continuously testy "cat."

An English test pilot made the following report about another aircraft he had flown that agreed 100 percent with my assessment of the Jaguar. He said, "The entrance to the cockpit of this aircraft is very difficult. It should have been made impossible!"

# Chapter 22

# The Toothless Tiger

## July 1954 to September 1958

The full story of the Grumman Tiger and Super Tiger has only been told in part by historians who wrote from second- or third-hand information. Although it is over 40 years later, this compendium has been written and documented by the principal Grumman test pilots and Blue Angel pilots who participated in the development of these aircraft, which came upon the scene in a very difficult but interesting era for both Grumman and the Navy.

### F11F-1 Tiger – A Race for Naval Supersonic Supremacy

In 1953 the Navy had two very important competitions that gave it supersonic capability until the 1990s. These competitions finally selected the F8U Crusader for the standard day-fighter role and the F-4H Phantom II for the night- and all-weather role. Grumman was a loser in both of these battles, probably because they were in full production of the F9 Panther and Cougar series of fighters and two other large production runs of aircraft, the S2F Tracker and SA-16 Albatross, plus miscellaneous smaller aircraft programs. Although, for losing these two juicy and lucrative contracts the engineering department blamed politics, I think the Navy considered Grumman too busy with present production and the other two contractors too low on future business. Grumman was not as lean and hungry as Chance Vought and McDonnell. There were also rumblings that Grumman top management thought that with ground-to-air missiles coming on, the day of the fighter was over. This surely lessened the necessary corporate resolve to win those two fighter competitions.

### The All-New Tiger Unofficially Steps In the Back Door

The Navy and Grumman knew that although MacDonnell had straight-wing jet production background in the Phantom I program, Chance Vought had no production jet background. Neither had built supersonic aircraft with complex avionics and missiles. The McDonnell F-4 would also have the untried General Electric J79 engine in a new aircraft. The Navy knew that both aircraft would require extended development times however optimistic the contractor's program projections were. Grumman officials also knew that the high-production Cougar program also had a very big and deep-pocketed budget.

Putting both of these premises together, Grumman management decided to form a top design team to interject a sole-source, interim, simple, small, supersonic, state-of-the-art day fighter with a known engine to put the Navy in the supersonic arena long before the F-8 and the F-4 could enter squadron numbers. Grumman still had their sterling reputation with the Navy for production ability of the Hellcat in World War II, the Panther in Korea, and the Cougar in the Cold War. Joe Gavin and Larry Mead, two top-notch engineers who could get anything done throughout the entire company, were named project and assistant project engineers and told to go to work and pull anybody needed into their group to make it happen.

Exceptionally thin wings were designed, thinner than those of the Bell X-1 supersonic research vehicle, and were milled from aluminum planks rather than from conventional sheet metal construction. The Whitcome NACA Coke-bottle formula was used on the fuselage for the first time to give the aircraft a predicted 25-percent reduction in transonic and supersonic drag. The team selected the axial-flow Curtiss-Wright J-65 engine, which had flown reliably in hundreds of North American FJ series and Republic F-84F production aircraft, but without the afterburner that was needed in the Tiger. We were not going to put an untried engine in our new aircraft, or so we thought, at the time. We had failed to take into account that Curtiss-Wright engines had always spelled trouble. This was their first jet engine, and they had never designed, built, or tested a jet engine afterburner. This last item is important because the average person thinks that an afterburner is attached to the rear of an engine and that is that. Not so. An afterburner has great pressure, temperature, and airflow interactions on the engine ahead of it. Both have to be tuned and tested to each other's eccentricities.

## The Tiger Is Official – Now the Problems Appear

Grumman sold the idea to the Bureau of Aeronautics and on 26 April 1953 the Navy ordered three prototypes. They now had their simple supersonic fighter. It would be their ace-in-the-hole in case the F-8 or the F-4 stubbed their toes. After losing the last two fighter competitions, Grumman was back in the fighter business with the F11F-1.

It was easy for the Navy to find the money for this development in one of Grumman's other pockets: the high-production F9F-8 Cougar program. Today it is difficult to believe that a totally new aircraft program could have been launched at the Navy Captain level in the Bureau of Aeronautics when all new programs today are decided at the Presidential level.

## Design Consideration Questions

I was selected to be the Tiger project pilot. I went to Edwards Air Force Base to fly the Republic F-84F and to the Naval Air Test Center at Patuxent, Maryland, to fly the FJ-3 Fury, both equipped with J-65 engines but without afterburners. The first J-65 I saw at Edwards was one that had some Foreign Object Damage to its aluminum compressor blades. All 650 blades had broken off and they never did find the foreign objects that had caused the problem. It looked like a corncob that had been stripped by a very enthusiastic eater. I was told that the USAF and the Navy were going to redesign the compressor blades so that the first three rows of both the rotor and stator blades would be made of steel. With this change the Foreign Object Damage problem went away. Before I flew the Republic F-84F, Republic's Chief Test Pilot, Carl Bellinger, was kind enough to tell me that the J-65 engine also had the bad genetic trait of greatly changing its normal vibration frequency in flight without changing aircraft attitude or throttle position. I found this to be true on my first flights in both aircraft. It was to become a source of nervousness to pilots because of all of the many other engines that we had flown had no such trait. One of my Navy friends described it as "having night noises in the daytime." The J-65 had a good name in both the USAF and the Navy as a very reliable engine. The problem that Grumman foresaw was that ours was the first aircraft to install Curtiss-Wright's first and still-to-be designed and developed afterburners to make our Tiger supersonic.

Our primary aircraft problems were that the transonic region aerodynamics between Mach number .95 and Mach number 1.05, and to a lesser amount the ensuing higher Mach numbers, were still considered witchcraft as far as performance predictions were concerned. The reason was that wind tunnel test throats, where the aircraft models were suspended, were relatively small because of the huge power needed to create and sustain supersonic wind speeds in them. Thus they would only take small models, which had large unknown scale effect. Shock waves, as they formed on the model, would bounce off the walls of the small throat tunnel and back onto the model, making the accurate measurement of transonic and supersonic data impossible. We were going to be as much in the dark as the supersonic North American F-100 and Convair F-102 performance aerodynamicists were when they designed the F-100 and F-102. On their first flights, these aircraft wouldn't even go slightly supersonic until major design changes were made and their afterburners developed to provide an additional 1,220 pounds of thrust.

The Tiger was designed to attain Mach 1.21 in level flight. We would find out all too soon that we were no better at this supersonic estimation witchcraft than all of our peers in the industry.

Although I had other flying chores to do during this period, I was named project test pilot, considered a member of the team, and cut in on all decisions.

## The Tiger Flies on 30 July 1954

The Tiger completed its ground tests early on 24 July 1954. Although Grumman usually did first flights without any notice to the outside world, we somehow had attracted many Pentagon Navy people who were interested in seeing the Tiger's first flight at our Calverton Flight Test Center. The weather was most uncooperative, however. The sun couldn't be seen through a cloudless but very hazy sky. The Navy wanted me to get on with it. I checked the weather in a Cougar several times that day and at 3,000 feet I couldn't see the ground. Jake Swirbul, noting my problem with the Navy personnel who wanted to see the first flight, suggested they go back to Washington and we would call them for the first flight. It was wonderful working with a leader like that who took the weather onus off my back at the right time.

Finally, on 29 July 1954, the weather cleared and I made two flights back to back without any problems. On the second flight I went supersonic in a shallow dive. We did have some unexpected problems. When I got to 40,000 feet on the second flight and had exceeded Mach 1 easily, I found that when I reduced the engine power enough to descend, the engine started having duct rumble and then with further throttle reductions made loud noises as if it were backfiring. This was not predicted. Nor was the very high aircraft buffeting when I opened the speed brakes to descend the first time from altitude. With the engine power retarded to the lowest backfiring I could tolerate and the speed brakes extended to the maximum buffeting I felt the structure could stand, I could only make a very slow let down. I soon became concerned about running out of fuel before I got to the ground. I just made it.

We put much bigger hinge gaps on both speed brakes, which eliminated their terrible buffeting, but it took us several more flights to locate the engine backfiring problem, which was caused by the blunt contour of the engine air-intake duct splitter plates. After they were re-contoured to a knife-edge like all the other supersonic aircraft I had flown, the problem was solved. You can now understand why new aircraft definitely should be tested only in clear weather for their first 10 to 15 flights.

After two weeks of opening the flight airspeed envelope, we decided that it was time for us to put on a high-speed demonstration for the Navy and the public. We invited the Navy brass, the news media, and a large number of Grummanites. The air show must have been a great success. The Navy increased their orders for the aircraft from 41 to 388 very shortly thereafter.

In the next two months the final speed/G build-up flight-test structural program for the non-afterburner aircraft and afterburning fighter were completed. The aircraft was now cleared to Mach 1.3 at altitude tapering back to Mach 1.0 from 10,000 feet to sea level. The Gs were increased to 7.5, or the buffet boundary, whichever occurred first at all altitudes. This also included full-pitch stick rolls and full rudder pedal deflections at all altitudes. In order to have good carrier landing characteristics and to get ready for the first NPE (Naval Preliminary Evaluation) we spent a lot of time tailoring the landing condition and stall characteristics to ensure a docile carrier aircraft.

Grumman always liked to have an NPE as soon as possible after the first flight so the Navy could help us solve problems that they had encountered testing other contractors' aircraft.

## An Almost Fatal Naval Preliminary Evaluation

On 20 October 1954 Commander Marsh Beebe, Director of the Flight Test Division, and Commander Tag Livingston came up from the Naval Air Test Center at Patuxent to evaluate our new bird. They flipped a coin and Tag received the honor of the first Navy flight. His evaluation would be within the flight

*Grumman gave a public flight demonstration to show their new "cat" on 12 August 1954. After the flight demo the group gathered here consisted of: the author, Admiral Apollo Souchek, Chief of the Navy Bureau of Aeronautics, LeRoy Grumman, Chairman of the Board of Grumman, Jake Swirbul, President of Grumman, and Joe Gavin, Project Engineer of the Tiger. History buffs may remember that Lt. Apollo Souchek attained the world's altitude record in a Wright Apache biplane in 1932. (Northrop Grumman History Center)*

envelope that we had tested but he was to perform a new but very unsuccessful test in the Tiger with only 20 minutes of familiarization flight time.

He flew the number one Tiger and I, coincidentally, flew the second Tiger at the same time. During my flight I inadvertently heard him say that he had a flameout and was descending over a small paved airport southwest of our Grumman Calverton airport while he was trying to get an air start. I happened to be over near that same field and soon I saw him spiraling down at a high rate of descent with his landing gear and flaps extended. For the first time in my life I couldn't think of what I should say to him that would help. I knew he had his plate full trying to get the engine started and/or planning for a flameout landing in a new aircraft at an unfamiliar field.

Finally, just as he started his 180-degree final turn, I "ordered" him, "Don't let your airspeed drop below 155 mph until you flare out," because I knew that was the minimum controllable speed at his aircraft weight. He said nothing, swung too wide of the landing strip, went into the scrub pine, and disappeared without an explosion. I figured he was a goner and called the field to tell them to send an aircraft over to get his body. I flew home in a state of shock. Less than 10 minutes later the rescue aircraft landed to meet Tag walking out of the scrub pine in a daze but with only minor injuries. He later told me that he heard my admonition very clearly and thanked me for that last-minute advice. We never did find out why his engine didn't start because the igniters were so damaged that they were unworkable.

## To Edwards Air Force Base for Engine Flameout Testing

We immediately decided to take the second aircraft to Edwards to determine why the engine didn't start, the top air restart altitude, airspeed, techniques, and limits for the Tiger aircraft/engine combination. After Tag's unhappy episode, it took a lot of self-persuasion for me to make the first intentional flameout even over the 10-mile diameter lakebed at Edwards. It did not take many flights, however, to determine a satisfactory all-altitude and airspeed air start envelope.

Because the Edwards lakebed runways were available, we prudently decided to perform some intentional engine-off landings to see that all of the control systems had sufficient hydraulic-boost power. And

The final resting place for the number one Tiger. As you can see, the pilot was shooting a landing on the abandoned Brookhaven airport runway. Although he didn't make it he walked out of the woods with only a lot of bruises and a very sore back. The trees that his wings cut down were six inches in diameter. (Northrop Grumman History Center)

to be able to maneuver the aircraft in rough air for landing with the engine off and windmilling while driving the two hydraulic boost pumps at landing airspeeds.

On my first engine-off landing I hit some rough air as I flared out well before my stick motions had the aircraft at the correct landing attitude. Both of the engine-driven hydraulic-powered flight controls froze up. I was immediately riding instead of flying. The aircraft bounded uncontrollably back in the air and bounced wildly two more times before coming to a stop. It was a very helpless feeling. I thanked my lucky stars for the long Edwards lakebed runways. It would have been a disaster if this maneuver had been performed at the Grumman airport. Although Tag was probably much too occupied with his off-runway landing in the scrub pine, I have always had the feeling that Tag had his controls freeze up at the last minute too. We changed the two 7-gallon-per-minute hydraulic pumps to 14-gallon-per-minute pumps and the controls worked very well even with much over controlling during several more engine-windmilling landings. We also tested the Tiger landing characteristics with the engine shut down completely and on the pilot-extended emergency hydraulic RAT (Ram Air Hydraulic Turbine), providing the only power source for the flight controls. It performed up to design standards under these conditions, too. It also had the capacity to make satisfactory landings in rough air.

## The J-65 Afterburner Disaster

During this same set of tests we had the first scheduled experimental afterburner shipped to Edwards. We were eagerly looking forward to the 50-percent increase in thrust that would greatly improve the inadequate rate-of-climb and high-speed performance of the Tiger. For the first test I went to 35,000 feet to see how rapidly this 50-percent increase in thrust would accelerate the aircraft to its contracted 1.21 Mach number supersonic speed.

The first time I lit the afterburner the aircraft started accelerating but not nearly as fast as other aircraft I had flown with afterburners. The F-100 would give you a belt in the backside and the aircraft would promptly accelerate through Mach 1 and not stop until Mach 1.25. I waited as the speed rose very slowly from Mach .92 to about 1.03. There was then a violent explosion in the aircraft. I immediately throttled back out of the afterburner detent to shut the burner off and assess the damage. My chase pilot reported that a very large ball of fire had come out of the back of the engine and he heard the noise from inside his aircraft about 100 yards off my wing! He said that my aircraft looked undamaged so we landed immediately. We found that a sizeable hole had been burned through the side of the afterburner shell that continued through the fuselage stainless steel outer protective shell and had been eating into the fuselage aluminum just over the fuel tanks. This was neither the first nor the last time I found that declaring an emergency, shutting down the engine, and landing as soon as possible was very prudent flight-test policy.

Because this was the first experimental afterburner that Curtiss-Wright had designed or constructed we knew that it would be months before they would have an improved and tested model to Grumman. We packed up and flew the aircraft back to Grumman's Calverton, New York, Flight Test Center.

## Grumman's Edwards Supersonic Test Education

Because there were so many of our competitors flying at Edwards, I made it a policy to find out what they were doing that might be applicable to the testing that I was doing or planning to do. I found both the military and the contractor test pilots most generous in informing me of the details of their programs. These were the golden years of testing at Edwards. There were 10 aircraft and engine contractors there. The USAF was testing at least 20 different aircraft, including the Century Series fighters and the ultra-high-altitude U-2 secret spy plane flying visibly at the North Base. The NASA High Speed Flight Station was also flying many experimental aircraft. It was a college education in high-speed flight-testing. I wrote a long report before leaving.

While I was testing the Tiger at Edwards, George Welch, the North American F-100 chief test pilot, was killed doing limit speed dives and pullouts at slightly over 1.5 Mach number, which was well over 1,000 miles per hour. On his last dive he pulled over 9Gs, the aircraft yawed more than 15 degrees, then the fuselage broke at the cockpit and the aircraft disintegrated instantly. The reason was twofold. To get more speed the North American engineers had designed a much smaller fin and rudder to reduce the drag. As the supersonic Mach number

increased, the directional stability decreased because of the shock wave effect, which blanked it out. This caused the huge angles of yaw that were recorded. The other factor that contributed to the accident was that the data reduction people were over 10 flights behind. George was going into a completely new region of flight-testing without anyone following the program. I cannot imagine why George didn't note and complain about the yaws that he had encountered on previous flights. When I did some of these supersonic investigative flights a month later in the Tiger I got to yaw angles of 5 degrees in pull-ups and I thought that I was flying sideways.

After that accident, North American installed a fin and rudder that was over twice the area, and flight-test engineering took a much greater interest in the detailed progress of limit speed determination. The revised F-100 with the increased area had over twice the directional stability and no further problems were encountered at the F-100's limit speed of Mach 1.5. North American provided me with enough data from their flights that Grumman immediately began to design a fin and rudder of 50 percent greater area to preclude this happening to the Tiger. You will soon

The first test flight to determine how well the Tiger could handle in-flight refueling on its 29th flight. Only minor and fixable problems were found. This early Tiger has the first 50-percent enlarged fin and rudder that was installed so that Grumman would not have to go through a fatal flight like George Welch did in the first North American F-100 at Mach 1.55. The amount we added was sufficient so that the Super Tiger did not require artificial stability augmentation at that speed to over Mach 2. (Northrop Grumman History Center)

see that the Super Tiger had excellent directional stability at twice the speed of sound gratis of North American, and directly as a result of George's demise.

## The Speed, G, and Altitude Build-Up Program

We flew the Tiger home from Edwards and resumed limit speed tests in dives as far as the non-afterburning engine power would allow.

This program had gone 10 flights without an incident until we were approaching the highest airspeed and Mach number combination to date, which was Mach 1.1 at 7,500 feet altitude. Without the afterburner, this dive would have to be made at a 45-degree dive angle and combined with a 7.5G pullout because the lowest altitude of the dive pullout would be at 5,000 feet. Mach 1.1 at that altitude was 825 mph and the rate of descent was over 1,200 feet per second. The ground was only four seconds away from the bottom of the pullout. I was soon

to learn that such a short time period did not allow much time for unanticipated mental agility.

I started the dive at 22,000 feet and attained Mach 1.1 at 16,000 feet altitude. My program was to jolt the stick twice in the pitch axis and roll-wise to see if any flutter ensued, apply full rudder pedal releases in both directions to check directional stability, and then pull 7.5Gs at 7,500 feet. All went well until about a second before I went through 7,500 feet when a very loud explosion occurred and the cockpit filled up with hydraulic oil mist. I couldn't see the instrument panel. I immediately pulled the stick hard aft to pull out of the dive, gain as much altitude as possible, slow down, and to determine what the hell had happened. The next thing I noticed was that I was going up vertically and the speed was decreasing rapidly. The cockpit vent system slowly cleared the mist in the cockpit and I frantically noted that if I didn't push over to level flight very soon I would go to zero speed in a vertical condition and tail slide

*An overall view of the Grumman Calverton Plant 7 production floor after Grumman received the order for 400 F9F-8T Cougar trainers. That production line was put in parallel with the Tigers. You will note how the Cougars are staggered in place next to the Tigers so that the folding wings of the Cougars can be exercised on the line. The rate of the combined production lines was 32 aircraft per month. (Northrop Grumman History Center)*

violently. I pushed over to about negative 2Gs, finally leveled out at 15,000 feet, and noticed that I had instinctively retarded the throttle to idle sometime before.

I eased the throttle forward and looked around for Commander Don Walton who was my chase pilot flying an F9F-8. He was nowhere to be found. It never occurred to me that my violent pull-up wasn't on the program. He later told me that I had disappeared from his view instantly. I then noted that I had pulled 9.2Gs on the accelerometer. Immediately after that the engine began to run very roughly. I tried to locate Don but there were clouds over the area and we never saw each other. I wanted him to give me a look over to see if he could find out what damage the explosion had done to the aircraft. I also wanted him to point me back to the field as the clouds were getting denser and we were still 10 miles out over the Atlantic Ocean.

As my engine began getting slowly but progressively rougher, I cruised in a direction I thought was towards the Calverton airport. Each time it got rougher I pulled the throttle back just enough until it smoothed out. I then noted with great relief that I was over the south shore of Long Island and on a course that would bring me over the field. The engine got rougher much faster with time and I retarded the throttle a little more each time to compensate. The speed was decreasing so I let the engine stay as rough as I could tolerate. I finally arrived over the field and I was down to 210 mph airspeed, which was the best glide speed for a flameout landing pattern. The roughness of the engine died down and as I moved the throttle forward I found out that it had quietly died. As you can now clearly see, it is always good to keep the engine running as long as possible. I had previously declared an emergency so I had the field all to myself.

I extended the wheels and flaps and set up the flameout pattern. I kept the speed until I was on a very short final and flared out for a landing. When I got close to the runway the aircraft was 75 mph over its landing speed. It kept flying with the airspeed decaying at a rate that made me think the engine was still running. I pulled at the throttle but it was against the rear stop. We had an arresting cable across the middle of the runway and when my hook picked it up at 195 mph, it decelerated me to a stop in 300 feet. I was very pleased for small favors. I would have surely gone out the other end of the field with blown tires if the cable or my tail hook had failed.

Inspection after the flight showed that the emergency hydraulic ram air turbine that was located right under the cockpit had come unlocked by itself, extended into the airstreams, and torn off the aircraft. When it ripped off it disconnected and broke the hydraulic lines just beneath the cockpit. That's where the hydraulic oil mist came from right after the explosion.

The 35-lb turbine had scored the side of the fuselage and made a big dent in the left-hand stabilizer. Had it gone six inches lower it would have torn off the entire left-hand stabilizer. We looked into the engine air ducts and saw several square feet of aluminum debris from the fuselage cover door of the departed hydraulic turbine pump blocking the air to the engine. But the real culprits contributing to the engine's demise were the two 3-lb steel uplocks to the hydraulic turbine that had been spinning against the front row of 90 engine rotor blades like balls on a rotating roulette wheel. They had almost completely damaged and eaten through the steel rotor blades. That was what was causing the engine to slowly die on me. If the air is disturbed on the front set of rotating turbine blades all the ones behind them have very badly spoiled aerodynamics for proper jet engine performance too.

*The Tiger is ready for launch. Note the catapult bridle "V" cable attached to the carrier shuttle just behind the nose wheel. It is attached to the catapult hooks on the bottom of the fuselage. This picture shows that the forces from the catapult go almost directly through the center of gravity of the aircraft, which is necessary to keep the aircraft from pitching during and after the shot. The catapult holdback fitting breaks when the catapult pressure is attained. It is the cable that appears to go into the left wheel. It is attached to the carrier. The tailskid is fully extended in this picture. (Northrop Grumman History Center)*

We also found that the locking mechanism did not conform to the drawings. The pull handle in the cockpit for emergency operation was not spring loaded to hold it in the "closed" position, as it should have been. It somehow vibrated open on this flight. The ram air turbine was completely redesigned, and I repeated the flight-test to the same limits of the Tiger flight envelope after it was ground tested again.

## F11F-1 Spin Tests

The Navy requires five-turn clean condition upright spins, two-turn clean inverted spins, and one-turn upright spins in the landing configuration both to the right and to the left. With build-up spin maneuvers, completing this program should take 40 spins and recoveries. Because our previous experience in the Panther/Cougar programs had shown that spins in jet aircraft were much more docile and less oscillatory than in propeller-driven fighters, we thought that spins in the Tiger would be a pushover. They weren't!

It was Grumman policy to restrict rudder and elevator angles to the minimum necessary for all air maneuvers in order to keep the spin as docile as possible and to have rapid recovery characteristics. On the first spin flight of the Tiger I noted that the rudder power in the clean configuration was much greater than it needed to be for any flight maneuver the aircraft would be required to perform. Accordingly, we reduced the excess rudder angle from 30 to 10 degrees. However, the aircraft did need 30 degrees of rudder angle for the slow-speed landing configuration because of the high adverse yaw of the swept wing at low speeds. We fashioned a device that increased the rudder angle to 30 degrees when the landing gear was extended. As a safety measure we installed a 10-foot-diameter anti-spin parachute in the tail of the demonstration aircraft in place of the normal arresting hook.

All required spins were demonstrated without any abnormal characteristics and were acceptable to the Navy. The spin chute was removed because this aircraft was going to be used to determine the source of a very high frequency and most annoying vibration at all transonic speeds at low altitudes. After trying several changes to the rudder control system without improvement, we heard from the Navy that another contractor had cured this problem by thickening the trailing edge of the rudder to one-and-one-half inches from its normal knife-edge shape. It cured the buzz on our first flight.

A week later one of the engineers said that I would have to repeat the spins because any change in a control system required a complete spin re-demonstration. He also suggested that since the rudder change was so small, the spins could be performed without going to the trouble of reinstalling the spin chute. Because of my Bearcat spin experience I disagreed, and the anti-spin chute was promptly re-installed.

The first spin that I performed was entered at 20,000 feet. The aircraft went wild on the first turn after the spin entry. It started massive oscillations about all three control axes. The accelerometer showed plus 4Gs to minus 2Gs, the aircraft rolled violently between plus or minus 60-degree bank angles, and it yawed plus or minus 20 degrees sideways, all at the same time! This was the most sudden and violent maneuver that I had ever experienced in any aircraft. This one lost me mentally in the first few seconds and physically several seconds thereafter. I felt that I was going to pass out because my eyes were graying out rather rapidly. Just before I lost consciousness I instinctively reached for the anti-spin chute handle and deployed it. I didn't even think to try any recovery techniques. (I found out later from recorded flight data that I had applied immediate opposite rudder and stick to stop the spin.) I came to and found myself at about 12,000 feet hanging straight down over the frigid Long Island Sound with the anti-spin chute deployed. I released the anti-spin chute

from the aircraft, recovered to level flight, and returned to base really shook up.

The only way I could appreciate the unbelievable aerodynamic flight limits the aircraft reached during the spin was that this data was recorded on the instrumentation in the aircraft. I had done hundreds of spins in my testing career. I had become used to unexpected and unorthodox spin gyrations and was easily able to mentally record the maneuver as it progressed, but I had never experienced anything this violent before. I was not finished with interesting flight experiences in the Tiger test program yet, not by a long shot.

Even after scrutinizing the flight records very diligently we couldn't find any reason why the aircraft went so completely out of control. We even rechecked the control surface deflections and the center of gravity position to see if they both had been set properly and found them to be correct. Nobody had any idea of what to do. Neither the NACA at Langley Air Force Base in Norfolk nor any of us had ever heard of any aircraft with such obstreperous spins. Going back to basics I decided to make a flight to check the directional stability and damping to see if any change had occurred with the thickening of the rudder trailing edge. Surprisingly enough, my flight-tests proved that the trailing edge change had made the rudder twice as powerful as the original rudder. We then reduced the rudder angle to 5 degrees in the clean configuration, flight checked it, and set out to re-demonstrate the spins.

Needless to say, I was not fully convinced that the problem had been cured. This was one of the smallest changes that we had put on an aircraft and it had the most unbelievable effects on the spin characteristics. I was very apprehensive during the climb to altitude on the next flight. I was hyperventilating somewhat, thinking of what might still happen. I decided to start these spins at 30,000 instead of 20,000 feet just in case.

When I tried to set up conditions for the first spin I couldn't get the engine speed, the start altitude, and the spin start airspeed into focus at all. Normally setting up these conditions was second nature and took no time at all. I had tried several times when my chase pilot asked me why I was floundering all over the sky. I told him to mind his own business and that I would get it straight shortly. After another few tries, the ground radio monitor, with whom I had worked with for many years, noted the change in my attitude and voice. He very diplomatically and propitiously asked me to check my oxygen breathing system. When I checked the blinker, which opened and closed with each breath, I noted that the blinker eye was not moving. I checked the oxygen pressure and found it to be okay. I then looked at my mask connection and found that I had forgotten to hook it up before takeoff.

I connected it and started to feel somewhat better so I tried another spin entry and found that I was still befuddled. I then decided to return to base. I well knew the lasting effects of anoxia (lack of oxygen). My chase flew formation with me and when we came over the field to the overhead break point I left him but found that the aircraft somehow wouldn't slow down. I set up another approach and it still wouldn't slow down. My chase pilot suggested that I use the speed brake and retard the throttle. I then realized that I was functioning very poorly so I asked him to fly formation on me for the entire landing pattern advising me as he saw fit. With his help the landing was anticlimactic.

The next day I tried spins again without any apprehension, but with oxygen connected before takeoff, and the aircraft spun properly in all configurations. These two excellent lessons paid off again in the near future.

The complete final demonstration at the Naval Air Test Center at Patuxent River, Maryland, went smoothly.

## Transonic Cross-Coupling – a New Phenomenon for Grumman

During my stay at Edwards Air Force Base for the flameout landing tests in early 1955, I started hearing from the USAF test pilots who flew chase with my test flights about cross-coupling at transonic Mach numbers, especially at the higher altitudes. They described cross-coupling as some very wild maneuvers that occurred if fighters were rolled over 360 degrees at full pitch stick deflections above .9 Mach number. They weren't very clear but they did refer me to Walt Williams, the director of the NACA High Speed Flight Facility at Edwards.

The importance of rapid, smooth, rolling capabilities is well known by combat pilots. High rolling power in a modern fighter makes it the sure-fire winner in both attack and evasive maneuvers. None of the jet fighters prior to the Century Series aircraft had any rolling limits beyond the fighter pilot's adrenaline-powered arm strength.

Walt Williams said that the cross-coupling phenomenon encountered by the supersonic USAF Century Series fighters occurred because the designs of this new breed of aircraft had changed the three axes' inertia ratios considerably from the older subsonic F-86 and F-84 designs. It was basically that the pitch and directional inertia were much higher and the roll or rolling inertia was much less. He also said that the inertia axes did not necessarily stay as close to the aerodynamic or geometric axes of the aircraft as they had formerly done. He amplified by adding that this was because engines now required afterburners, which made their fuselages longer and weightier than the subsonic fighters. This caused the location of the fuel, weapons systems, and cockpit weights to be much further from the center of gravity than in the subsonic designs. He also said that their wings were much shorter in relation to their fuselages, further aggravating the problem.

Walt also pointed out that the only recovery known was for the pilot to instantly release all the stick and rudder pedal forces and let the controls return to neutral. He said that the aircraft were gyrating so fast that it was impossible to use the controls with the right timing, possibly causing ever-wilder excursions. He did impress upon me that we should proceed very slowly in our flight-test program. In looking over our new enlarged fin design, he agreed that this would help delay the onset of cross-coupling greatly, compared with the smaller fin with which we had started our flight-testing program. He was kind enough to provide several NACA reports so our engineers could be brought up to date with their efforts, too.

As I had performed several high-speed continuous 720-degree rolls in air shows with no trouble, we decided to start our flight-test program at 25,000 feet from a fairly low speed and increase our speed by 25 mph at a time. Our tests showed that 720-degree rolls could be safely performed to about .9 Mach number. At .925 Mach we met cross-coupling instantly after 360 degrees of roll had been accomplished. After about 420 degrees of full-stick roll the nose of the aircraft pitched up to 5Gs without any effort on my part and the rate of roll, at the same stick deflection increased instantly from 180 to 400 degrees per second. The G was still increasing as I released the stick and rudder pedals. The aircraft recovered to 1G level flight immediately. I did not know how high it might have gone,

nor did I want to know, if I hadn't released controls until a second later. It was like the aircraft had changed from a smooth roll to a raging high-G snap roll without any input from me. We never did any testing beyond the first onset of cross-coupling because it was clear that these excursions were well beyond a pilot's ability to control the aircraft. I had been forewarned, but it was still a real eye-opener. I landed immediately. We inspected the aircraft and the recorders. To our relief we found that no structural load limits had been exceeded. We probed the limits in a similar fashion at all altitudes and found that the Tiger was limited to 1.1 Mach number for 360-degree full stick rolls at all altitudes. Up to 1.3 Mach number, full stick roll was limited to 180 degrees of bank angle change. Above Mach 1.3, bank angle change was limited to 90 degrees. Needless to say, I became most proficient at releasing the controls when the Tiger met its cross-coupling foe. This was duly noted in the Pilot's Handbook.

## The Blue Angels Select the Tiger Over Other Fighters

The Blue Angels Flight Demonstration Team was formed in 1945 with the Grumman F6F-5 Hellcat to assist Navy recruitment of pilots after the end of World War II. The Blues were a success in Grumman fighters: the Bearcat F8F-1 and -2; the F9F-2s and -5 straight-wing jet Panthers; the F9F-6 and -8 swept-wing Cougars; and the F11F-1 Tiger in 1957. They flew first-contract and then second- contract Tigers until 1969, which is the longest any one Navy fighter has been flown by the Blues. It was long after the F-4D Phantom II, the F8U-1 Crusader, and the A-4D-1 Skyhawk were operational. Leader of the Blues, Commander Bob Aumack, said that they kept the Tiger so long because it was much easier to fly, train in, and maintain than any of the newer fighters.

# Chapter 23

# A Super Tiger Emerges From the Tiger

## May 1956 to February 1957

The Tiger design team was dedicated to keeping it in the forefront; thus a design was presented to the Navy in January 1955 with the J79-GE-3A installed. The Navy accepted it on 18 August 1955. The last two Tigers of the contract were designated to have the J79-GE-3A installed, replacing the J65-W-18. The two engines were approximately the same length and diameter. The J79 dry weight of 3,250 pounds was 250 pounds lighter than the J-65 engine. To show how much General Electric was ahead of the industry in engine thrust development, the J79 engine had 2,600-lbs more non-afterburning thrust and 3,750-lbs more afterburning thrust than the J-65 in the same size but much lighter package.

The redesign of the basic fuselage structure was relatively simple. Only the ducts had to be redesigned to accept the greater airflow requirements of the GE J79. Except for the engine installation and ducts, the main difference between the Super Tiger prototypes and the Tiger was an extended and enlarged nose section to house the 24-inch disk of the Westinghouse APS-50 search radar.

The Navy approved Grumman's Super Tiger design for another very good reason. On 18 October 1954 the Navy had ordered two prototypes of the F-4H-1 Phantom II for its new missile-armed all-weather fighter powered with the same General Electric J79-GE-3A engine. The Navy purposely wanted to get that engine airborne with as much development flight-testing as possible in the already developed Super Tiger before it would be installed in the new engine/new aircraft, complex twin-engine F-4H-1.

The Super Tiger first flew at Edwards Air Force Base on 25 May 1956, just nine months after the contract was signed. The

*The raw power of a full afterburner run of the first Super Tiger at Edwards AFB. A Douglas SkyRay delta aircraft can be seen on the right. This was the General Electric test aircraft with the J-79 installed. The engine was never installed in the SkyRay in production. (Credit Northrop Grumman history center)*

first flight in BuNo 138646 on 7 May 1956 was a "hot aircraft" fiasco. Because of the very high thrust of the main engine of the J79, I had to light the afterburner after I started rolling or I would have skidded the tires and probably blown them. After I started rolling with full military power, I moved the throttle to the left into the A/B detent, but nothing happened. I tried it again and again until I was nearly out of runway. It finally lit and we were off. By that time I finally noticed that the pressurization air coming in the cockpit was up to 140 degrees and was rapidly increasing. I was forced to open the canopy and land immediately. Something was really wrong.

The engineering team tried to tell me that such heat was normal in a high-powered aircraft. I wouldn't buy it, because I had flown several of the Century Series fighters and their cockpit cooling systems worked great. Using less emotional engineering and better inspection of the system revealed that a certain balancing air valve in the pressurization system had been wrongly located in an exterior vented area. Because of a high differential pressure, which built up, it could not close. It was relocated and our "hot aircraft" cockpit cooled properly. The delinquent A/B throttle switch was replaced.

Our first flight was to determine the optimum full power afterburner climb schedule and high-speed level flight Mach number for the J79-GE-3A Phase 0 engine. Our climb performance showed that the Super Tiger had a rate of climb three times greater than the Tiger. The maximum level flight speed at 35,000 feet was determined to be Mach 1.61, which we built up to by the fifth flight with very satisfactory supersonic stability and control characteristics.

Directional stability in other supersonic aircraft usually decreased as the supersonic Mach number increased. Our flight-test results at Mach 1.61 showed that because we had doubled the original fin size we could be confident of a satisfactory level of stability to Mach 2. We also looked forward to the arrival of the second prototype with a much more efficient engine air-intake duct boundary layer removal system.

## The Super Tiger Dedicates a New Runway at Edwards

The lakebed was still very wet from the winter rains and was closed to flight. The new 18,000-foot runway was completed but also not yet in use. Thus we were forced to use the 8,000-foot runway at the old base. The new runway was very tempting, but because of traffic on a road between the old and the new base, which crossed the runway at the midpoint, it could not be used. I decided to put our radio truck at that intersection for all of our flights so that they could close the runway temporarily if I needed it for an emergency. On the third flight on 28 May 1956 I had experienced some heavy aircraft vibrations in a speed range that I had previously been through several times. I decided to use the new, longer runway for an emergency engine-off landing. I called our truck, the runway was promptly closed, and I landed. I just got back to our office when an upset General Holtoner, Edwards Air Force Base Commander, called me on the carpet because I had used the runway without USAF permission. I suggested that I was not as skilled as his pilots but perhaps he should station one of his Air Police officers with a radio so his pilots and I would have that same advantage. A short silence ensued when he replied that my idea was so good that it was now his. Simple ideas are sometimes easy to sell. An inspection plate that had blown off the aircraft caused the vibration. It was easily repaired.

## Grumman Solves a Major General Electric Argument

Sometimes, even a large company's right hand doesn't know what the left hand is doing. To illustrate, two separate areas of GE were trying to determine the correct fuel pressure for air starts in the J79. From the beginning of the indoctrination with the engine we had, we used 5 psi as the correct fuel pressure for ground starting, and for several flights we perceived no problems. This was the fuel pressure specified for the engine that had been delivered to us. During a casual conversation with Roy Prior, the chief test pilot for GE, he mentioned that the two latest crashes of Lockheed F-104s were caused by the inability of the Lockheed test pilots to make air starts with only 5-psi fuel pressure.

I asked him what GE flight-test had determined from actual air starts to be the correct fuel pressure for air starts. He answered that the correct pressure was 15 psi and added that the GE Service Department didn't agree with them and were still pushing 5 psi. I immediately grounded our aircraft until GE flight-test could get a single answer from their top management. Very shortly thereafter I received a call from one of Grumman's vice presidents who had received a call from a high-level GE bigwig. He wanted to know the reason for my impertinent and unwarranted decision.

When I told him the full story he fully agreed with me. He called his GE counterpart back and very soon I received an official decision from GE top management to change the fuel pressure to 15 psi. So did Lockheed. Roy Prior thanked me, too.

## The Second Prototype Flies

The second prototype (BuNo 138647) had the new, untried but wind-tunnel-tested bump/suction-type ramp method of removing the boundary layer air from the engine air-intake duct. We knew from the wind tunnel tests that it would have much better duct efficiency for the engine intake air than the Tiger-type splitter plate of the first prototype. Furthermore, supersonic engine thrust and aircraft top speed would improve. The new ship also had 60-degree wing leading-edge fillets and a 13-inch after-body extension installed to further reduce supersonic drag.

The second prototype made its first flight on 16 August 1956. We checked its entire subsonic and supersonic flight characteristics to Mach 1.61 and found no problems. We then increased the level flight Mach number speed to the new limit Mach number of 1.85. We were happy to find that the 60-degree wing fillets and the new ducts reduced the supersonic drag much more than predicted. Our flutter speed limit was a torsional weakness at the stabilizer connecting yoke and we had not yet received the nod to fix it. It is interesting to note that we still used the Phase 0 engine while Lockheed had Phase I engines that had more thrust. The predicted directional stability degradation that we expected did not occur. The yaw damper was also found to have sufficient power for the aircraft in supersonic rough air. We had now proved that the Super Tiger didn't require stability augmentation for any of our three control systems up to Mach 1.85. We were to be the first and only Mach 2 fighter in the world, before or since, to make this design breakthrough.

## The New Attack Fashion – Zoom Climbs

Zoom climbs were the rage by the other manufacturers of supersonic aircraft, so we decided to try one to see how proficient our Super Tiger was in this maneuver. A zoom climb is performed by getting the most kinetic energy in the aircraft by going as fast in level flight at as high an altitude as possible then converting that into potential energy by pulling up to a ballistic flight path of 30 to 40 degrees climb angle and letting the aircraft climb to the highest point in its trajectory. Obtaining the correct angle of climb was most important for attaining maximum altitude.

To perform any maneuvers above 45,000 feet altitude, the pilot must be equipped with a partial or full pressure suit. These suits looked like fictionalized space suits. They were very clumsy to wear unpressurized and almost impossible to move in when automatically pressurized in case of cockpit pressurization loss. Without such a suit on, however, the pilot would die instantly if the canopy broke or the cabin pressurization was lost. They were also very claustrophobic and limited one's vision considerably. I was not looking forward to this flight.

In the zoom trajectory, the afterburner usually flamed out or was predicted to flameout at about 65,000 feet. If the engine flamed out at higher altitudes it had to be relit when the aircraft descended to its upper relighting limit, usually below 40,000 feet. Speeds at the apogee of zoom climbs fell below 100 mph because the aircraft was in an engine powerless ballistic trajectory. The aircraft couldn't be maneuvered because it was well below its normal stall speed. At best it was a difficult maneuver for both the pilot and the aircraft. It was useless as a tactical ploy, both because it was difficult to re-aim the aircraft and there were very few missiles that could operate in that rarified atmosphere. On my first and only zoom climb I didn't attain the proper climb angle and I only reached 61,500 feet. We considered the flight satisfactory as a systems check. I was happy that only the afterburner blew out. I was expecting the engine also to flame out, as the J79 had not made any zoom climbs

before my attempt. I tried relighting the A/B as I descended and found that it easily relit on the first attempt at 46,000 feet.

On 27 October 1956 we installed a Phase I J79 engine in the number two prototype. This engine had a 600-lb increase in A/B thrust. I flight-checked it and found that the aircraft accelerated much more rapidly to Mach 2 (1,320 mph at 40,000 feet) after we had replaced the stabilizer yoke and no longer had a limit on the flutter speed of the horizontal stabilizer.

## The Super Tiger Program Sets a New World Altitude Record

During this time period Commander George Watkins brought the World's Altitude Record back to the United States from Russia by zoom climbing to 75,550 feet on 12 April 1958. This record was measured by the Edwards Space Positioning Unit and verified by the Federation Aeronautique Internationale in Paris, France.

## The Naval Preliminary Evaluation at Edwards

As the Super Tiger had completed its full flutter flight envelope, we immediately invited NATC Patuxent to perform an NPE. We still had high hopes that the Super Tiger's performance would excite Navy and USAF fighter procurement personnel.

The following is a portion of their five-page evaluation by Commanders Tom Gallegher Jr., head of the Flight Test Branch, and George Watkins, project pilot. Both of these pilots were associates I had known and had flown with for many years.

"Project TED No. PTR AC-22003.1; Naval Preliminary Evaluation of Model F11F-1F aircraft, Report No.1 28 November 1956 ABSTRACT

1. A Naval Preliminary Evaluation of the model F11F-1F aircraft was conducted at Edwards Air Force Base, Mojave, California, during the period 31 October through 8 November 1956. The evaluation was completed in 23 flights totaling 25.7 flight hours.

2. Except for the insufficient mission time and within the mission envelope investigated, the general flying qualities at subsonic speed and the exceptional performance with and without afterburner, make the F11F-1F aircraft an outstanding day fighter. Present unacceptable items include afterburner light-off and blowout altitudes, pitch trim change associated with flap/slat extension and retraction, and insufficient mission time. Unsatisfactory items include aft field of view, magnitude of pitch trim change in the transonic region, inadequate stall warning, angle of inclination of the pilot's seat, light rudder forces, roll sensitivity in configuration PA (Power Approach) below 160 mph, pitch sensitivity in all clean conditions, buffet boundary below .9 Mach, and the complexity of the present engine controls.

3. It is recommended that all unacceptable items be corrected at the earliest date and that because of the great potential of the F11F-1F (Super Tiger) aircraft as a superiority day fighter a study be made in an effort to increase the mission time to be consistent with current fleet requirements."

The Navy report did not find anything that we couldn't fix. It praised the aircraft much more effusively than we had ever seen in other NPE reports. We were sure that we could now change the Navy's mind about the Super Tiger's future procurement.

Twelve flights totaling 10 hours and 50 minutes were flown between 7 and 10 November 1956 by three USAF test pilots. They were: Major Stewart Childs, Director of Fighter Test, Captain Ivan Kincheloe, Project Pilot, and General Stan Holtoner, Base Commander. Their report was as glowing as the Navy's, even though they compared it to the much lighter, smaller, and more agile F-104A, also with the General Electric J79-GE-3A Phase 0 engine. Their conclusions and recommendation are as follows:

*The number two Super Tiger on a landing rollout on the Edwards lakebed. This picture depicts the very large vertical tail, which kept this aircraft out of directional stability troubles that other Century Series supersonic fighters demonstrated. The full span flaps and slats on the wing are the reason that the Super Tiger had such docile takeoff and landing speeds. (Credit Northrop Grumman history center)*

"The Grumman design 98J, which was flown under the Navy designation of the F11F-1F, can satisfactorily perform the mission of air superiority interceptor or day fighter against aircraft comparable to those presently operational. The favorable characteristics of the aircraft are:

1. Simplicity of cockpit and aircraft control designs.

2. Excellent low-speed handling characteristics, with the exception of oversensitive roll control and stall warning in the power approach configuration.

3. Generally desirable stability and control characteristics over the entire speed range of the aircraft. Roll rates decrease with increasing Mach numbers such that roll control is marginal at high Mach numbers. It should be noted that inertia-coupling tendencies were not investigated over 1.1 Mach number or during less than 1G flights."

We were very appreciative of their high praise of the fundamental flight characteristics of the Super Tiger. The reason the stabilizer yoke flutter was highlighted twice was that General Holtoner accidentally flew faster than the low altitude speed restriction by about 50 knots and entered the flutter range. He was a sharp enough test pilot to turn the instrumentation on and record the frequencies. This was a

great help for our redesign. He and we were also very fortunate that, although the flutter had large amplitude, it was not catastrophic.

General Holtoner was so impressed with the Super Tiger that he persuaded General Al Boyd, who was the Commander of ARDC (Air Research and Development Command) to come to Edwards to evaluate the aircraft. General Boyd was even more pointed in his remarks. He stated that the Super Tiger could handle the MiG-19s and -21s that would not become operational behind the Iron Curtain for several years. This was high praise coming from the USAF. General Boyd and his people were very helpful to my upcoming job change to Super Tiger salesman.

## The Super Tiger Fights the Lockheed F-104 Starfighter

### February 1957 to January 1960

At the completion of the Navy and USAF evaluations in November 1956, and because of the upcoming worldwide German fighter competition, I left test flying to become a full-time Super Tiger salesman. I just couldn't see such a great fighter going into the trash basket. The

The number two Super Tiger with two 150-gallon tanks and one 1,000-pound bomb. The flashy color scheme was not designed by the public relations department of Grumman. It was that color to be able to be seen by the chase aircraft and to help locate the wreckage in the event of a crash. A silver airplane disappears in a blue sky very rapidly. (Credit Northrop Grumman history center)

Lockheed F-104 Starfighter was the USAF offering to the Germans. The Navy put the Super Tiger on the list. I received permission to evaluate the F-104 to check on our competition. My F-104 checkout pilot, Captain Joe Jordan, said that they had already received the USAF cancellation notice on my flights (requested by Lockheed) but they would not tell me until I finished my second flight. The following is my flight report written 7 October 1957.

## C. H. Meyer's F-104 Flight Report

Our first customer appeared to be the USAF. Although the Super Tiger did not have quite the performance of the Lockheed F-104, it did have a combat radius of over three times that of the Starfighter and was reported by the USAF to be a much simpler aircraft for pilot acceptance. It should be noted that four F-104s had been lost to accidents by this time and there were still many fundamental problems to solve. An illustration of one of the many differences between the two aircraft was the flameout landing characteristics and patterns. The Super Tiger had a 360-degree overhead pattern that started at 12,000 feet and 210 mph with the landing gear and flaps down. Its flare-out and landing were normal. The F-104 had a 20,000-foot start altitude with a 255-mph speed with flaps only. Flare-out altitude was 5,000 feet and the landing gear extension had to be delayed until the last few seconds before touchdown or there wouldn't be enough elevator power to make the flare-out. After several crashes from this maneuver, F-104 pilots and the USAF brass decided that ejection was the only sane solution in this situation. We saw two of the disastrous attempts at flameout crash landings at Edwards.

In early 1957 I received permission to fly the F-104. As I got into the cockpit for my first flight I was told to complete my two flights immediately because Lockheed had persuaded USAF officials to cancel my clearance. My check pilot informant also said that they would hold its effective time back until noon. I had friends in high places. Those two flights convinced me that any pilot who flew it would surely forgive its many ills in light of its spectacular performance. I now knew our main competitor most intimately and fully understood why Lockheed was interested in cancelling my evaluation flights.

## FLIGHT REPORT F-104A
## 9 OCTOBER 1957
## CORWIN H. MEYER

SUMMARY: The F-104A has a very short range. It has, however, several more serious limitations that will make it difficult to employ as an Air Defense Command weapons system and it is almost impossible to employ as a Tactical Air Command weapon system. The limitations are basic enough to restrict growth potential.

This aircraft design has sacrificed acceptable flying qualities and safety too much in favor of very high performance.

Acceptable items noted in the F-104A:

1. Performance.
2. Roll and pitch control harmony.
3. Cockpit size, layout, and visibility.
4. Speed brakes.

Unacceptable items:

1. Very restricted roll control power for high altitude maneuvering in order to prevent dangerous T-tail pitch-up.
2. Very high takeoff speed—210 mph. Very high landing speed—195 mph.

3. Very short radius of action—55 nautical miles.
4. Very low rolling performance restriction because of inertial cross-coupling.
5. Small flight restriction envelope after three years of flight-testing.
6. Poor duct-afterburner operation at high speeds—strong duct rumble.
7. Poor directional stability, damping, and breakout forces at all speeds.
8. Poor pilot psychology for engine-out landings. USAF does not recommend it, bailout is recommended.
9. Poor gun platform because of 1, 4, 6, and 7.
10. Complicated pilot's harness and downward ejection seat.

SUMMARY: Permission was granted the writer to make two flights in the F-104A at Edwards Air Force Base. Two 35-minute flights were made 7 October 1957 in F-104A-734. This aircraft was being used in Phase IV (Service Test) during the time of the flights. F-104A Number 56-1734A is a Block One aircraft.

Five Super Tiger engineers and I took on the three-year sales program. In Germany, Canada, Japan, and Switzerland the Super Tiger won the first round. Lockheed had previous sales knowledge that bribes would win the competition so they did so and received an okay for a second round of flight evaluations with different foreign test pilots. Grumman wouldn't allow me to provide bribes, so Lockheed won the second round in Canada, Japan, and Germany. Lockheed President Dan Houghton and Chairman of the Board Robert Gross were both fired for the bribes, but Lockheed sold over 3,000 Starfighters before the end of the program.

The accident rate in fighters is directly proportional to the takeoff and landing speeds of the aircraft. The F-104 had a takeoff and landing speed 80 to 110 mph faster than the Super Tiger. Its accident rate was horrendous. In the USAF 47 aircraft were lost in a 238-aircraft program. In the German Air Force 110 pilots were lost in the first two years of its operations. One of the pilots was the son of the Minister of Defense. Japan had an accident rate of 51 aircraft in the first two years of their operations with the F-104. As in all politics, once a decision is made it is kept.

After it was all over I learned that Jake Swirbul had sent a message to the Navy after the receipt of the first German message of our win in December 1957 saying that Grumman would not accept that program. I asked him why he did this to all of our hard work to get the decision. He said that he knew that Grumman was going to win the contracts for the A-6A Intruder, the E2A Hawkeye, the Army OV-1 Mohawk, and 400 additional F9F-8T Cougar trainers later in that same month. His high-level Navy friends said that if he accepted the German Super Tiger program Grumman could not receive these four programs. The EA-6B Prowler and the E2C Hawkeye are still in Navy inventory 48 years later. Time surley demonstrated that it was the proper decision.

I then asked him why he encouraged me to stay three more years in the Super Tiger program until the end. He said, "Corky, Mr. Grumman and I believed that you could never get better sales training in any place else except in an actual international program with the Super Tiger."

Chapter 24

# A Jet Jockey Tests a World War I Fokker D-VII

## January to April 1964

During the latter half of 1916 and all of 1917 the Albatros series of beautiful biplane fighters was produced in very large numbers to supply all of the German Jasta-fighter squadrons on the Western Front. Fokker's Eindecker (monoplane) E-I to E-IV series had become the Fokker scourge to the Allies in 1915 and 1916 by having the first synchronized machine gun that fired through the propeller. His designers failed, however, to produce the increased performance needed to combat the newer SPADs, Sopwiths, and SE5-A fighters. The higher-performing Albatros

*Baron Korwin Heinrich von Meyer searching for enemy fighters over Long Island in 1965. This aircraft was a delight to fly and it was quite obvious that Anthony Fokker and Rheinhold Platz made a great team for the design and production of German fighters. Fokker delivered 407 D-VIIs by July 1918 and 775 before Armistice Day 11 November 1918. (Corwin H. Meyer Collection)*

238

CHAPTER TWENTY-FOUR

biplanes had, therefore, supplanted the Eindecker. The famous Baron von Richthofen had gained the majority of his victories in his red Albatros. At the end of 1917, Albatros aircraft were the undisputed best fighters in German aviation.

Another fighter competition occurred in January 1918 at the Johannisthal flying field, near Berlin, to determine which design would win new contracts. Nine different contractors brought 31 prototypes for the top fighter pilots to evaluate and to select the winner. Fokker attended with nine different prototypes. Von Richthofen was a fierce competitor and was not going to miss being the leader of the lucrative German fighter business again.

One of his prototype fighters was the V-11. This was the model that he pinned his hopes on. Fokker test flew it the day before the competition began and found that its roll and directional stabilities were grossly lacking. He knew that the top German fighter pilots would desire good characteristics in combat. So, he had a 30-inch extension welded into the fuselage that night just behind the pilot to give the rudder and horizontal stabilizer a longer lever arm to increase both stabilities. After testing he was satisfied with this new configuration. The German fighter pilots unanimously decided in favor of the extension for mass procurement. Only von Richthofen requested even more directional stability. A fixed vertical fin installed in front of the rudder solved the problem in short order. The V-11 was declared the winner. In production this design became the D-VII. (In German "D" stands for Dopple Dekker or biplane.)

The pilots' enthusiasm for the Fokker D-VII was unanimous. Although it was not as fast as the allied fighters it would meet in combat this new Fokker could climb faster, turn tighter, and hang on its propeller for the fatal belly shot under complete control at high altitudes where maneuvering was more critical. None of its competitors had that ability. It also had very agreeable and easy handling characteristics in all other flight conditions. Pilots reported, "It would make good fighter pilots out of mediocre material." Late in World War I the German fighter trainee pool did not have sufficient numbers of satisfactory pilot applicants. The growing shortage of gasoline also drastically limited the number of flight training hours available to each pilot. A fighter with less amenable qualities might have decimated their poorly-trained fighter pilot supply even further. Experienced squadron leaders like von Richthofen well knew what kind of a fighter was needed for the coming months.

The uniquely simple Fokker D-VII construction philosophy was also well-liked by the German High Command, who now quickly needed very large numbers of a new aircraft for the upcoming final push of the war. They directed two other major aircraft producers to be subcontractors to Fokker to assist in the required production rate buildup. The Albatros Werke GmbH at Johannisthal and the Ostdeutsche Albatros Werke of Schneidemuhl were immediately authorized to gear up for large Fokker mass production. This decision resulted in the fantastic in-service availability of 407 Fokker D-VII machines by July 1918 and 775 by November 1918. This number resulted in 49 squadrons being so equipped by the time the armistice was concluded 11 November 1918. It was a marvelous aircraft and a fabulous production record.

These three German aircraft corporations were able to gear up fast because Fokker utilized the very new and unique welded steel tube fuselage and tail surface construction process, which could produce aircraft much faster than the wood and wire and/or the labor-intensive laminated wood fuselage construction of the Albatros fighters.

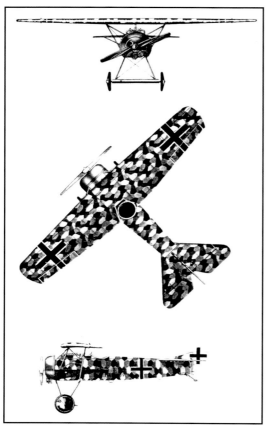

This is a three-view drawing of the last Fokker design built for the Great War, the Fokker D-VIII. Because of the great shortage of gasoline at that time, Fokker only used a 110-hp Oberussel rotary engine but he took off the additional drag of a biplane wing to enable it to have a top speed of 125 mph on such small horsepower. It thus had a comparable speed with most allied fighters in late 1918. (Corwin H. Meyer Collection)

## My Lifelong Introduction to the Fokker D-VII

The Fokker D-VII was the Lockheed F-22 of the 1930s era in which I grew up. It was the model aircraft of choice for my generation. Its clean and elegant lines and much better flight characteristics appealed to us much more than the bull-dog look of the French SPAD. The Fokker's mystique was doubly enhanced in our minds by the fictional battles pub-

lished in pulp magazines like, "G-8 and His Battle Aces," where the round-goggled Phillip Strange heroically and successfully fought off the square-goggled Baron von something-or-other's Fokker D-VIIs at 10-to-1 odds.

I had another incentive to be enamored by the Fokker D-VII. In the ancient Mechanics Machinery Building at the Illinois State Fair Grounds in my hometown of Springfield, Illinois, hung a stodgy Curtiss Jenny JN4-D trainer and a real live Fokker D-VII. The D-VII hung suspended so near the balcony railing that I could touch the lower wingtip. Its magnificent BMW 185-hp engine resided in a glass case on the balcony adjacent to the Fokker. I spent hours every year staring at it, wildly imagining that I was flying many daring and successful air battles against it.

## Epilogue For That Fokker D-VII

About 20 years after the end of World War II, I asked my brother, who continued to reside in Springfield, if the Fokker was still hanging there. He called back and related that fair officials had deemed it a useless, archaic exhibit, taken it down, and stored it outside in the weather until it rotted and rusted, and then trashed it just a few years before I called. I was also trashed.

## A REAL Fokker D-VII Enters My Life

In 1962 I heard that a person was building a Fokker D-VII about a mile from my home on Long Island, New York. Needless to say, I was at his door ASAP. I met Fred Berg, a quiet but direct gentleman, who was a tenured professor of manual training arts at a local college. He showed me the half-completed aircraft that he was building in his four-car garage. It was obvious from first sight that he was a first-class craftsman. His work was impeccable. When I asked him just why he chose a Fokker D-VII to construct, he replied that his father was a mechanic in a Fokker D-VII squadron during World War I. Reason enough.

I occasionally made my way to his home during the following seven years as construction progressed. I diplomatically suggested several times that if he needed a professional test pilot to fly it I would be pleased to do so. He replied in a very polite but forthright manner that he was going to teach himself to fly in that very aircraft, a subtle inference that I could only be a spectator to his Fokker flights.

As the time for the first flight neared, Fred discussed this with the FAA and found that they were similarly forthright in that he was not going to fly his Fokker over the heads of taxpayers without an FAA-approved pilot's license. My worth suddenly became more apparent and he asked me to fly his magnificent machine. My offer to test fly it at Grumman's 10,000-foot Calverton runway, instead of a cow pasture, may also have appealed to his sense of safety for his aircraft's long-range future.

Fred had done a great job of research before he started work building the Fokker. He had obtained much specific material from Wright Field archives on the static and flight tests they had performed in 1920 on several of the 142 Fokker D-VIIs that had been previously shipped to the United States as war reparations. The static test report on the wings stated that at 5.2Gs a very loud snapping noise was heard. It was further reported that the load was increased to 8Gs without any further noises or breakage. They never did determine just what caused that recalcitrant noise at 5.2Gs. Fred had also made a trip to the Aeronautical Museum in Munich, Germany, where he had taken many measurements from the only original remaining Fokker D-VII. Fred even constructed two exact replica

Spandeau machine guns. Most of his instruments were original from that time period, but with English markings.

Fred apologized that he did not adhere exactly to Fokker's specifications. He modernized his Fokker with wheel brakes and a steerable tail wheel instead of a tailskid. Tailskids were required for grass field flights by providing braking and directional stability on the ground. Most aircraft did not have wheel brakes until the mid 1930s, when hard runways came in vogue. Fred knew that a tailskid would cause disastrous skidding on a smooth, hard runway. He also used 4130 steel tube instead of the original mild steel and modern resorcinol adhesive instead of horsehoof glue used in 1918 Fokker construction. He also installed a small windshield where there evidently had been no requirement for it by the German Air Force. As far as I was concerned, Fred's well-thought-out, newer specifications would greatly improve my comfort and flight-testing longevity.

After it was completed, Fred towed it on a trailer behind his truck on back roads 20 miles to the Grumman Calverton airport, assembled it single-handedly in a very few hours, and persuaded the FAA to certify its airworthiness. During the FAA inspection they listed over 40 "restrictions that must be removed before flight," such as the fuel cap that must have a label stating that the tank could only be filled with 25 octane gas or higher, etc. Amazingly, they asked not one question concerning important major items such as weight and balance calculations, structural limitations, flight envelope determination, or engine integrity.

The engine was a six-cylinder 160-hp Hall-Scott, which was an Americanized version of the Mercedes used in the wartime Fokkers. Fred had located it in someone's barn. He completely rebuilt it in order to have a thoroughly accurate and reliable Fokker. He even reworked the

*Twenty-six-kill World War I ace of aces Captain Eddie Rickenbacker stands next to a French SPAD-7 that he flew against the fabulous Fokker D-VII in 1918. No other American topped his score until World War II when Richard Bong shot down 40 Japanese aircraft in his Lockheed P-38 Lightning. (Corwin H. Meyer Collection)*

cam system so that the propeller would rotate in the correct direction. He installed an impulse ignition system, which required only a 6-inch hand motion of the propeller similar to 1918 German ignition designs to start the engine. It didn't require the macho "propping" that was required by all other aircraft of that vintage. The engine performed like a charm for all of the nine flights that I made in it. The only precaution necessary was to monitor the engine coolant temperature during cold January flights. It was a most docile engine. With only one magneto, the only run-up testing required was to see that the engine would obtain 1,150 static RPM before takeoff (the wheel brakes came in very handy here) and to check that

the coolant was warm enough to fly. It would have been a dream for wartime interception scramble starts.

I officially entered the cockpit on 25 January 1969 with all my persuasive arguments now in cold storage. After a walk-around check and engine start only one major unexpected state-of-the-art problem was to rear its ugly head and spoil my exciting, sunny horizon.

My first takeoff was into a 10-mph wind. I was caught off guard by the Fokker's very light, Piper Cub-like, 9.4-lb-per-square-foot wing loading compared to the jet fighters I had been flying. They had wing loadings over 100 pounds per square foot. I had just lifted the tail for forward visibility and was ready to lower it in order to leave the ground when I found that I was about 15 feet in the air after a ground roll of only five aircraft lengths that equaled only 115 feet! Torque effect had been so minimal and so easily controlled with the very large rudder and its 40-degree deflection limit that I failed to anticipate such spectacular takeoff performance possibilities. I may have been daydreaming just a bit, too.

I had selected a climb speed of 80 mph, and the aircraft went up like an express elevator. Visibility was excellent except over the long nose, and handling characteristics were as gentle as a Piper Cub. I soon noted that although the Fokker had adequate aileron for flight it did not have the crisp rolling qualities that were paramount in fighters that I was acquainted with. The rudder and elevator had smooth and positive feel. I then remembered that Fokker pilots got directly behind their adversaries and pumped lead, spraying their targets with the sensitive and positive rudder motions available. They never did develop the curved approach, lead-pursuit gunnery runs that were popular in World War II fighters. They required much greater rolling power.

I performed many stalls to explore the behavior of the Fokker with various aileron and rudder inputs. I wanted to see for myself how the aircraft would perform in the hands of a clumsy student pilot. I was pleased and amazed to find that the Fokker had no wing-dropping vices at all. Stall occurred at a low 38-mph indicated airspeed. Just before the aircraft stalled, it gave adequate buffeting for warning and the nose slowly dropped to the horizon for fast, easy recovery. Accelerated stalls showed that the wing design was without vice. I could see the great benefit to stall speed and handling characteristics from the highly cambered airfoil on the tips of both the upper and lower wings. Few World War I fighter aircraft knew such gentle stalling characteristics. I could easily see how novice pilots could mistreat the forgiving Fokker D-VII and keep their landing rolls well within the confines of the small fields that they operated from. I immediately felt at home in the Fokker.

Reed Chambers, who was Eddie Rickenbacker's executive officer in the 94th Aero Squadron, was a friend of mine for 25 years before he died. He related in great detail the not-too-gentle stalls that he experienced in the French Nieuport 28 and the miserable stall characteristics of the SPAD 7 and 13 because their wings had very sharp leading edges. He further stated that because of these bad habits near the stall speeds, pilots approached much faster than they should have, causing many more landing overrun accidents than necessary.

Flare-out and touchdown was a piece of cake in the Fokker using an approach speed of 55 mph. I was congratulating myself long before the rollout had finished, however. This is a well-known no-no in all tail draggers and it caught up with me—big time! The Fokker started leaning with its left wing down, which started a beautiful ground loop without even a crosswind for me to blame it on. After a sharp swerve to the left I caught it by nearly standing the bird on its nose, but my honor was tinged with the aroma of Limburger cheese.

Because it had been so much fun to fly I thought I should redeem my ineptitude. I decided to take off again immediately before my audience caught on. The next circuit was great until I settled into the three-point position. The Fokker "headed for the barn" again but in the opposite direction. I caught it again with the rudder and brakes after another swerve but I was greatly perplexed at my inability to tame such a docile aircraft from its only bad habit.

Because the wingtip of the aircraft had dropped slightly both times just before the ground loop started, it finally struck me that the landing gear shock cords might need adjustment. We tightened them somewhat and I took off for my second flight to calibrate the airspeed and to gradually increase the pullout G limit to 3.5Gs. I was not going to probe that 5G snapping regime in the air. I very warily

*Major Reed Chambers (a friend of Corky's) standing next to his later SPAD 13 with the 220-hp Hispano-Suiza engine. After the armistice they were told to paint their aircraft in sharp colors for the occupation of Germany. Chambers shot down seven Fokkers and nine observation balloons, which were difficult targets because they were surrounded with anti-aircraft guns. (Corwin H. Meyer Collection)*

pulled Gs in half-G increments up to 3.5Gs and decided that was enough of this nonsense. Thankfully no unusual noises were noted. During the dives I noticed that the Fokker's fixed pitch propeller over-speeded to 1,500 rpm at 125-mph indicated airspeed with the throttle fully retarded. Thus I couldn't dive it any faster without seriously damaging the engine. The timed airspeed calibration from 60 mph to 105 mph along the two-mile length of the Calverton runway was completed without a hitch. I also made some stabilized climbs from 1,000 to 3,000 feet to determine the speed for best rate of climb. These climbs demonstrated to me that I was way out of touch with reality on guessing the best rate of climb speed in anything but highly wing-loaded jets. The best climb speed proved to be 65 mph.

## A Very Unexpected State-of-the-Art Problem Arrives

The landing was uneventful until I was almost stopped when Herr Ground Loop started again. I could stop it more easily now that I was getting used to it, but it seemed to be way out of character for this otherwise mannerly fighter.

After the flight when I debriefed concerning the tenacious ground-looping tendencies, Fred suggested that we talk to a pilot friend of his who had learned to fly in World War I. He might be able to shed some light on our problem. This old but wise pilot immediately asked how we had tested the shock chord tension before each flight. When we told him that we didn't think it was necessary and just guessed at their needed tension, he gave us

*Without all the cross bracing of flying wires between the wings like all other biplanes had at the time, this aircraft looks quite simple to manufacture. It was because this was the first time welded-steel tubing fuselage, tail assembly, landing gear, and engine mounts were used in aircraft construction. This new fabrication method took less than half the time to construct as the 100-percent wooden trussed aircraft that were built by both air arms until then. (Corwin H. Meyer Collection)*

quite a lesson from his World War I days. He said that a 180-lb pilot must sit on the wingtip of any shock-cord-using aircraft that he is going to fly before every flight. If the wingtip goes down by more than 2 inches the shock cords are way too loose. Eureka! I sat on the wingtip of the Fokker and it went down eight large inches. When we tightened the shock cords to our pilot friend's specifications, the ground-looping tendency disappeared as if by magic. So much for my knowledge in shock cord state-of-the-art.

On the next flights I did loops, slow rolls, Immelmanns, and snap rolls. They all could be performed easily except slow rolls. The ailerons needed more roll capability for that maneuver. I, of course, did not consider my lack of ability as any part of the slow roll problem.

I then made a climb to 10,000 feet to see what the fuss had been about the Fokker's great ability to maneuver while standing on its tail with full control at 45 mph indicated airspeed. I could pull it up to a 45-degree angle with the horizon and slow down to 45 mph with full power and the aircraft was steady as a rock. It could be maneuvered easily with both the ailerons and/or the rudder in simulated firing runs. It was unbelievable. I now understood why the British Handley Page bomber pilots and other allied pilots of World War I were so afraid of this fighter and kept a look out for bottom attacks.

On the next flight we measured take-off and landing distances in a calm wind by having people line up on the side of the runway to determine exact points of liftoff and touchdown. Takeoff was noted to be four lengths of the aircraft (91 feet), and landing, with the use of brakes to simulate tailskid drag, was four-and-a-half lengths (103 feet). It really had a great combination of slow approach speed coupled with very short ground rolls.

As my flights had been made in the depth of winter temperatures, Fred decided to put the Fokker in storage until spring. With its drafty cockpit and very small windshield even my winter flight gear was not sufficient to avoid freezing to death.

When spring weather arrived I partook of an aerial photo flight from a grass field where Fred achieved his FAA permission to fly his Fokker, by way of his required Private Pilot Certificate. I know he related that he found the Fokker to be even more clawless than the ubiquitous Piper Cub he had trained in because he had his Fokker propeller come off its shaft while flying one day, and made a very successful off-airport forced landing with no damage to either his pride or joy.

## Conclusions and Another Sad Fokker D-VII Epilogue

The Fokker D-VII was a fabulous fighter. While it wasn't the fastest machine in level flight, its amazing rate of climb, turning abilities, and benign handling qualities throughout its entire flight envelope made it an unbeatable aerial weapon. It was able to dogfight successfully, above the altitudes of allied fighters, in the hands of pilots with as few as 20 hours total flight time. Its demonstrated superiority prompted the Allied Armistice Commission to demand that all Fokker D-VIIs be turned over to them immediately after the cessation of hostilities. It was the only weapon of that war so honored specifically by name.

Their operating squadrons had burned many D-VIIs. Tony Fokker has surreptitiously shipped six trainloads to Holland, unbeknownst to the Allied Armistice Commission. Nonetheless, the United States Army Air Service received 142 Fokker D-VIIs in 1919 as partial reparations from the war.

The Navy was given six Fokker D-VIIs from the reparations batch taken from

Germany. In 1921 the Navy transferred them to the Marines for use at Brown Field at Quantico, Virginia. From their records (listed below) they were only flown between six months to a year and a half during 1921 to 1923. There is no record of their flight times.

On the strike report of serial number A-5844 there is a note that states: "Sec Nav letter 3239-75 July 19, 1921, to S&A directs sale of this deteriorated aircraft to the State Museum, Springfield, OH for $1.00." I will always wonder if this is the aircraft that went to the State Museum Springfield, Illinois, and could have been the one that I enjoyed so much.

U.S. aircraft contractors found much to learn from Fokker. The 1921 Curtiss PN-1 fighter had tapered wings, horn balanced control surfaces, and upper wing/fuselage strut designs similar to the Fokker D-VII. Follow-on aircraft, the Curtiss P-1 to the famous P-6E series, had tapered wings. Huff-Deland and Boeing aircraft used tapered wings and welded steel fuselages in their postwar fighters. Fokker did make an impression on American designers.

I'm sorry to relate that Fred Berg's meticulously constructed Fokker still languishes in his basement even though I have tried to get him to place it in one of the many museums that would be proud to present his work of art to the public. I hope that someday he changes his mind. His masterpiece deserves better treatment and the world deserves to appreciate that unique aircraft with such a historical significance.

## Epilogue – Biography of Anthony H. G. Fokker

Contrary to popular belief, Tony Fokker was a Dutch national all of his life. He designed, built, and taught himself to fly in his first aircraft, the Spinne (Spider) when he was 21 years old. It was powered with a 50-hp Argus automobile engine. Because it had no rudder or ailerons he only flew it in straight "hops." On 16 May 1911 he passed the test for his pilot's certificate in his much-improved Spinne number two. By 1912 he had gone to Russia to demonstrate his aircraft and he sold an M-3 to the Russian aviatrix Ljuba Galanschikoff. In July 1912 he delivered his first aircraft to the German Army at Doberitz Airfield. After winning a competition for four aircraft that could be transported dismantled on a lorry for the Army in July 1913, he soon won an order for 10 more. He was constantly in the Berlin newspapers because of the new and appalling "loop-the-loop" maneuvers he performed during the acrobatic demonstrations required to sell aircraft in those days.

Before World War I broke out, Fokker had started an Army flying school at Johannisthal near Berlin, using his M-7 aircraft. In 1915, after the famous French ace Rolland Garros and his Morane aircraft were captured with a machine gun that had been rigged to fire through the propeller (with steel deflectors mounted on the propeller to deflect bullets that might hit the propeller), Fokker decided to find a way to synchronize the machine gun mechanically to fire only when the propeller was not in the way of the bullets. After Lieutenants Butlar and Wintgens had successfully tested his mechanism in actual combat, he built it into all of his production aircraft. Fokker was now in the real fighter production business, obtaining orders for 625 of his E-I to E-VI series monoplane fighters ("E" was for Ein Dekker or monoplane). His record of building 3,350 aircraft during the rest of the war is history. In order to continue building aircraft after the war, he smuggled six trainloads, filled with over 200 complete Fokker D-VIIs and much machinery from his several factories in

*From this angle it is easy to see the laminated propeller of basswood and mahogany that Fred carved to construct an exact Fokker D-VII propeller. He made this entire aircraft to the plans that Anthony Fokker used in 1918. Fortunately, he was a teacher of manual arts in a local college and had many years of excellent talents in wood and metalworking. (Corwin H. Meyer Collection)*

Germany, into his home country of Holland.

Fokker started up slowly in Holland by building both military and commercial transports. In 1923 his 10- passenger, single-engine, Liberty-powered Fokker T-2 purchased by the U.S. Army made a world-acclaimed record by spanning the United States from east to west flying non-stop in 23 hours. Because he believed that the western hemisphere airline executives would require that he have a plant there, he located his Atlantic Aircraft Corporation plant in Teterboro, New Jersey, in May 1924. His American-made F-VIIb-3M trimotor was a global sensation when it completed a 7,000-mile trans-Pacific flight piloted by Sir Kingsford-Smith in May 1928. Pilots who demanded Fokker aircraft

made many other record long-distance flights during the time period before and after Lindbergh's flight in 1927. His four-passenger, single-engine Universal and Super Universal designs, followed by his F-VIIa-3M trimotor, soon became the standard transport aircraft for many airlines worldwide.

His business expanded rapidly. His several corporations received large orders from Europe, China, Japan, South America, and 12 U.S. and Canadian airlines. His order for 350 engines from Pratt & Whitney and Wright was, at the time, the biggest commercial order ever for commercial aircraft engines.

The CAA grounded all of his many airliners after the 31 March 1931 crash of TWA's Fokker Trimotor, which killed all onboard, including the famous football coach Knute Rockne. His fabric-covered fuselage and especially the wooden wing construction came under detailed scrutiny by concerned airline and government officials. This accident, coupled with the advent of the all-metal 10-passenger, twin-engine Boeing 247 transport, followed by the even faster Douglas DC-3 all-metal transport, soon spelled the demise of Fokker's wooden-wing airline transport business.

His Dutch factory continued to turn out transports and military aircraft, developing a total of 211 models of fighters, amphibians, and transports since Fokker first flew his fragile Spinne monoplane in 1911. Quite a record for a very young entrepreneur to attain, beginning only eight years after the Wright brothers' flights.

Fokker died of an infection received in a New York hospital in 1939, but his Dutch Fokker company has continued to prosper until the present date, albeit disappearing into a multi-national conglomerate similar to the fate of many other pioneer aviation company names, including Grumman.

# Chapter 25

# Retirement Is Even Busier Than Working

## January 1991 to January 2005

Still being hung up on aviation at the age of 71, I decided to find a private aviation community in Florida (for a good reason—no income taxes). I surveyed 10 of them and decided to build a home on Leeward Air Ranch. With its 6,000-foot runway, and many aviation people who built and/or restored their own aircraft, the Ranch proved to be a very good move for me.

I had just emptied my van with my belongings into my rented home when a Luscombe tail-dragger taxied down my street and stopped. The pilot got out, lifted the tail and turned the aircraft around, introduced himself and said, "You look like you need to fly an aircraft. Get in, I'll hand prop it so you can see your new surroundings from the air." I did and Ralph

*In December Dorky and I spent a week in Africa. She suggested that we fly over to visit Idi Amin in Uganda to sell him a new Grumman Gulfstream III to replace his Gulfstream II business jet. We did, had lunch with Idi and his family, saw the entire country by helicopter, and flew home in it instead of on East African Airways. We didn't know it at the time but our son Peter had previously instructed his pilots through their Airline Transport Pilot ratings. (Corwin H. Meyer Collection)*

Braswell and his wife Judy became my closest friends for over 20 years. What a neat welcoming committee.

To give you an idea of Leeward's growth, my home, built in 1986, was the eighteenth built. In 2004 there are over 160 homes and more are still being built. Over 350 aircraft are based there.

I purchased a Mooney 201 and enjoyed visiting friends all over the East Coast. It didn't take long at Leeward to get into the aircraft-rebuilding mood, so I purchased a Grumman Avenger to restore. Other Grumman combat aircraft cost four to five times the $75,000 price I paid for the Avenger. When it was delivered I didn't have enough space in my hangar, so I asked a friend if I could store the fuselage in his brand new wooden hangar. He was kind enough to store it for me but it was in there for only a very short time. I was in Albany, Georgia, finishing up my job with Old Man's Aircraft Company (OMAC) when I received a call from Ralph saying that the hangar burned to the ground at 2AM that morning and that only a few steel parts remained. My Avenger's aluminum fuselage now was a 14-foot-long puddle on the hangar floor! My Avenger was not insured, nor was his hangar, so I took a $75,000 loss and looked for another fuselage.

I found one in Connecticut and started driving up the day I heard about it because the owner said that, although he had another buyer, he would hold it 24 hours for me. At 9 o'clock that evening in a cold and drizzling rain my car engine began to get rough enough that I pulled into a lighted but closed filling station out in the country to call the police, who arrived 45 minutes later. During my wait, a young man came out of the dark, walked up to me shoving a sawed-off shotgun into my stomach, and said, "money mon, money mon." It seemed like it took me a half an hour to get my wallet out and give it to him. He disappeared back into the dark and that was the last I saw of him and my wallet. After I gave the police

*The only completely stripped fuselage available in the United States being dropped off at my hangar after making the trip from Connecticut. It had no rust or corrosion but it needed some damage repair. I spent the next six months finding all of the hundreds of missing parts necessary to make it a flight-worthy aircraft. (Corwin H. Meyer Collection)*

*The first takeoff with Corky at the controls after three-and-a-half years of Corky and Art Miller slaving 60 hours a week to complete it. Although I had not flown an Avenger in 51 years, 7 months, and 2 days I felt completely at home in it as soon as the wheels left the ground. (Corwin H. Meyer Collection)*

my report I found that I had no more engine roughness so I drove on, finally stopping for the night at Emporia, Virginia, because of engine roughness again. When I told the motel keeper that I had just been robbed and that I would like to call home to get another credit card number so I could pay her, she immediately went to the phone. It was only a few minutes later that two cops arrived and kindly asked me to face the wall of the motel with my hands in the air while I told them my story. I stood that way for another 20 minutes until they had called the Rocky Mount, North Carolina, police to verify my robbery story. They then said that I could go into the motel. The next morning I looked under the hood and found that I was missing the tube that connects heat from the exhaust to warm the carburetor to prevent icing. This was what had happened twice during the freezing and rainy night before. A $2 tube fixed the problem.

When I arrived in Connecticut I found that the fuselage was completely stripped of everything and had some dents in the skin. I had been unable to locate a fuselage for the previous three months, so I purchased it immediately. To get it out of the field it had been residing in for the last 20 years, I had to saw down five large trees that had sprouted up during that time. I was soon to find out that my dilemmas were par for the course for rebuilding a derelict World War II aircraft.

The fuselage remained in my hangar for several months while I tried to locate the 250-plus pieces, including an engine and propeller that I needed, to fill the fuselage with the required equipment. My luck was about to change. One day I decided to make a project of removing the tail wheel assembly from the fuselage to clean it up as a first step in the restoration. I spent 1 hour and 15 minutes in a very cramped tail wheel retraction compartment trying to get four large, rusted bolts off to remove the assembly from the fuselage. I had used foul language, had many nicked knuckles and elbows, and had not gotten one rusted nut off its rusted bolt when someone knocked on the fuselage and said, "Hello." I got out and found

Art Miller, a very well-known aircraft inspector and mechanic who lived at Leeward. He asked what I was doing. When I told him he asked to crawl into the hole to look at the problem. Wanting to stay clear of that torture hole forever, I readily agreed. Less than 20 minutes later, to my great amazement, he had removed all of the four rusty nuts and bolts and lowered the tail wheel assembly to the ground. He then asked me if I would like to hire him to help me complete the restoration job. I couldn't get "yes" out fast enough, and for the next three years and four months we both worked six eight-hour days a week to complete it. Art knew every aspect of aircraft restoration and worked very quickly at every task he performed. I did a lot of rough clean-up jobs under his auspices and had the dubious pleasure of spreading 200 gallons of paint stripper to remove four acres of paint (one coat was house paint) from the aircraft. I have never had a nastier job before or since. I spent a lot of time finding parts and getting them to Leeward. I found an engine in Arkansas and drove a truck there and back to the engine overhaul location in less than 24 hours.

When we finally finished its restoration I made several lift-offs and touchdowns to check its brakes, engine, etc., like a good test pilot, but I had a few misgivings about flying it. I checked my logbook and found that the last Avenger I had flown was only 51 years, seven months, and two days ago—so I decided to fly it. The very second I felt the landing gear hit the lock-up after takeoff I felt like I had test flown another Avenger only a few hours before. The smells, noises, vibrations, and the picture view from the cockpit all came back to me and it was spellbinding. This was another first flight for my logbook.

Art Miller and I only had one argument in the three years and four months we worked together. Art always had Rush Limbaugh playing loud on the radio and it nearly drove me nuts. But trying to be diplomatic I put up with it for many months while he was listening to it. Finally one day I said, "Art, what has Rush said in the last two hours?" He answered, "I don't listen to him. I only have him on to drive you crazy." We both had a great laugh and Rush magically turned into music from then on.

Many friends asked me if I was going to fly it in air shows. I told them no, because I had previously been paid by the government for all the air shows that I had ever put on and it was too darned expensive now. I must have sounded like a party pooper, but I had my fun restoring and test flying it. I sold it to Steve Hay in Syracuse, Indiana, who flew it to Oshkosh, Wisconsin, in 1985, where it won a Silver Wrench Award. After flying

*After demonstrating 19 new Navy military fighters in my 36-year career at Grumman, I was made an Honorary Naval Aviator at NAS Pensacola on 9 May 1997. The Commander of Naval Operations, Admiral Jay L. Johnson, pinned on my gold wings. I was only the 23rd person since 1911 to receive that honor. (Corwin H. Meyer Collection)*

*Immediately after the flight a Leeward friend brought a bottle of champagne for the heroes to drink while standing in front of that big, beautiful monster. It was a typical Grumman aircraft. It required that a pilot have at least 35 hours of Cub time to fly solo in it even after 51 years. And as a bad test pilot, I didn't break anything on its first flight. (Corwin H. Meyer Collection)*

it for 10 years he sold it to another Avenger enthusiast in California who fully believed that he bought the Taj Mahal of all warplanes. I'm still quite pleased that it made two other pilots even happier than it had made me.

## My "Hobby" Changes

A few months later a former associate, Captain Paul Stevens, USN (Ret.), called me and asked why I didn't write some stories regarding the test piloting of Navy aircraft. He further said that I should call Captain Earle Rogers, USN (Ret.), who was the editor of the Pensacola Navy Museum Foundation publication, with that suggestion. After talking with Earle for a short time it was obvious that Paul Stevens had made that suggestion to Earle before calling me. Earle has published 14 of my articles in subsequent Foundation magazine issues so far and is still asking for more. Soon after, another acquaintance, Paul Koskela, a famous aerial photographer who had seen my articles in that Navy periodical, suggested that I call Tom Atwood, Editor of *Flight*

*Journal* magazine, to suggest that I write for them. My call to Tom Atwood had the same delightful results as my call to Earle Rogers. I have now published 82 articles in four publications including Steve Ginter's "Naval Fighter Series" booklets and a French publication, *La Fana de l'Aviation* (The Aviation Fanatic). Having published only a few articles in 1998, I was even more amazed when Dave Arnold, the owner of Specialty Press, called me out of the blue and asked if I was going to write a book. I sent the first copy of it to Dave Arnold, who in turn published it.

I am enjoying my retirement and it surely has been an exciting time of life for me. I plan to keep all of my flight ratings as long as the FAA and I sleep well at night under those conditions. I have firmly decided, however, that I am not going to attack more subjects like World War II military aircraft restoration, weight-lifting, portrait painting, driving in the Indianapolis race, or mountain climbing for my future entertainment. I'll find something interesting to do to keep me out of too much trouble.

# Chapter 26

# Divine Intervention – My Entire Life

Over 1,000 years ago Confucius said, "If you really like your profession you will never work a day in your life." He described my career perfectly. I never worked a day in my life. I was allowed to open up my childish obsession from building and flying model aircraft to test flying and building full-scale aircraft at Grumman.

Carl Alber, who you met previously in this book, said several years after we both retired from Grumman, "Corky, you are without a doubt the luckiest man I have ever known. You had more near-fatal flying events combined with 11 crashes during your lifetime than all the rest of Grumman's test pilots put together." The word luck has many synonyms: happenstance, good fortune, chance, fortuity, windfall, fluke, the breaks, advantage, and godsend. I now believe God-sent was Carl's definition of my luck.

After the following list of events happened, however, I knew for sure that I had been either unwise enough or unable to take the actions necessary to provide the God-sent results that were required to keep me alive.

The recovery from the P-40 spin that I got into so foolishly over the Grumman airport was an early one. Aerodynamically, I had performed exactly the wrong action by unknowingly shoving the throttle to

full power. That had to be a God-sent miracle. He made the recovery; I couldn't have. The P-40 example is clear, but what about all the rest of the miraculous events of my life:

My mother successfully arguing with my father to get permission for me to learn to fly in a barn-storming era of aviation when only one out of 1,000 mothers would let their sons even take an aircraft ride.

Craig Isbell's insistence on teaching me to fly, which allowed me to find out that I could fly cross-eyed even after Dr. Morris had said that flying under such conditions would kill me.

My late arrival to Boston Airport that kept me out of the Stinson aircraft, which I saw reduced to rubble by the P-40 crashing into it, killing the student pilot whose seat I would have been in.

My visit with Pan American Captain Mike LaPorte, who sarcastically suggested that if I wanted to use my technical background in engineering, I should get a job as a test pilot.

The stranger on the train who directed me to an unknown-to-me Grumman Aircraft, my final, but successful opportunity to be hired as an experimental, not production, test pilot with no military flight experience.

The spine problem I received while performing the first rolling pullouts in the

Wildcat in 1945, which three doctors had predicted would result in painful and grave back and neck problems before I was 40 years of age. My shrunken and bent-over spine problems all waited until I was 82 years old—and I still don't take any prescription pain medication!

My first air show in the F9F-5 Panther, whose wings had been designed without sufficient anti-twist strength, that caused me to push the stick with both hands to keep the Gs from exceeding nine. Only 2Gs more would have broken the wing.

My unbelievably wild spin in the Tiger after I had over-ridden the engineer's decision not to install an instantly needed anti-spin chute recovery on that flight.

These and scores of other events, including Bob Hall's and Bud Gillies' many strong diciplinary actions, I have experienced in my life were all God-sent. Many times these angels were dressed and spoke as humans.

It still amazes me that I waited for five long years after the P-40 spin until I began praying the simple words of the tax collector in Luke 18:13 before each takeoff. He said, "God, be merciful to me a poor sinner." I finally realized that I needed His assistance, as well as that of engineers and mechanics. He had taught birds to fly millions of years ago—why shouldn't He teach me? There is no question that God forced His way into my life. I didn't come to Him, but why?

Let's go back to my childhood. I was baptized shortly after birth. I went to church every Sunday, we gave thanks before and after each meal, my mother taught us the Lord's Prayer and the Apostle's Creed, and I spent the eighth grade in a Lutheran school to be confirmed as a member of the church. All this education, however, seemed mechanical to me because no specific benefits from my memorization of lots of catechism pages had been revealed to me at the impudent age of 14 years. I had heard a lot of "Hellfire and Damnation," however, if I didn't do the things I was taught. I guess that it was assumed by my elder teachers that God's benefits should have been as obvious to a youth as they were to their years of maturity. I don't remember being taught that I needed to ask for God's protection and wisdom, and to thank Him every day for the blessings He had and would bestow upon me so I would make choices as close as possible to the Ten Commandments. I do not mean to suggest that I have made no wrong choices in my life. As you have seen I have made all too many big ones, but I was not taught to ask God for wisdom before making choices until I heard a "Wisdom Prayer" sermon one Sunday in church in 2004. I finally realized that wisdom and patience, which were good enough for King Solomon to ask God for in all of his choices, are what I needed to ask God for each day, not things, fame, money, or passing grades.

The point of this book is: don't wait until it is almost too late in your life, as I did, to finally understand that beginning today you should pray for God's protection, wisdom, and thank Him for the many past blessings you have received every day of your life.

Divine intervention is available to everybody. God will prove himself to be a faithful Father any time we ask. It is up to us to want to be his trusting children. Studying the Bible is the best flight-instruction manual you will ever read. It will fly you to heaven on angel's wings.

In clear hindsight I will always wish I had had less technical "affliction" success and had given my family much, much more consideration, attention, and love. I hope that God and my family will forgive me for this belated wisdom I now understand so clearly.